Confessions of a Counterfeit Farm Girl

·SUSAN McCORKINDALE·

NEW AMERICAN LIBRARY

NEW AMERICAN LIBRARY
Published by New American Library,
a division of Penguin Group (USA) Inc.,
375 Hudson Street, New York, New York 10014, USA
Penguin Group (Canada), 90 Eglinton Avenue East, Suite 700, Toronto,
Ontario M4P 2Y3, Canada (a division of Pearson Penguin Canada Inc.)
Penguin Books Ltd., 80 Strand, London WC2R 0RL, England
Penguin Ireland, 25 St. Stephen's Green, Dublin 2,
Ireland (a division of Penguin Books Ltd.)
Penguin Group (Australia), 250 Camberwell Road, Camberwell,
Victoria 3124, Australia (a division of Pearson Australia Group Pty. Ltd.)
Penguin Books India Pvt. Ltd., 11 Community Centre,
Panchsheel Park, New Delhi – 110 017, India
Penguin Group (NZ), 67 Apollo Drive, Rosedale, North Shore 0632,
New Zealand (a division of Pearson New Zealand Ltd.)
Penguin Books (South Africa) (Pty.) Ltd., 24 Sturdee Avenue,
Rosebank, Johannesburg 2196, South Africa

Penguin Books Ltd., Registered Offices:
80 Strand, London WC2R 0RL, England

First published by New American Library,
a division of Penguin Group (USA) Inc.

First Printing, October 2008
3   5   7   9   10   8   6   4

Copyright © Susan McCorkindale, 2008
All rights reserved

 REGISTERED TRADEMARK—MARCA REGISTRADA

LIBRARY OF CONGRESS CATALOGING-IN-PUBLICATION DATA
McCorkindale, Susan.
Confessions of a counterfeit farm girl / Susan McCorkindale.
p. cm.
ISBN: 978-0-451-22493-4
1. McCorkindale, Susan. 2. Marketing executives—New York (State)—New York—
Biography. 3. Country life—Virginia. 4. Career changes—Virginia. 5. Virginia—Biography.
6. New York (N.Y.)—Biography. 7. New Jersey—Biography.   I. Title.
CT275.M416A3 2008
975.5'043092—dc22
[B]   2008016258

Set in Palatino with Giddyup Display • Designed by Elke Sigal

Printed in the United States of America

Confessions of a
Counterfeit Farm Girl

To my sons, Casey and Cuyler,
and my husband, Stu.

There's nothing counterfeit about
my love for you McMen.

Contents

Part Five
EPILOGUE

Author's Note

If anyone had ever told me I'd leave my big-city job and suburban home for rural country living I would have declared them a few bristles short of a brush. But here I am, living proof that, while it isn't pretty, one can learn to survive without Starbucks and New York–style bagels.

This book is based on the past few years of my loony life. It is founded on a series of e-mails I sent to my friends after my family and I moved from beautiful, bustling Ridgewood, New Jersey, to beautiful, anything-but-bustling Upperville, Virginia, where we now reside on a five-hundred-acre beef cattle farm.

In Ridgewood, my husband tended our less than a quarter acre of "land" with a grass mower he pushed around our small patch, and the only wildlife we encountered were squirrels, the occasional rabbit, and our friend Rich, who developed a penchant for setting off fireworks in the middle of our heretofore quiet suburban street on the Fourth of July.

In Upperville, the cattle cut the "lawn," our wildlife companions have grown to include twenty-six hens, a rooster, two dogs, several foxes, innumerable groundhogs, deer, box turtles, and black snakes, and if we wanted to we could launch fireworks and full-scale mortar attacks from our fields, and no one would ever be the wiser.

In chronicling this bizarre turn my life has taken, I've stuck to the old adage "Never let the facts get in the way of a good story." So kick back, relax, and take my tale with a grain of salt. Preferably on a margarita. Or better yet, a bagel. Oh, what I wouldn't do for a nice, New York–style salt bagel right now.

Confessions of a Counterfeit Farm Girl

Part One

Days of Whining Big Wigs

Chapter One

SUSAN MCCORKINDALE, M.D.

The M.D. doesn't mean what you think it does. But had they published this entire book in my handwriting you'd be certain I was some kind of doctor. That, or a kindergarten dropout.

No, it stands for *marketing director*, specifically the marketing director for *Family Circle* magazine, which is what I was before I was lured away from the land of power suits and Jimmy Choos and into the land of chickens. Not to mention cattle, deer, foxes, groundhogs, turkey buzzards, and box turtles.

But I'll get to my new life in the sticks in a sec. For now I'd like to tell you a little about my hotshot past.

There were lots of things I loved about being at *Family Circle*. I had a big salary and a big bonus, which allowed me to have a really big closet stuffed with big-name designer clothes. I had a big office, with big sliding glass doors that opened onto my own big conference room. I had a big staff and a big budget. I also had one really big problem: The actual job gave me a big, fat headache.

If you don't know anything about the marketing function at a magazine, allow me to shed a little light. Marketing supports the advertising sales staff. Without us, the sales people don't have too much to sell with. Except the magazine. Which you'd think would be enough, considering that's where the advertising runs, but it isn't.

No, these days it's all about programs. You've got to have a Big Program in order to pitch, say, Hewlett-Packard. Because if you don't—horrors!—they're going with *Good Housekeeping*. Or *Better Homes and Gardens*. Or, God forbid, *Redbook*.

What's a Big Program, you ask? It's something that promotes the advertiser's product outside the pages of the magazine. It's also something the advertiser doesn't get charged for because they're doing the magazine the honor of advertising in it, and not in one of its competitors. It's roughly the equivalent of going into a supermarket and saying, here's the deal: I'll pay for the stuff from aisle five but not aisle one. That you can throw in for free or I'm going to a different grocer.

And you wonder why great magazines like *Life* and *Mademoiselle* didn't make it.

As you can imagine, top program development people are in serious demand. I was lucky. I had two of them. On any given day Rich and Kim would dream up a half-dozen different ideas, and four of them were deal makers. Between my two creative geniuses, the magazine raked in hundreds of ad pages and hundreds of thousands of dollars. And because they were—and still are—two of the industry's thriftiest multitiered platform[1] pros, the programs they pitched didn't cost us a lot to execute.

---

1. That's magazine industry gobbledygook for "program with more than one component," i.e., a Web site *and* a direct mail effort.

Believe me when I tell you that I loved Rich and Kim. And their internists did, too.[2]

There were seven other members of my marketing team, all of whom did about a million jobs, including executing the programs Rich and Kim came up with. There were the glamorous Cory and Whitney, and the brilliant and talented Barbara and Noel. There was sweet Lisa, whom we saved from Sales, and, of course, New York sophisticate Janine, and J. Crew catalog–cute Ryan (whom I expect will get married at any minute). I'm not going to bore you with the intimate details of their job descriptions, but suffice it to say that each was more than a dozen bulleted lines long.

And that was before I divvied up my job nine ways and gave them each a chunk of it to do, too.

Hold on, hold on. This isn't going to be one of those self-centered, boss-behaving-badly books. I was a good manager. I loved my staff. It was my actual job that I hated. Why? Because I just couldn't get my natty Anna Sui knickers in a bunch about getting or not getting a particular piece of business. I didn't see the whole thing as crucial to keeping the world spinning on its axis. I just couldn't drink the Kool-Aid and elevate magazine marketing and program development to cancer-research status.

I was burned out, apathetic, and bored. Stealing the Pampers business from *Parenting* no longer made me so happy I could've wet my own pants. And the extra effort involved in getting an extra spread[3] from Clorox (which

---

2. Please note that if you're considering a career in magazine publishing, the program development field is not for sissies. Or for those with an aversion to antacids.

3. A *spread* is magazine lingo for an ad that runs on the left and right sides of the magazine. Way back in my salad days as a secretary I worked for a particularly funny salesman whose motto was "A spread for a spread." QW, no wonder you always made your quota.

involved kissing the butt of that account's asshole head honcho) made me so sick I might as well have poured bleach on my brain.

I'd simply reached the point where I couldn't get worked up about a big win or a big loss. It didn't matter to me. It hadn't fed a starving child, stopped the ethnic cleansing in the Balkans, or made my boobs bigger. (And hey, if that had happened just once, it would've definitely renewed my appreciation for my post.)

Nope. I was fried. But I couldn't just quit. My husband and I had two kids and a mortgage to pay. And I had a very serious addiction to the designer department at Neiman Marcus. We'd miss my big paycheck in a big way. I had to do something, but what?

And then one day it hit me. I had nothing but stars on my staff, people who'd no doubt one day be marketing directors. Why not give them a taste of the position . . . today?

I went in, divvied up my job description, and doled it out. And nobody blinked. In fact, they were thrilled. Every single one of them was smart enough to realize I'd just made them eminently more employable. And for much bigger bucks. All I needed to do now was manage them managing my tasks.

Problem was, they really didn't need me.

And so I was left trying to find ways to kill the hours between eight thirty and five thirty. At first it was tough. But after a while, I got good at it. So good, that I began spreading the "No work at work" news to anyone (outside of *Family Circle*, of course) who would listen. Ultimately I developed a patent-pending list of ten ways to pass the work day. Yes, you have my permission to use them.

Suzy's Top Ten Ways to Pass the Workday

1. *Exercise*

I have a confession to make: I'm a fitness freak. The whole time I was a "powerhouse" marketing pro, I taught kickboxing classes at night. As you can imagine, being stuck at work pretending to do my job left me little time to prepare my routines, so I did what any reasonable human being would do: I put my staff through my sets. I dragged them into my office and got them jabbing, jogging in place, high kicking, lunging, and leg lifting. At the end of one month, we'd lost a collective twenty-five pounds and sixteen pairs of pumps. If I'm ever a marketing director again, I'm putting a line for Reeboks in the budget.

2. *Manage Your Minibar*

If you've got a big job, chances are you've got a big office. And if you've got a big office, you've probably got a refrigerator. Sure, you could let staffers keep their stinky leftover chipotle salads in your sweet KitchenAid, or you could do your entire team a favor and keep it stocked with fine wine, lite beer, fruit, cheese, and chocolate. After all, what's more important—tuna that hasn't turned, or the chance to get buzzed after a big meeting? Right. Now send your assistant out for ice.

3. *Decorate*

Nothing says "I'm too busy to bother with bullshit" like a hammer in your hand. Shop the Pottery Barn catalog for wall vases, mirrors, and paintings of oversized poppies, then spend a good portion of each day putting them up.

And taking them down. And moving them to a different spot over your desk. And calling office services to work their magic patching the wall. If this tome teaches you nothing else, let it be this: Those who don't want to deal, decorate.

4. Clean

Cleaning works almost as well as fussing with your furnishings, only here your weapons are a box of Clorox wipes and a bottle of Windex. The combination of those two acrid aromas will keep most bosses at bay. Throw in the sight of you scurrying around with a Swiffer and a DustBuster, and I can almost guarantee that entire fiscal periods will pass before you're forced to make a meeting.

5. Plan a Party

We've all heard of bosses who spend all day online planning their weddings. Or their parents' fiftieth anniversary party. Or their boyfriend's "Finally Sober!" soiree. Big whoop-dee-do. The party to plan and throw is an office party for those who work for you. After all, they're doing your job. Or at least my staff was doing mine. So the least I could do was order several cases of La Crema chardonnay, five hundred dollars' worth of food, and a DJ. Once every six weeks. Oh, and I had a disco ball installed in the conference room ceiling. Just my way of saying thanks for their willingness to hustle.

6. Attend a Pretend Power Lunch

The pretend power lunch is a terrific way to shoot almost an entire workday. Why? Because it starts midmorning and doesn't end till almost dinnertime. At about eleven a.m., you stop what little you're doing to organize your brief-case. First you ask your assistant to find certain Important Files. Since they don't really exist, this will cause a bit of a ruckus, and soon everyone will be rushing about, trying to help you "get to your lunch on time!" After thirty minutes or so, you say, "Forget the files," you'll muddle through without them, and head to the ladies' room to touch up your makeup. Twenty-five minutes later you emerge, re-freshed and fabulous. You grab your coat, bag, and empty briefcase, tell your assistant you could be "gone a while," and hail a cab. Fifteen minutes later, the nice ladies at the St. John store are fawning all over you, taking your lunch order and your measurements. Three hours after that, you check your "CrackBerry," return a few e-mails, then text your team to say you're heading home with a migraine. Sure, the power lunch was bogus. But the headache's real. Waiting for a seven-hundred-dollar skirt to be altered is enough to give anyone an aneurism.

7. *Catch up on Your Reading (aka, "I'm working on the budget")*

The budget was the one part of my job I didn't give away. And that's because I didn't actually do it. My business manager did. Twice a month my financial guru and dear friend Marilyn would stroll into my office, plop a spread-sheet on my desk, and point out the ways in which she'd once again saved my bacon. "OK, you've blown through your sales materials budget," she'd say, "but you had thirty-five thousand stashed in presentations, and another fifteen thousand in in-store promotions, so I moved money around and you're golden again." Of course nobody knew it was this simple,[4] so I was able to use "working on the budget" as an excuse to hide behind my frosted-glass double doors and spend half the day devouring multiple issues of *Cosmo* and massive amounts of peanut M&M's.[5]

8. Take a Meeting

This might sound suspiciously like work, but you don't really do anything. Other people do. Simply schedule all the Web site developers, ad agencies, and public relations firms,[6] the sales incentive companies, point-of-purchase display makers, caterers, and party planners who bombard you twenty-four/seven with their phone calls, postcards, sales brochures, and e-mail blasts to come in on the same day and make their pitch. Politely pretend to listen, take the occasional note, and say such insightful things as "I really don't see what use a consumer magazine has for a refrigerated truck, but tell me, is your top Tahari?" You won't buy anything, but you might be sold on several new designer brands by the close of business.

9. Watch a Movie

This was one of my favorite ways to waste time. Why? Because I was expected to do it. In order to conduct one of our most successful Big Programs, Family Circle Family Movie Night (to which readers were invited to sneak pre-

---

4. It was also simply wonderful of her. Thank you, M!

5. In case you're wondering, the day after budget day was typically "exercise in the office" day.

6. When I was really bored, I'd book a full day of meetings with public relations firms. Nobody knows the hot restaurants, clubs, nail polish colors, local movie shoots, up-and-coming fashion designers, and chic boutiques like the chain-smoking JAPs, sorority sisters, and social X-rays who run these outfits. A few hours with them is worth more than a month of *New York* magazine.

views of brand new movies), someone had to screen the features first. And that someone was me. Most of the time I got to see the film under consideration.[7] But other times, when the film wasn't finished, I was forced to see the movies it was compared to. "It's like *Scary Movie* meets *Titanic*," said my contact at one of the major movie studios, "only it takes place on a plane." When this happened, I'd have them send me copies of both films on DVD, as well as the shooting script. Then I'd whip up some microwave popcorn[8] and settle in for a four-hour film festival. The best part was hearing my assistant tell callers, "Sorry, Susan's tied up today. She's greenlighting a picture for Paramount."

10. *Take Your Team on a Field Trip*

When you work in a city like New York, your field trip options are endless. And when your job is marketing director for a major magazine, a huge part of your position is finding fabulous client gifts. Sure, I could've shopped solo, but it's much more fun with friends. So every now and again I'd schedule a team field trip day and we'd all take off to places like Bliss or the Avon Spa. After all, you can't confidently recommend a four-hundred-dollar sea salt pedicure and complimentary fruit platter if you haven't actually sampled it yourself.

Now, I don't know about you, but I can only go so long feigning enthusiasm for something. And after three years I was exhausted from pretending to give a damn about beat-

---

7. Don't get excited. We're talking *The Brothers Grimm*, not *The Godfather*.

8. In my own, personal microwave. OK, so it was cushy to be the queen.

ing *More* for the Almond Board business, and casting about for ways to steal the Catfish Farmers schedule from *Cooking Light*. It didn't matter how much money I was making or that I was dripping in Donna Karan (and tripping in my ridiculously high Manolos); I was miserable.

The commute from my home in New Jersey was killing me. The filth and noise and general madness of my beloved Big Apple were killing me. The only reason I got up and went to work every day was to see my staff. Otherwise I was so beat from faking it, I could barely get out of bed in the morning.

I just wanted to stay home.

Why, when my house is about as relaxing as a trip to the dentist, I have no idea. But I did.

Chapter Two

THE ONLY GRASS THAT'S GREENER IS THE STUFF YOU'RE SMOKING

You know the old expression "The grass is always greener on the other side"? Well, that's how it was with me and being home. I'd climbed the corporate ladder for so long, my calves were killing me.[9] I no longer gave a crap about cracking the glass ceiling. I simply wanted to go home, stare at my own ceiling, and maybe even give it a fresh coat of paint.

Obviously I was at DEFCON 4 on the sleep-deprivation scale, or else I'd have realized that being in my house all day—available to root for my writer husband ("Go, honey! Finish that book!"), help with homework ("Go, honey! Finish that 'new' math worksheet I've no clue how to do!"), play with my sons, maybe even join the PTA—was just the twenty-four/seven version of what it was like to come home to it every night. And that was not pretty.

Like millions of working moms, I came in from the office each evening to a house that looked like horses in

---

9. Sure, a break from heels would've helped, but nothing says "Out of my way! That big office with the full bath is mine!" like stilettos and a skirt.

digestive distress blew through. (Look at that. A little farm foreshadowing. I never realized it until now.) And while I'd never assume others respond as I do to anything,[10] particularly something as personal as a mess that's spread like a rash from room to room, I refuse to believe I'm the only mother in America ever to do what I call the Clean Sweep.

Starting in the kitchen, I wipe down the counters, cleaning off crumbs from breakfast and lunch, and wonder, "If I saved them up for a week, then used them to coat chicken cutlets, would anyone be the wiser?" Deeming this idea too *Mommy Dearest*, I turn my attention to the dishes in the sink and escort them to the dishwasher *next* to the sink. It takes ten seconds tops, but I guess between leaving the sports section strewn about (my husband) and setting up and abandoning every board game they've got (my kids), nobody else could find the time.

Warming to my mission, I sail into the dining room, where I tuck the chairs into the table (yet another task only Mom can tackle), check the centerpiece for tennis balls (why must they use the decorative accessories for slam dunks?), and scoop a mound of crumbs from my husband's spot. (Frankly, that cutlet idea may have some merit.) Pleased with my touch-ups, I turn to the living room and stop cold.

You know the other old expression "The lights are on, but nobody's home"?[11] Welcome to my world. Every lamp

---

10. I mean, anyone who comes up with a list of the top ten ways to pass the workday and not one of them is *work* isn't exactly normal.

11. I swear, I'll stop with the old expressions. . . . Soon.

in the room is ablaze. The TV is on at a deafening decibel. Soda cans and snack packages clutter the coffee table. Small green army men line the arms of the loveseat, and every pillow in the room has been recruited to make a barracks for "the boys." Crumbs dot the carpet. A teaspoon peeks out beneath the kick pleat on the couch. And my family is nowhere to be found.

For a moment I simply stand there, stunned by the mess before me. And then I do what any normal mom would do. I completely flip out. Five seconds into my outburst, all three men in my life have surfaced and are scrambling to secure their toys (lest I toss them in the trash); turn off the television (lest I remove the batteries from the remote, permanently nixing the sports night they planned); and generally clean up the newspapers, leftover junk food, and other assorted flotsam they've flung everywhere. They're moving at a good clip, which is pretty impressive, but you know what's even more amazing? Not one of them can understand what I'm so upset about.

This same scenario took place every night, so why I wanted to be home, I have no idea.

Except that I liked my home. And I missed my kids. And sometimes, when I wasn't so ticked at my husband for launching his literary career before I could launch mine, I actually missed him, too.

I hadn't always worked in the city. For ten highly profitable but natural light–free years I worked in our basement as a copywriter, churning out headlines and taglines for some of the biggest brands in the country. Schick. Redken. Tetley. Purina. MasterCard. Maybelline. Dove. Duracell. It was as much fun as you could have and still call it work. I was at it seven days a week, fifty-two weeks a year. At home. During the holidays. In hotels. I loved the rush of finding the right words. Or, more to the point, the right three-to-five words.

Copywriting is a lot like that old game show, *Name That Tune*.[12] Remember how the contestant who could name the tune in the least amount of notes won? Well, copywriting works the same way, only with words. The copywriter who can make the consumer respond—in five words or less[13]—is the one who works.

And I guess I was pretty good at it, because I was always working.

I cranked out taglines for Sunlight Dishwashing Liquid from Disney World, and marketing plans for Colonial Homes from Hilton Head. I wrote an entire ad campaign for Liz Claiborne's men's line from my cousin Lisa's beach house in Long Branch, and drafted a series of sweepstakes headlines for Heinz on a plane bound for Houston. No matter where life took me, I took my laptop. Hell, I even racked up billable hours from my bed in the maternity ward at Hackensack University Hospital. I checked in, had Cuyler, and then, between feedings, crafted a brand new advertising strategy for Children's Claritin allergy medication. (Frankly I think the Percocet they gave me for pain improved my performance, but let's not let *that* get around.)

---

12. If you're too young to remember *Name That Tune*, put this book down. Now. Go turn on *Total Request Live*, or better yet, take a *CosmoGirl* "Battle of the Boys" survey and let me know how Drake Bell does.

13. Some of my all-time favorite taglines that I didn't write include: Nike's "Just Do It," Motrin IB's "We've Got Your Back," and Cotton Incorporated's "The Fabric of Our Lives."

Speaking of maternity, this might be a good time to tell you about my sons. I have two. Casey,[14] the eldest, was born the year before I launched my business. Cuyler[15] was born seven years later, at the height of its success. I'm not joking when I say that I had the kid on a Monday and was back at my desk on Thursday. My poor doctor really didn't want to release me (like Case, Cuy was a "C," which meant the health insurance gods granted me permission to stay in the hospital a whole twenty-four extra hours), but the twice-daily bedside FedEx deliveries finally forced him to.

So there's seven years between my kids, and twelve between me and the old man. That would be my husband, Stu. He was on his way to being a Master of the Universe when we got married—you know, big job, big office, big bucks—and then sometime after Casey was born he decided he really wanted to stay home and be . . . Hemingway. Of course, he's not exactly like Ernest. He doesn't drink (at least not to excess) and he doesn't play with guns (he uses them only to scare chickens from window boxes and "off" rabid foxes, but really, the farm stuff's coming in a sec, I swear. . . .). And while he likes cats, he accepts the fact that he's limited to three (and not forty-three).

I've got lots of nicknames for him besides Hemingway. Sometimes I call him Corky or Mac, which are relatively self-explanatory. But other times, like when I'm annoyed at

---

14. Named for Casey Stengel, Hall of Fame baseball player and former Yankees manager.

15. Named for Hazen "Kiki" Cuyler (pronounced Kyler), the Hall of Fame baseball player who hit the winning home run for the Pirates in the 1925 World Series. Just call me Saint Susan.

the mess he's left me in the bathroom, he's the Dean of the Directionless Discharge, and the Titan of Urinary Untidiness. Not exactly pet names for public consumption, but you get my drift. And he leaves me his. Which is how this whole thing started.

Most of the time, though, he's simply hon.

As in "Hon, the recession decimated my copywriting business. And since we still want to pay the mortgage and eat more than macaroni and cheese, I'd better hightail it back to magazine marketing for whoever will pay me the most. Did you hear me, hon?"

That's actually what happened. In February 2001 my billing was so far down, I knew something was up. As it turned out, the entire country was nose-diving into a recession. And that terrible, splattering sound you heard as the economy connected with the ground? That was my business.

By May, one of my three top accounts folded. Another laid off ninety percent of its employees. And my largest account, the one worth just under a hundred grand for each of the previous four years, pulled everything in-house. I think I billed them seven thousand big ones in '01. OK, I know that's all it was; a fact like that you never forget. No matter how much sangria you swill.

Hon and I cut out the extras: highlights and haircuts and dinners out and magazine subscriptions and Netflix memberships and weekends away and any kind of credit card with a usage fee over five dollars. Our goal was simple: make the mortgage, and keep the kids in Ridgewood's five-star school system.

In July my hair began falling out and panic attacks set

in. We'd blown through our cushion and were borrowing against our life insurance; I knew it was time to bite the bullet and go back to the Big Apple.

And all I wanted from my first day there was to come home. To my messy house. My hon. My boys. My basement.

Take Suzy's Clean Sweep Survey!

You didn't actually think I could end this chapter on such a sappy note, did you? Trust me, that is so not my style. Oh yes, poor me. I hated working in the city. I wanted to come home. It was such a hardship earning in the high six figures during a frigging recession. Please. Somebody slap me. The toughest part about being at *Family Circle* all day was pulling cleaning duty all night. And since I know I'm not the only wife and mom tagged with that task, the real question is, do you do the Clean Sweep too?

- **First comes the cramping** . . . The Clean Sweep comes on like a contraction the minute you walk in the door. Which might not be so bad if you could just arrange for an epidural during your commute.[16] The key is that your husband and kids have been running amuck sans adult supervision, and the pain upon viewing the destruction is akin to being at ten centimeters on two Tylenol.

- **Assess your risk** . . . The Clean Sweep is triggered by the dynamic duo of marriage and children. If you've checked both these boxes there's a good chance you frequently wield the family-size bottle of Fantastik and a jumbo-size roll of Bounty. With one hand.

16. Note to auto manufacturers: Now, *this* is a little something to make standard.

• *'Til death do you dust bust . . .* If you're married and your husband is like mine—his idea of straightening up the kitchen is putting the newspaper in the recycling pile, he thinks he's tidied the bathroom simply because he put the toilet seat down, and his approach to making the bed means pulling the duvet up over the dog—you do the Clean Sweep.

• *Congratulations, it's a wrecking ball (er, boy)!* If you've got kids and your kids are like mine—their backpack contents cover the entire top of the bed; their toys overtake every room in the house; their bathing habits rival those of Charlie Brown's old pal Pigpen; and they possess the ability to scarf down every snack food in the fridge in less than fifteen minutes and leave the empty containers in such far-flung locales as in the closet, beneath the bed, in dresser drawers, and my personal favorite, under the pillow—you do the Clean Sweep.

• *Prognosis:* The Clean Sweep is not a particularly debilitating ailment, though it can be painful for family members who find themselves in the sufferer's path.

• *Treatment & Support:* Believe it or not, fellow Clean Sweep sufferers, you can learn to curb your clutter-conquering tendencies and embrace the mess your loved ones leave you like a gift. And you can do it all without a prescription. Simply join your local Clean Sweep Support Group. It's completely anonymous, so when you tell them (as one woman I know did) that your kids typically join the cat in using the sandbox as a Portosan, and that their idea of rainy day fun is freeing the hamster in the house, then following its feces to find it, you don't need to further embarrass yourself by providing your name. We know who you are. You're one of us. One of the millions of harried moms desperate to step off the treadmill of tidiness. To welcome the chaos you come home to. To learn to find joy in the jumble, relaxation amidst the mayhem, delight in the disarray. And a recipe for those crumbs you've been collecting. Cutlets, anyone?

A note from the blonde in the boonies:
Hold onto your $2,600 Louboutin bag.
It's gonna be a bumpy ride.

Now that our relationship's a little further along and you've put up with my kvetching about work and commuting and cleaning, and alluding to chickens, cows, and rabid foxes for a bit, it's time to tell you how, in the space of a single Sunday afternoon, I went from hotshot (but miserable) marketing chick to counterfeit farm girl.

If I'm honest, I have to admit that my descent from publishing diva to reluctant pasture princess didn't actually occur in the prick of a cattle prod (because nothing—other than a pimple; cold sore; or jumbo jet–size hive the day of your huge job interview, date, or photo shoot for the book jacket of your first book—happens *that* fast), though it sure did feel like it. But you know what? I just don't feel like being all that honest.

I feel like bitching about the bill of goods my guy sold me, blowing things out of proportion, and pouting. (Admit it: Sometimes nothing satisfies like a good pout.) But before I get ahead of myself, I invite you to see for yourself what happened next.

Ready? Kick off your Tod's, pull on a pair of Timberlands (or don't; God knows I won't), and come with me back to August 2004. . . .

Part Two

SUZY IN STICKSLAND

Chapter Three

"DARLING, I LOVE YOU, BUT GIVE
ME PARK AVENUE. . . ."

"*It looks like Nathaniel Hawthorne's house.*"

We were standing side by side, staring at a red, four-square-style farmhouse with a white porch, situated on a five-hundred-acre beef cattle farm, when my husband, aka Hemingway, aka hon, aka Mr. History, pulled that little factoid out of his well-read head.

"Don't you think?" he prompted, with a grin so wide my hackles shot straight to the skyscraperless sky. "Sue, don't you think it looks just like Nathaniel Hawthorne's house?"

Now, how the hell would I know what Nathaniel Hawthorne's house looked like? If it was featured in *In Style Home*, I might have a fighting chance of having this chat intelligently. But alas, it hasn't been, and frankly I'm a little out of the whole "birthplace of American literary giants" loop.

"I see Nate didn't have any neighbors," I cracked.

"That's part of its country charm," continued my bizarrely ebullient better half. "It's quiet."

"Quiet? It could be the setting for the *In Cold Blood*

sequel." Was he kidding? Except for our conversation and the occasional moo, it was as silent as a toddler in a Benadryl-induced nap.

"Don't be so dramatic, Susan. It's peaceful, not desolate. Don't you remember we talked about this?"

You know how some people can recall a conversation verbatim? Well, I'm not one of those people. Unless it's something life-or-death, like whether I'll be getting a $35,000 bonus and stock options, or a $45,000 bonus and company car. That conversation you can bet I'll recall (and I'll hold you to it, too).

But when it's something like my husband droning on and on about some trip to Home Depot that he needs to make to buy mulch or fertilizer or primer or pipe or caulk, and I just don't give a crap, you can bet I won't remember a word of it. Except maybe that he said he was going to a store, and that I wondered if there was a Starbucks nearby.

So as far as the accuracy of the conversation I'm about to recount to you goes, on a scale of one to ten, I'd give it a seven, which is pretty good because, as you'll see, the subject matter is rather weighty. Having said that, you'd think I'd recall it word for word. But I don't. This either means I've repressed it, or I'm stereotypically blond enough to make big life decisions without paying too much attention to the details.

Hmm. That sounds about right.

Anyway, what I remember most about the day I decided to give up my high-profile, high-paying, headache-inducing position in magazine publishing; sell my lovely home in suburban Ridgewood, New Jersey; put six hours' driving between myself and my mother; and wrest my kids from their best friends (and me from mine) to follow my crazy husband into, of all things, farming, is that it was brilliantly sunny. Just the kind of cloudless, happy day I adore. The kind that makes me want to drop the top on the Mustang and drive to the mall for a little shopping, a little lunch, a makeup session, and a manicure. What can I say? I'm just an outdoorsy kind of girl.

On this particular perfect shopping day, we'd left the boys with my mom and driven to no-man's-land, aka Upperville, Virginia, where my husband hoped I'd finally buy the lifestyle change he'd been pitching for three years.

"But there's no people, no stores, no hair salons, and no Starbucks," I pouted.[17] "What part of that description doesn't scream *Deliverance* to you?"

"Would you stop with the movie references already?"

"Don't talk to me about movies. I bet there isn't a theater for thirty miles." One hundred and thirty miles was probably more like it. And from the looks of things, there was an excellent chance it would be one of those wretched dollar theaters that showed *Shrek* and other, non-first-run family films, seven nights a week. What were we going to do for entertainment? Tip cows? It was time to go for the jugular. "What if we can't get cable? How will *you* survive without *The Sopranos*?"

"We'll get a satellite dish."

Hmm. I hadn't thought of that. A massive satellite dish

---

17. I have a confession to make: I'm a pouter. Not all the time, of course. Just when it suits my purpose. And when kicking my four-inch heels and cursing is overkill.

just might make my death by cinematic starvation a little less painful. "A plain one, right?"

"What do you mean?"

"One without Mary or Jesus painted in the center. You know, like we saw in Pennsylvania."

"I didn't see that."

What is it with men and eyesight? They can't see dust bunnies. They can't see billboards. But beer in the back of a packed refrigerator? That they can see. "Then I guess you didn't see the GOT GOD? signs in West Virginia, either."

"We passed a sign that said GOT GOD?"

"Four of them." I paused and looked at my husband, who had finally taken his eyes off the innumerable farm buildings, all of which were painted the same red hue that graced Nate's Place, the rolling fields, and the huge black cows mooing and pooping wherever they damn well pleased, long enough to look back at me.

"You're exaggerating," he said, still smiling like we'd just hit the lotto jackpot or were at a huge party—a huge, people-free party, I should add—in our honor.

"I'm telling you, Toto, we're not in New Jersey anymore."

"And here I thought that was the plan."

This is probably a good time to tell you about The Plan.

After the recession claimed my business, and the terrorist attacks on the World Trade Center and the Pentagon claimed the lives of thousands, Hemingway and I put The Plan in place.

Phase one involved my going back to work in magazine marketing. Not something I really wanted to do, but since I enjoy feeding my family and prefer not to be on a first-name basis with bill collectors, I took one for the team and accepted the first job I was offered.

I was one of the lucky ones; I landed the position I've been bellyaching about at *Family Circle* because a million years before I was a copywriter, I was a marketing director.[18] People knew me. And for some reason, they liked me. In no time I was commuting into New York City and life was back to normal.

Kind of.

Sure, I traipsed through Ann Taylor on my lunch hour, held meetings over manicures, and ducked out for facials whenever I felt I could get away with it. But I was always looking over my shoulder, jumping at the sound of a truck backfiring, and breaking into a sweat at the sight of a jumbo jet soaring overhead. In short, I was scared.

Phase two of The Plan involved just one thing: selling the house we'd worked so hard to hold on to, and getting our family of four out of what we called the Tri-State Target Zone. There were some parameters, of course: Wherever we wound up had to have good schools for our sons, Internet access, and a Starbucks.[19] And so, with those rather broad specifications settled, we began to look around.

Thirty-six months later, we'd researched every facet of every town in every state in the continental U.S. We knew

---

18. Right before I launched my writing business I held the top spot at *Popular Mechanics*. Laugh if you want, but I loved that job. A half-dozen good-looking sales guys, annual meetings in Miami Beach, and monthly features on THE NEW FLYING PORSCHE! REALLY! COMING SOON TO A SKYWAY NEAR YOU! Serious fun and a six-figure paycheck. What's not to like?

19. Frankly, "OK" schools would have been fine, but there was no way I was going without my morning mocha.

which high schools scored highest on the SAT, and which fielded the best football teams. We knew which elementary schools offered Japanese as a language option, and which actually took kids to the Land of the Rising Sun. We knew if the banking, dining, and shopping pickings in a particular area were plentiful or pitiful, and you can bet I knew its Starbucks status. We even knew which towns had a five-to-one church-to-tavern ratio, and knew we'd never fit in. What we didn't know was where we wanted to move.

"Earth to Susan," Hemingway teased, snapping his fingers in my face. "Please tell me you're thinking how unbelievable it is that there's a fox practically in front of us."

He was right. What looked like a small red dog was making its way across the field dead ahead. Studying it, I suddenly flashed in horror at the memory of a fox wrap my brothers and I bought my mother one year for her birthday. I was ten at the time, too young to understand that not only was a dead black fox with rhinestone eyes not the height of fashion; it probably freaked the hell out of the poor woman. In any case, I didn't think it was related to this fellow. But I didn't want to find out.

"To be honest," I said, "I was thinking we should look around a little longer."

"Three years isn't long enough?"

"Well, maybe there's another house someplace else with . . . people . . . and maybe a Panera Bread . . . and a Designer Shoe Warehouse. You know, I didn't see a single DSW on the way down here. And they say Southern women are so chic."

"Enough looking. It's time to pull the trigger."

"Wonderful. We're not in the country five minutes and you're ready to go gun shopping."

"I'm ready to make a decision, and I say we try it. Just until Doug retires, twenty-four months tops. If we're not happy then, we'll move."

Doug, in case you're wondering, is Stu's older brother. Doug is wildly successful, a scratch golfer, and he tells the kind of fabulous, funny stories that make me want to kill myself for not having a life like his. And I don't mean "Once upon a time" type stories. I mean the kind of stories that start, "So, I was having dinner with [insert name of major movie-studio head here] at [insert name of fabulous four-star restaurant on the East or West Coast here], when suddenly [insert name of famous late-night television show host, hotshot NFL quarterback, best-selling author, or MLB franchise owner here] walks in, joins us, and . . ." And blah, blah, blah. But you get the picture.

Like many of his ilk, my brother-in-law has the wherewithal to buy it all. And at the top of his shopping list is land. Lots and lots of land. Which of course has everything to do with how we came to be standing on this particular parcel, staring at Nate's Place and three additional empty tenant houses, plus the aforementioned innumerable farm buildings, an old grain silo, a spring house, and a smokehouse where I guessed they once cured ham and hoped I wouldn't be expected to do the same. What Doug wanted was to buy this farm and live on it upon his retirement. But as that was at least two years down the road, and an investment of this magnitude would require full-time management in the interim, he called his little brother and basically said, "Hey, you've been looking to move and I have a place that needs moving to. What do you think?"

And so here we stood, considering not just relocating from the burbs to the backcountry, but a whole new career for Stu, who'd be catapulted overnight, sans experience, into the world of farm management of this and Doug's other, "smaller" estate,[20] Oakfield.

"Your brother realizes you're a writer and not a farmer, right?"

"I'll learn."

"And what'll I do?"

"I don't know what you will do, but I know you *won't* have to commute to New York anymore."

"Farewell fabulous *Family Circle* paycheck and 401(k) plan."

"And two-hour bus rides, occasional anthrax scares, and subways that smell like feces."

"Please. I wouldn't use scent in your sales pitch right now. I'm not sure the grass agrees with some of the 'girls.'"

"I kind of like the smell."

"You didn't when you had diaper duty."

"Did I tell you there's nearly fifty acres that's just woods? And the other four hundred and fifty are filled with streams and ponds. The boys are going to love this place."

For Pete's sake. Did he actually mean *our* sons? "You mean the boys who don't play on the quarter acre we have now? Whose idea of open space is an available TV on which to hook up the PlayStation? Casey is going to take one look at Nate's lonely abode and these rolling hills and hyperventilate. God, I hope they have 911 out here."

"Oh, come on. I think Nate's Place is kind of quaint."

---

20. Only ninety acres. Boo hoo.

"I guess it does have a certain je ne sais quoi."[21]

"It's a hundred and ten years old."

"Older than you. Who knew such a structure existed?" I paused. "Please tell me it has indoor plumbing."

"And an eat-in kitchen."

Now, this was a surprise, and a plus in the Nate's Place column. We didn't have an eat-in kitchen in our house in Ridgewood, and I really, really wanted one. Not because I cook. I don't. I prefer to order dinner and have it delivered, a little talent I perfected while pregnant with Cuyler, going so far as to call in a three-hundred-dollar order for Chinese take-out Christmas morning, just eleven days after the kid's birth, and serving it to my very shocked Irish-Italian family for dinner. To this moment, the memory of the "What, no lasagna and meatballs?" look on my three brothers' faces is one of my favorites. But I digress. I wanted an eat-in kitchen because I was sick of eating every single meal in the dining room. I might not have minded as much if our antique chairs weren't the world's most uncomfortable seats this side of the electric chair, but they are. And my heinie has had it with them.

"An eat-in kitchen? Now, that I'd love to see."

"And I'd love to show it to you. Except Doug doesn't get the keys until the closing."

"And of course there won't be a closing, at least not one that involves him, if you don't decide to move here and manage the farm."

"That's right."

"And live in this house."

---

21. That's French for "farmhouse in the middle of fucking nowhere."

"You got it."

"The one I can't see until after I decide to move into it."

"That pretty much sums it up."

Unbelievable. We'd driven six hours to see the *outside* of a house. Had my husband never heard of photographs? Or did he think a camera wouldn't quite capture the "magic" of being there to watch a phalanx of turkey buzzards disembowel a groundhog?

I was seriously considering killing him (let's face it, it's not like anyone was around to stop me) and tossing his lifeless body to the aforementioned buzzards, when I realized his lips were moving. Fighting my way back from the brink of homicide, I heard words like "good-size rooms," "two full baths," and "the perfect spot for a piano," and it dawned on me that he'd actually been inside Nate's Place. Not that he wasn't past making a pigsty sound like a palace, but I knew he knew if he sold me on what was essentially a frat house, there'd be hell to pay.

"OK, OK," I said, unable to take his telemarketer-on-happy-pills patter a moment more. "The house is habitable. I get it. Just tell me the truth. How much work does it need?"

"Nothing I can't do myself."

"Deal breaker." Maybe he didn't recall the mess he made installing the Pergo floor in Cuyler's bedroom, but I did.

"We were close to a deal?"

"*Were* is the operative word."

"Alright, we'll hire a contractor."

"And who's going to manage the contractor while you're becoming Farmer Brown and I'm packing the house, showing the house, caring for the kids, and working?"

"Nancy."

Bingo! Now I knew Nate's Place had potential. My sweet sister-in-law had obviously assessed the renovating and decorating situation and deemed it worth doing. This was definitely another surprise plus in the "let's move to the country" column. What to do? I looked around. There were cows in my future front yard. But look at the size of that yard! The boys could get dirt bikes or ATVs, and I could toss the Play-Station into the huge pond in the corner of the property. The mere prospect pleased me so much, I smiled. And of course, Hemingway caught me.

"We're going to do it, right? Right?"

I couldn't breathe. I couldn't speak. A true rarity for me. So my future farmer plowed forward.

"Come on, Susan, you know you want to. We'll close in October, hire a contractor, and by the time you and the boys arrive in January, the job will be done."

The final glitch. I mean, who the hell works over the holidays? And contractor types, they work for four hours and then disappear for four days. But it was too late.

"Never happen," I said weakly.

"It'll be done."

"What if it's not?"

"We'll spend a few days at Oakfield."

I should've realized right then and there that my husband was born to live on a farm. 'Cause, boy, can he sling the bull.

Suzy's Top Ten Immediately Noticeable Differences
between the Sticks and the Suburbs

1. **No traffic.** This makes Hemingway happy. To me it just means there's no place to go.

2. **No Catholic churches.** No Jewish temples, either. If I discover lion farms, I'm going to freak.

3. **Lots of religious signage.** Don't Southerners know there are certain subjects you just don't discuss? Maybe secession wasn't such a bad idea.

4. **No malls, but a nice big Cabela's.** We're hurtling down barren Route 78 when suddenly this Mecca for outdoorsmen shoots up like the price of a pair of Pradas. Inside there are fully stocked ponds and stuffed bucks, an unsurpassed selection of blood-trailing spotlights, and "camouflage for the whole family!"

5. **Santa Claus Syndrome.** With their bristly mustaches, full beards, and immense bellies, a good percentage of Southern men bear a striking resemblance to St. Nick. It was Cuyler who brought this to my attention when he attempted to give his Christmas wish list to one of Mr. Ho Ho Ho's "helpers."

6. **"Honey, there are people on our property!"** It's OK, though; they're on horseback. And "hacking through" on your pricey steed is totally permissible. It's shambling across on foot that'll get you shot.

7. ***Folks speak really, really sloooooowly to me.*** Which makes me want to reach out and shake them, and shout, "I'm not retarded! I'm from New Jersey!"

8. ***No sidewalks.*** What, I'm supposed to speed walk through the meadow muffin–filled fields? That's just how I like my $200 cross-trainers; covered in cow crap.

9. ***Plenty of fireworks stands and adult video stores.*** Further proof there ain't a whole lot to do out here in the hinterland.

10. ***"Yes, ma'am. No, ma'am."*** Wham, bam, I'm going to pop the next person who calls me ma'am. How is it that making a woman feel ancient is what passes as Southern politeness?

Chapter Four

LIVING IN (E)STATE OF SHOCK

$\mathcal{I}$'m sure it comes as no surprise that not one, not two, but three weeks go by, and we're still in Virginia, and specifically at Nancy and Doug's weekend house, Oakfield. Not exactly the brief stopover somebody (eh hem, Hemingway) promised me, but I'll get to that shortly.

I've never actually lived in a house with a name, though had I given our Ridgewood home a moniker I might have called it, as my former neighbor and dear friend Lois did, Fort McCorkindale. Seems our extensive exterior lighting—comprising front, side, and back-door overhead fixtures, two strategically placed megawatt lampposts, and several motion-sensitive floodlights that were tripped on and off all night by raccoons rummaging through our garbage—enabled Lois, her husband, and their three kids to read in bed and find their way to the bathroom in the dead of night without ever flipping a single light switch. What can I say? When it comes to electricity, we're shockingly generous.

Of course calling my sister-in-law and brother-in-law's country home a house—weekend or otherwise—is akin to calling a BMW a car. The ultimate driving machine, meet the ultimate living quarters: Oakfield Estate.[22]

Simply put, Oakfield is like a palace, and my two princes have taken to it like rednecks to rifles. They've got their own room, their own bathroom, and a playroom outfitted with comfy furniture, a fridge, and a brand new flat-screen TV purchased just for their enjoyment. In addition, and as if they weren't bringing an entire Toys "R" Us with them, my sister-in-law ran out and got them sleds, CDs, DVDs, books, board games, and several supermarket aisles' worth of snacks. What does she get for her loving largesse? The opportunity to watch her wacky nephews send their brand-new remote-controlled race cars sailing off the landing atop her spectacular spiral staircase, through the middle of the crystal chandelier that probably cost more than we cleared on our house, and onto the imported marble floor in the foyer.

While I beat the boys, Nancy beat it back to McLean, which is where she and Doug reside (and at this point, hide) from Monday to Friday. Hopefully by the time they return next weekend we won't be here to greet them. Not that I don't want to see them; I'm just antsy to get my third-class kids out of their first-class house. We were only supposed to be here a week, which turned into two weeks, and

---

22. At this point, I feel it imperative to bring to your attention the fact that, around here, all the homes have names. Things like Seven Chin Grove and Old Maid Manse. Maybe it's my marketing mind working overtime, but I have to wonder if the people who own these places selected these particular names as some type of passive-aggressive promotion ploy. I mean, does an old maid actually live in the aforementioned manse? Do seven people named Chin—or one person with seven chins—live at Seven Chin Grove? And what am I to make of homes named Gold Hill Farm and Silver Mountain Manor? That Bronze Run is somewhere nearby, or just that each of these hundred-plus-acre estates is owned by spectacularly affluent former Olympians?

now, well, we're looking at a month, people. With any luck, by Friday we'll be in the refurbished and fabulous Nate's Place, which, contrary to my prediction, did not cause Casey to hyperventilate.

Instead he fainted.

We took the kids to see the farm during a driving snowstorm. Maybe not the best idea, but they were desperate to see their new home, and we were equally as desperate to get them out of Nancy and Doug's (if just for a short while), so we went.

Big mistake.

Everything was white. The trees and bushes and buildings and cattle. And of course Nate's Place. The only thing whiter was my tall, sweet, thirteen-year-old son's complexion when he stepped out of the car and saw for himself how far from suburbia we really were.

He looked from the snow-covered house to the snow-covered fields to the cows noshing on snow-covered hay for about ten seconds before he turned to me, mumbled what I think was "How could you do this to me, Mom?" and collapsed into a snowdrift. It was probably hearing his little brother lay claim to the video games that revived him ("If he's dead, I get the PlayStation, right? Right?"), though it might have been Hemingway pelting him with snowballs that did the trick. To be honest, I was only half paying attention, as I was busy looking around to see if a Starbucks had sprung up since the last time I'd seen the place.

No such luck.

I guess it was too much to expect that Casey would be excited to see the farm, especially since he was emotionally and physically exhausted from the drive down.

After making about two hundred trips in and out of our old house to pack the Durango (my car) and the Mustang (Hemingway's car), and waving good-bye to the massive moving truck containing all our worldly possessions, we got on the road sometime around nine fifteen. Hemingway had Cuyler, Inky the cat, and Jerry, the small hamster with the big stink. I had Casey, my coffee, a box of Kleenex, everything we could possibly need for our "few" days at Oakfield, and hunger pangs. What can I say? When I'm happy, I eat. When I'm miserable, I eat more. And since I hate to eat alone, I forced my eldest to join me.

Between the two of us we scarfed down four bagels, a package of Twinkies, twelve chicken strips, innumerable French fries, one large vanilla milkshake, two jumbo-size Three Musketeers bars, and a six-pack of Poland Spring water. And, just in case my driving buddy didn't find consuming all that junk food distracting enough, I challenged him to a rousing game of "spot the religious billboard," which, despite his matricidal state, he won quite handily.

Over the course of the trip, Casey caught all four GOT GOD? signs, spied several spiritually themed satellite dishes, including one Impressionist-style rendering of the Three Wise Men I totally missed the first time, and two obviously new placards that implored travelers to JUMP FOR JESUS! Six hours, four bathroom stops, and two big bellyaches later, we arrived at Oakfield.

As for the reason we're still here, well, it's very simple. Nate's Place isn't ready. Which of course I knew it wouldn't be. I love my husband, but he thinks everything takes fifteen minutes. "We'll close, hire a contractor, and boom, it'll be done." Might as well call in the mice that made

Cinderella's dress, dear, because you are living in fantasy land. Sure, the closing occurred in October, but we didn't find a contractor until sometime in November, and they didn't start ripping out the kitchen until late December. So the fact that it's February and Nate's Place is basically un-inhabitable really isn't a surprise.

What is a surprise is that I suddenly don't hear my sons. In my own house this would make me happy. But here at Oakfield it gives me hives. Last time they were this quiet I discovered Casey caressing the plasma screen TV in the den with his Rastafarian-length fingernails—why that boy won't use a nail clipper I'll never know—and Cuyler playing aquarium with his Aunt Nancy's $5,500 Herend dolphins. An improvement, I guess, over the day I found them playing hide-and-seek behind the custom Scalaman-dre drapes in the dining room, but not by much.

We need to get into our house before we wind up in the poorhouse. Because replacing whatever it is they just broke (the crashing sound followed by shouting, tears, and recriminations is a pretty good indication it's something pricey) is probably going to put us there.

Suzy's Oh-So-Brief Book of Estate Etiquette

The rich really are different, and they don't like that fact pointed out to them. So if you want to hang with the Cartier crowd, bite your tongue when the following bon mots threaten to tumble out.

Mind if I help myself to one of your dog's Fiji waters?

There are more pet beds in this place than we have people beds.

Are those Kohler fixtures in Secretariat's stall?

Six sinks and two dishwashers. You people must eat like pigs.

I think I went to college with your cleaning lady.

Did you get your flat-screen TV at Wal-Mart, too?

I've never seen so much cashmere in one closet.

Beige is a brave choice for a kid's bedroom rug.

You know, those Waterford Lismore goblets look just like Mikasa.

The only antique in my house is my mother-in-law.

That's a Stark carpet? Looks pretty luxurious to me.

Funny, I thought Oneida made French fries.

We've got a La-Z-Boy recliner that looks a lot like your Ralph Lauren.

Hey, we picked up that Picasso print, too! Posters.com, right?

Chapter Five

A TALE OF TWO TURTLENECKS

$\mathcal{L}$iving at Oakfield has not only been giving my sons a serious case of the DTs (as in "Don't touch!"), it also has me questioning my hip, New York–honed sense of style. Why? Because the dress code here in affluent horse country means the women wear one turtleneck *on top of* another.

Since I can't wear a single turtleneck without turning into a pool of perspiration before I even step out of my bedroom, the thought of wearing two starts me shvitzing[23] from my scalp to the soles of my feet.

From what I've seen among the social elite in my sister-in-law's circle, the first layer is always a crisp white cotton number. And the second one, the "show" turtleneck, is always something fabulous, like a periwinkle blue, apple green, or pale pink cashmere sweater.

Now this is a lovely look if you don't break into a sweat with every breath, as some of us older folk have begun to

---

23. That's Yiddish for sweating. Of course no one down here speaks Yiddish, and every time I say *schvitzing* they think I've said *shitting*, and I end up having to apologize and explain myself, and wind up once again wondering where the hell I am and how do I get home?

do, or if you don't mind being choked to death all day. Unfortunately I do, and I do. So while the style is rich and sophisticated, this is one time I'm glad to be poor and trashy (by comparison, of course).

I've noticed a few other questionable fashion favorites, as well. Like bright pink corduroys embroidered with lime-colored poodles, worn with a pair of four-hundred-dollar emerald green Gucci slides (with pink and green socks, I swear), and a navy blue cashmere crewneck. The whole ensemble probably set the woman wearing it back a thousand bucks. Money I would've suggested she spend on glasses, a personal shopper, and some fashion magazines, but that's just me.

Speaking of fashion magazines, it's as if no one around here reads them. Or even knows they exist, for that matter. I can find no other reason for the millions of women wearing too-tight khakis or, worse yet, "mom jeans"[24] paired with ballet flats, and accented with custom-made belts emblazoned with photos of their favorite horses and hounds.[25]

The other thing I've noticed is that the women around here like to wear riding pants. You know, the skintight, Lycra-like jobs that look a whole lot better on stick-figured eleven-year-olds and women with bodies like Angelina Jolie than on most adult females. My mantra is, "If you're not willowy, you shouldn't be wearing 'em!" Apparently,

---

24. Ankles exposed and so high at the waist you can rest your boobs on your belt. You know, for a little added support.

25. It's freaky how many women are walking around with pictures of their million-dollar mounts and rescued mongrels on their shoes, belts, and handbags. You've got to wonder if Seventh Avenue is aware of what's happening below the Mason-Dixon Line, and if there's anything they can do to stop it before it spreads.

though, I'm the only one of that opinion, as everywhere I look women of all shapes and sizes are parading around Middleburg[26] in riding pants so snug they appear ready to pop off and blind anyone walking behind them. I'm also of the opinion that going blind would be a blessing if that happened.

Needless to say, in my low-rise, boot-cut jeans, spike-heeled black boots, and endless, straight-from-working-in–New York City selection of sweaters, tees, and tops also in basic black, I stick out like a sore thumb. And you know how I hate to stick out.[27] I like to fit in, be part of the crowd, just another one of the girls. You know where this is going, right? No, I didn't try to squeeze my ample Italian ass into a pair of riding pants. But I did, however, attempt to wear two turtlenecks.

Yes, I, the Sultana of Sweat, the Princess of Perspiration, and my husband's favorite, the Mistress of the Instantaneous Migraine, got it into my obviously empty head that I should try to step it up style-wise and go for all the *Town & Country* class I could muster. This in turn led to the Great White Turtleneck Search—as I only possess two

---

26. The equestrian capital of the country and favorite haunt of Jackie O., one of the few women in the world who looked primo in jodhpurs.

27. Calling Dr. Freud! This business of needing to fit in began when I was a kid. I had really, really, *really* light blond hair, and I took a ton of abuse for it. The popular girls, all nine-year-old brunet babes wearing bell bottoms and belly shirts and wielding watermelon-flavored Bonne Bell Lip Smackers, called me Suzy Claus and Whitey and occasionally Albino. This completely flipped me out, as I didn't know what an albino was. I ran home, looked it up, and promptly convinced myself they were right and I was going to spend the rest of my wretched light-blond life indoors. I didn't, of course, but I did use every cent of my allowance to buy scarves and hats to hide my freak-of-nature head. By the time I hit middle school, my collection was so extensive the local hospital called and asked if I'd donate it to their oncology department. I did, but only after my mom threatened to send me to self-esteem camp if I didn't.

items of white clothing, both of which are sweat socks[28]— which led to a trip to the Fun Shop.

Now, the Fun Shop is a small boutique bursting with all manner of lamps, picture frames, plates, placemats, throw pillows, martini glasses, coasters, wall calendars, wine carafes, funny cocktail napkins, clocks, kids' books, toys, hand towels, tablecloths, magnets, mints, soaps, bath salts, body lotions, paintings, plaques, planters, teapots, and of course women's turtlenecks.

Of course.

You wouldn't know this unless you shopped there with a local, so I dragged my sister-in-law along after confessing my desire to take a stab at this fashion feat. (Me: "What do you think if I try the two-turtleneck trick?" Nancy: "You? You can barely wear a bra beneath a T-shirt." Me: "You know what they say. When in Rome . . . " Nancy: "Yeah, wear riding pants." She paused. "OK, I'll help you with the turtleneck. But remember, we don't do jodhpurs.")

Half an hour later I was the proud owner of a bright white PB&J brand turtleneck, and a jumbo-size bottle of Excedrin, which we got at the Safeway across the street.

Ahh. I wasn't just going to have a headache. I was going to have an aneurysm. Time to confirm we're still covered by Blue Cross.

Matters of health insurance handled, I proceed to wear my new PB&Jer topped by a luscious chocolate brown

---

28. You thought I'd say bras, right? I'm a buff girl (buff colored, that is, not flapping-in-the-breeze free; you need actual breasts for that). White bras bother me. And women who wear them under peek-a-boo black tops should have their *Harper's Bazaar* subscriptions rescinded.

cashmere turtleneck Nancy gave me for my birthday. And in no time I'm in a full-on, hair-frizzing, makeup-melting, body-soaking shvitz the likes of which you'd expect to experience if you lived someplace really warm. Like the sun.

To make matters worse, if indeed there is anything worse than being able to quench your thirst by sucking on your sweater, I also began to choke from the garments' vice-like grip around my throat. No matter how I pulled and tugged and yanked and stretched the necks of both those shirts, they simply snapped right back—just like the Play-tex 18-hour girdle my grandma used to wear. The one that forced her spleen to the top of her spine.

I was about to black out into my breakfast when it came to me like a mild stroke that it didn't matter if I ever achieved *Town & Country*– or even *Southern Accents*–style sophistication. What matters is that I'm me. Blond, blue-jeaned, and black-topped, and able to give dead-on directions to the Stone Pony in Asbury Park while smashed on mojitos at the height of a hurricane.

What was I thinking wearing two turtlenecks so tight my skull was about to explode? And besides, if I want my head to pop off, I simply need to squeeze into a pair of riding pants. One glimpse at my butt in those babies and I'm certain to need a neurologist. Or at least two Excedrin.

Good thing I bought the big bottle.

Saturday Night's Alright for Sweatpants

My sweet, beautiful sister-in-law Nancy lives the life of my
dreams.

Last weekend she and Doug were out at a white-tie dinner with the President. And Dick Cheney. And Condi Rice.
And the guys who made JibJab. (Just kidding.)

To be honest, what got my attention was not whom she
was out with, but the fact that she was out. On a Saturday
night. Dressed like an adult in a dress, heels, hair, and
makeup. And where was I? Curled up on the couch at
Oakfield, in a pair of hot pink sweatpants bedecked with
red cherries and hearts and the words SPLASH OF LOVE
splashed across them everywhere. She's resplendent in
Ralph Lauren, and I looked like a mental patient dressed for
a party (at which the guest of honor was the ever lizardlike
Joaquin Phoenix in Ladder 49, and the menu consisted of
Klondike bars and beer).

Now, I'm not making fun of mental patients. They deserve to go to parties. But so do I.

Maybe if I encourage the kids to finish driving me mad,
Hemingway will institutionalize me. Then I can enjoy
some really red-hot Saturday nights at the asylum.

After all, I already have the outfit for it.

Chapter Six

COCKTAILS WITH CARMELA

$\mathcal{M}$y indoctrination into the lifestyles of the rich and rural continues to leave me feeling like I never should've left the Tri-State Target Zone. So what, I could be killed by terrorists? At least I'd die surrounded by friends, wearing a miniskirt, midcalf boots, and just one turtleneck, thank you very much. Up North I fit in. I could make cocktail conversation. And nobody cared that I sound like Carmela Soprano.

To be fair, folks in this neck of the woods don't make that big a deal of my regionalism. They simply hear me speak, slap their hands over their mouths (as if to prevent catching what's obviously a communicable communication disease), and burst out laughing. Once they get their breath, they usually say something sweetly Southern like, "My, but you do sound like that Mrs. Soprano, don't you!"

Yes, I do, and to my way of thinking it's a whole lot better than sounding like a six-year-old sucking on a helium balloon.

But moving on to my inability to make cocktail conversation.

Talking to total strangers is my forte, and I can land a new "best" friend in just under two martinis. But when the topic's drinking and deer hunting, like it was at a party Hemingway and I attended last weekend,[29] I have a tough time doing anything other than looking aghast.

"You need to absolutely, positively, outfit both your boys in bright orange parkas and ski pants during hunting season." This from a wiry-haired, makeup-free mom with a rock as big as one of my butt cheeks on her manicure-less left hand.

"Red's good too," added a short, hippy woman in a crushed velvet Juicy Couture tracksuit that had clearly never been paired with anything this side of a running shoe.

"Our kids wear yellow. Every year, yellow," yawned an exhausted-looking pregnant woman whose four Hanna Andersson–clad horrors were alternately crawling beneath the table and trying to decapitate the dog. "With black snow boots, so they look like bees," she concluded sleepily. "My husband keeps bees." If he also keeps birds, all bets are off.

"Let me see if I've got this straight," I interjected, covering my mouth a bit in a halfhearted attempt to soften the honking nasal sound Mrs. Soprano and I seem to share. "We grant permission to people to hunt on our land *and* we

---

29. We don't have any friends of our own yet, so Nancy and Doug drag us around to social events they've been invited to. This particular shindig, at a cozy little twenty-thousand-square-foot "weekend cottage" called Prosper Hill, was actually a Super Bowl party. Only none of the guys wore torn rock concert T-shirts or team jerseys with jeans (pastel yellow sweaters paired with dark-colored cords and loafers without socks were the preferred look), kept personal-size coolers at their feet, or even watched the game. In fact, they eventually ditched it in favor of golf. I don't get it. Sure, Tiger Woods is cute. But he's no Tom Brady.

have to outfit our kids in a particular manner to keep them from being mistaken for deer by some overserved marksman and shot?"

Lots of nods, serious looks, and nods. No one speaks, though. It's as if they've been beaten mute by my New Jersey–by–way–of–Brooklyn timbre and need time to recover. For a split second I stand there, not so much speechless as terrified of speaking and bursting blood vessels in the brains of my fellow party guests. Finally I err on the side of shutting the hell up (not something I'm good at, but I'm getting there), and sneak off in search of Hemingway.

"Unbelievable," I whispered when I found him at the bar, nursing some kind of fancy British lager (a tough break for a Budweiser guy). "We moved here to get away from the madness of Manhattan, only to risk getting popped on our own property. What do you think of my forming my own MADD spin-off called Mothers Against Drunk Deerhunters? You think any of those babes in there'll be board members?"

"Don't count on it, Carmela."

The death-by-deer-hunting diatribe was surpassed only by one woman's dissertation on the area's best private schools. There are several, and almost everyone we meet wants to know which institution of exorbitantly overpriced education our kids attend. You should see their faces when we state, proudly, that both Casey and Cuyler go to public school. They look at us like we're religious zealots denying our kids measles, mumps, and rubella vaccines, not to mention Internet access, video games, and the chance to spend every waking moment wearing khakis, but of course that's not what they say.

"You can get a very solid education in public school," said the wiry-haired mom with the diamond I'd willingly die for.

"My oldest, Robert, spent a full year at one before he went back to boarding school in Switzerland, and it didn't hurt him a bit," said the Juicy Couture chick.

"My husband went to public school," Preggers yawned.

Hmm. Private school may have some merit.

Of course the funniest conversation I had that day began with this simple query: "Do your kids ride?" To which I can only reply, How did I not know she meant horses?

Maybe I'd had too much wine. Maybe I was dumbfounded by the discovery that the sticks might be no safer than the suburbs. Maybe I was simply exhausted from trying to master a flat Midwestern accent on the fly. But when Juicy Couture asked, "Do your kids ride?" the only thought that came to mind is the one that came out of my mouth: "No. I make them take taxis. The subway's just too unsafe."

I guess if Juicy had been wearing jodhpurs I might have realized what she was referring to. But she wasn't, and I didn't, and the whole thing went from the sublime to the seriously insipid really quickly.

"I meant horses."

"Oh, sorry. Of course you did. I'm so used to riding the subway," I replied, my fingers making those stupid air quotation marks around the word *riding*. "But to answer your question, no, they don't. Yours?"

"Yes. My girls study at Miss Patty's over in The Plains.

Lots of boys train there, too. You might look into it for Casey and Cuyler."

"Maybe I will," I said, smiling hard and hoping my brilliant pearly whites made up for my sounding like a moll. "We're football people, though, you know?" I continued, "Tackle in the fall, flag in the spring, speed camps in the summer." I paused, waiting for her to say her son plays, too, or her husband's a diehard 'Skins fan, or something. Playing football, watching football, bitching about the Giants; that's all common conversation up North. So I'm figuring it'll work its magic and in just under a case of merlot (not my usual two-martini triumph, but I'll take it), I'll have made one of those best friends I was bragging about earlier. But no. She simply stared at me, her face a combination of disbelief and condescension. So I stammered on. "Stu[30] coaches, the boys play, and I'm in charge of ice packs."

"Isn't that dangerous?"

"Ice packs?"

"No, football," she practically spat, as if I used lead paint like mayonnaise in my kids' lunches. "So many players get paralyzed!"

And riding horses is safe? Hello? Anybody else remember Christopher Reeve?

Now I'm ticked. I'm working hard here to find some common ground. I'm doing my best "like me" dance. And I'm still a day late and a dollar short (make that a few million dollars short) for this chick. Juicy doesn't want to chat;

---

30. I try to remember to refer to Hemingway by his real name whenever I meet new people. This works well early in a party when I'm still sober, but later on it's often "Stu who?"

she wants to pontificate. Not something this Jersey girl and
her Carmela Soprano twang take kindly to. And so I let
her have it. Lock, stock, and two smoking North Bergen
barrels.

"Yeah, spinal cord injuries are the pits," I said, hitting
her with my best Valerie Harper–meets–Fran Drescher delivery. "But they're not nearly as frequent in football as they
are in riding. Horseback riding. Not riding the subway.
Don't want to make that mistake again! Although, you
know," I added, leaning in conspiratorially, and channeling
every ounce of Manhattan-meets-Moonachie melodious-
ness I can muster, "with the way those cars jerk back and
forth, sending people flying, I'm surprised there aren't more
broken necks." I pause to catch my breath and enjoy the fact
that she can't seem to get hers. "But really, when it comes to
football, it's so much safer than soccer or rugby or horseback riding. At least my boys are covered in pads. With serious helmets on their heads. Your kids are wearing what, a
hubcap? I've got to hand it to you, though. You Southern
gals don't raise no sissies!"

A direct hit. And all without Tony's (or even Hemingway's) help. I can't imagine we'll be invited back, but I
don't care. Kudos, Carm. You're now a made mom.

Hot News from Hicksville

TO: Friends & Family
FR: Starstruck Suzy
Date: Tuesday, 11:30 a.m.
Subject: Hollywood in the hinterland

Hey, all,

Who knew Virginia was a hotbed of Hollywood types? Certainly not me. I toiled for ages in New York City without ever seeing so much as a Rockette outside Radio City Music Hall, and now, just weeks into our Virginia adventure we run into Robert Duvall.

That's right, dining in the Rail Stop Café (an establishment, we've come to find out, he used to co-own) was Tom Hagen himself. You know, Marlon Brando's *consigliere* in *The Godfather*.

Hemingway, Casey, and I played it cool and kept the bumping into each other, whispering, furtive glances, and finger pointing to a minimum. Cuyler, on the other hand, completely flipped out. Seems he recognized Mr. Duvall from *Lonesome Dove*. He and Hemingway have been watching the miniseries on DVD, and Cuy's so completely enthralled that for a minute we feared the family madman would run up and bellow, "Did you *have* to kill your horse?"

To our great relief he simply stood there staring, then dashed to our table, where he threw a spectacular fit over the lack of French fries on the menu. We thought it was a particularly Oscar-worthy performance; one that earned him the not-so-coveted Swat on the Ass award. I don't think Mr. D. noticed, but as long as the maitre d' missed it there's always next time.

—Susan

Chapter Seven

TOSS ME BACK, I BEG YOU!

Between the bizarre cocktail party blather and the styles that pass for fashion around here, I find myself flopping around feeling like a fish out of water. The kids are doing fine; making friends, forgetting their homework, and generally showing us that the trauma of the big move is behind them. And Hemingway's gotten into his groove, too; attending cattle sales, lunching at the Livestock Exchange, and taking seminars on such curious subjects as manure management and cattle breeding basics.

Of the four of us, I'm the most adrift and disorganized. I've got a million things to do, and yet I often waste the day wandering around Oakfield, making lists, losing them, and trying to avoid the kitchen.

Not because the kitchen isn't gorgeous; it is. And not because it doesn't contain every gourmet goodie imaginable; unfortunately it does. It's just that it's home to the massive pile of (to my way of thinking) bad news Nancy and Doug devour on a daily basis.

OK, OK. I have a confession to make: I am not a newspaper reader. This probably doesn't come as a huge surprise, considering my background in magazines, but my preference for glossy pages has more to do with the fact that what's inside most women's books[31] is fluff, and what's inside most newspapers is hard, cold, frightening fact.[32]

Anyway, since we're still living with my brother-in-law and he's in the newspaper business, there's no escaping them. They're piled high on the kitchen table, competing with my kids to see what will kill the two-hundred-dollar, dry-clean-only, cream-colored tablecloth from Crème de la Crème first: crushed Count Chocula or newsprint.[33]

I do my best to dodge the myriad dailies that are delivered every morning, but sometimes, like today, we run head-on into each other over coffee and I catch a headline that sends me reeling.

Ready?

WHITE SUPREMACISTS SEEK RECRUITS. And I was worried there wouldn't be enough clubs here in cow country for my kids to join. Silly me. Who needs the Boy Scouts when you've got skinheads?

Or how about this one: PANEL RAISES PENALTY FOR DRUNKEN HUNTING. According to the article, it's now a Class One misdemeanor (punishable by a $250 fine and confiscation of your cooler) to get totally soused and run around with a rifle. (Whew. Not only is this good news on

---

31. Industry speak for magazine, because "magazine" simply takes too long to say. Thanks, MTV.

32. You know: death, destruction, and really bad news like they might close Bergdorf Goodman.

33. Go, newsprint! Go, newsprint! If my kids destroy one more thing in this pristine decorator show house we're calling home, I'm going to drown myself in one of the four lap pools masquerading as tubs.

a personal level, it's also the perfect conversational tidbit for the next cocktail party. *If* we ever get invited to one again.)

Frankly, the local newspapers are enough to keep me wondering what kind of world I've entered. But just to make sure I stay completely shell-shocked, Hemingway's subscribed to more than a couple of popular rural publications. His new favorite? A monthly manual called *Grass Farmer*.

Now I ask you, who the hell farms grass? You cut grass. You water grass. You fertilize grass. But farm it? And why didn't he tell me this was what he wanted to do? Had I known, we could have stayed in Ridgewood, stocked up on Scotts Turf Builder, and perfected the patch in front of our house. But no. We had to pack up everything we own and move to Two-Turtleneck and Too-Tight-Pants Land. All this just so he can farm grass? Maybe I should simply start smoking it.

The other tome he's tucked into lately is *Shotgun News*. Casey discovered this font of firearm intelligence, ammo, and camo ads at, of all things, the gun show. Yes, the gun show frequented by a bunch of weird Waco types wearing fatigues[34] and pretending to be in the military, and folks like my brother-in-law, Hemingway, and Casey, who know they're not in the military and wouldn't dream of costuming themselves to the contrary.

Even my husband's bedtime book reading has gotten bizarre. Right now he's alternately plowing through both *The Plot Against America* and *Storey's Guide to Raising Chick-*

---

34. That they probably bought at Cabela's.

ens. If I find he's stockpiling feed, I'll know for sure he's hatching a plan to use pullets[35] to take out terrorists.

I've got to hand it to Hemingway, though. For a Dumont boy whose closest contact with wildlife was the keg parties he hosted in high school, he's totally into this agriculture stuff. At this point he's read two years' worth of back issues of a magazine called *Progressive Farmer* and can speak knowledgeably about the best bull[36] for a small herd of cattle, essential tractor accessories,[37] and several "fabulous ways to freeze your garden's bounty!"[38] He's also attended a couple of seminars on something called rotational grazing,[39] mastered the ins and outs of cattle auctions (at which it seems you cannot bid on your favorite bovine if you're not wearing a John Deere or New Holland baseball cap, a mistake he'll never make again; he learned the hard way that his Giants cap doesn't cut it), and attended several farm safety and equipment-repair workshops at places like Tractor Supply.[40]

Sometimes I'll catch him late at night on his laptop, drawing up grand plans for Nate's Place. "The goal is to be totally organic and self-sustaining, Sue." "Uh huh, hon. Sure thing." (An even surer thing is that I've no clue what

---

35. A baby hen. Hemingway wants to raise his own poultry. I'm sticking with Perdue.

36. A bovine multitasker that can "service" the heifers and cows, and cut grass, too. Sounds like the poor boy's going to be beat. For a definition of *heifer,* see *cow* in the Impractical Girl's Guide to Farm Speak glossary.

37. Stuff like soil pulverizers, dirt scoops, and bale spears, but not a single pair of stilettos.

38. So I guess *he's* planting one.

39. A fancy phrase for "moving cattle from one field to another."

40. The Bloomie's of the boonies. Again, see the glossary.

he's talking about.) "We'll get chickens so we can have eggs, and you can plant a vegetable garden."

I can plant a vegetable garden? I'm unsure we've met. Hello, my name is Susan, and I'm a manicure addict.

"We're also going to get goats. They're tough to fence in, but the milk's great." Goat milk? OK, then. You tell the kids we're going goat. I don't want them smothering me in my sleep.

"What if we keep pigs," he continues, "and bees?"

"Sounds good," I reply, hopping into bed with the Pottery Barn catalog, a mega-pack of Post-it notes, and the memory of Cocktail Party Preggers flashing through my mind. (Thank God one of us had the good sense to get our tubes tied.) "We can grow honey-glazed ham!"

One patented McLook[41] later, I'm consumed by my catalog and several copies of *Coastal Living*. In addition, I've come to two conclusions: one, that as soon as Hemingway has this "self-sustaining" farm stuff out of his system we're moving to the beach, and two, if I still feel like a fish out of water on the water, it might be time to bite the bullet (and buy a bulletproof vest) and go back to the Big Apple.

---

41. A withering glance that conveys "Knock off the sarcasm" and "Don't be stupid" in a split second; as natural to the McBoys as breathing.

Saturdays in Suburbia vs. Saturdays in the Sticks

If my mentioning the gun show earlier got your attention, here are several other Saturday in suburbia vs. Saturday in the sticks comparisons that will really blow you away. Surprisingly, at least to me, I'm not completely anti–the country stuff. In fact there are several rural activities I prefer to their more cosmopolitan counterparts.

• *Car Show vs. Tractor Show*
Men in dress shirts and jeans, or men who dress prettier than I do? Hmm. I'm going with the guys in the jeans (and the John Deere–logoed baseball caps). They've got just as much money as the Brooks Brothers contingent at the car show, and some of those closed-cab Mahindras are as sexy as any Maserati.

Best way to spend a Saturday: Tractor Show

• *Seventh on Sixth vs. the Swineway Speedway*
One Saturday I'm applauding the collections at the annual fashion week in New York's Bryant Park; the next I'm cheering on a passel of squealing pigs racing around the Swineway Speedway at the Fauquier County Fair. The difference is night and day, blond and brunet, Balenciagas and work boots.

Best way to spend a Saturday: Seventh on Sixth

• *Potluck Dinner vs. Pig Roast*

I love foraging through my fridge, grabbing whatever's not too moldy to make a decent dinner, and gathering at a friend's for a little potluck and Pinot Grigio. But what I really love about it is that there's no pig involved. Which means there's no chance I'll discover a decapitated hog head propped up on a platter with an apple stuck in its mouth, and pass out. Again.

Best way to spend a Saturday: Potluck Dinner

• *Westminster Dog Show vs. Poultry Show*

I feel about dogs at the dog show the way I do about men at the car show. If they're prettier than I am, that's a problem. Birds, on the other hand, don't bother me. Why? Because it doesn't matter how beautiful their coloring or impressive their lineage; their ET-like feet beat mine in the ugly department any day.

Best way to spend a Saturday: Poultry Show

• *Hair Show vs. Hog Show*

At one you're treated to the latest in cut, color, style, and shine. At the other you see it on humans. While enjoying champagne and caviar in a four-star hotel, and surrounded by people who smell like a million bucks. Not a million boars.

Best way to spend a Saturday: Hair Show

Chapter Eight

SUPER SUZY

Greetings from snow-covered Oakfield Estate,[42] where right this instant six beautiful, hungry deer are digging through the drifts surrounding our Dodge Durango, looking for breakfast. (If I'd known they were going to come this close, I'd have encouraged the boys to drop food outside the car, instead of just in it.) It's a nice change, though, from the Dachshund-size rodents I used to see running along the subway tracks, toting chunks of discarded cheeseburgers, French fries, and once, a huge stalk of broccoli I watched a mama rat excavate from a crushed container of Chinese food. She dragged it over to her kiddies, and they chowed right down. I was so impressed. Even rat babies know to eat their greens. But my sons? Please. They much prefer something picked from their proboscis than any kind of produce.

Speaking of litter, do you believe there's no garbage pickup here? None. Nada. Nyet. So folks store it all up—the meal scrapings, magazines, newspapers, plastic

---

42. Wish you were here! And we weren't!

bottles, cardboard, clear glass, and green glass—and make weekly runs to the recycling center to dispose of their refuse.

This works fine until you can't get to the dump. You're sick. Snowed in. Have a flat tire, or can't get to your car because it is surrounded by famished fawns. Then those Hefty Cinch Saks seem to multiply overnight. The bags of glass and plastic begin reproducing pretty quickly, too, and before you know it the rising mountain of wine bottles makes you wonder if Betty Ford and not Nate's Place is where you really belong. Soon your garage[43] is filled to the rafters with waste. But amazingly, it doesn't smell like a trash scow off the Jersey coast. Why? Because the frighteningly stinky stuff is stored in the freezer.

It's ingenious, actually. And it works. Until the kids pull apart a plastic Food Lion bag frozen solid with last night's chicken instead of the chocolate ice cream they were looking for.

Having been in Virginia now six weeks, all of them at Doug and Nancy's, as progress on our house is moving with the speed of flowing molasses, we decided on Friday to see some more of our new state. So we visited Fauquier Hospital in Warrenton. Specifically, the emergency room. A wan shade of green, if you're wondering, with seats that could use a bit more padding, unless you pack your own as I do.

See, earlier this week Casey was sick. Coughing, sneezing, body aches, runny nose, and watery eyes. The poor kid was just oozing from every orifice, and at some point

---

43. Because where else are you going to keep garbage?

he oozed onto Cuy. Because by Friday Cuyler was sick. He was OK in the morning, so I took him to school, and then I took Case to the doctor, where he was diagnosed with a major sinus infection.[44]

OK, so I drop Casey at school[45] and head to the pharmacy to have his prescription filled. After driving what feels like a hundred miles, I'm not back at Oakfield five minutes when the phone rings. It's the nurse at Cuyler's school, asking me to please come retrieve my disease-ridden offspring.

So I race to school and there's my younger son, coughing, nose running like a pair of hose, and so hot you could fry an egg on his forehead. I fly immediately into Super Suzy mode[46] and call the doctor. They can't see him. They're completely booked. Oh, wait, they've had a cancellation. He's in!

Cut to Cuy on the examining table, where this wonderful, gentle nurse is trying to take his temperature. Since Super Suzy uses a Braun Thermoscan, her kids have never had to hold a thermometer under their tongues, and Cuy's in no condition to get the hang of it now. To further prove this point, he bites down and breaks it. This rattles the nurse and Super Suzy, who both rush to rinse his mouth out with water and confirm the mercury is still where it's supposed to be and that there's no glass going down the kid's gullet. The second thermometer meets a similar

---

44. So *that* accounts for what looks like creamed peas packed in the kid's nose.

45. In my book, a sinus infection does not equal a sick day.

46. You'd love my costume; purple parachute pants and black leather bustier. Kind of a Ronald McDonald meets Cat Woman combo; sexy but accommodating.

fate, and finally we give up and take his temp the old-fashioned way.[47]

It's a hundred and three. And the doctor keeps listening and listening and listening to Cuy's lungs. And checking the oxygen meter on the kid's thumb. And doing a dozen other doctorly things. And finally he says to me, "You know, when kids present with symptoms like this we usually admit them."

As Super Suzy mode has begun to fade, leaving me freaked out and fatigued, I have no clue what he means. Admit them to what? College? The kid's not even old enough to tap a beer keg. What fraternity will he pledge?

And then it dawns on me. We're going to the hospital. Time to call Super Stu.[48]

With Super Stu at the wheel, we rush to the emergency room. They're actually expecting us (yay!), but they can't take us (boo!).

See, it's begun to drizzle, and according to the admitting nurse, that means no one in the state of Virginia can control the pickup trucks they're all tearing around in. So the ER's quickly getting overrun with all manner of car accidents. And of course those who arrive with a steering wheel protruding from their solar plexus need to be treated before kids who may or may not have pneumonia.[49]

So we wait. And wait. And soon the ER is SRO. And

47. This not only gets the job done, but guarantees there'll be no further thermometer chomping in my child's future.

48. See? I don't always call him Hemingway or hon, or any of those mean-spirited pee-pee monikers I mentioned earlier. Sometimes, like when the kids are sick or I'm giving birth to one, he's simply Super Stu. Because really, he's super. Love you, hon!

49. I'm not being sarcastic here—well, not too much. I'd want my family member's skull sewn up before little Charlie got his chest X-ray, too.

just about four hours after our arrival, they come to get Cuy.

Three chest X-rays, one IV—administered while Super Stu has him in a headlock—six vials of blood ("Can I have that back? What if I run out?"), three new stuffed animals, one dose of amoxicillin, and two and a half more scary, exhausting hours later, the verdict is in: Cuy has a serious virus but no pneumonia, thank God. He doesn't need to be admitted. We're home free.

Not so fast, folks.

Remember that rain I mentioned? Well, the good news is it's stopped, so we don't have to play adult bumper cars on our way back to Oakfield. But the bad news is its friend fog has rolled in to wreak further havoc on our lives.

It's as if a shroud of cotton gauze surrounds the car and we can't see two feet in front of us. Cuy's completely oblivious to the situation and keeps asking me to turn up the volume on the Rolling Stones CD I happen to have in the CD player. Super Stu, who has years of experience driving in a fog—unfortunately usually alcohol induced—is concentrating on driving ohhhhhh sooooooo slooooooowwly while Mick Jagger is describing the overall visibility by wailing "Paint It Black." As for me, I'm sharing the front passenger seat with GUILT and PANIC, so it's pretty crowded. PANIC keeps screaming that we're going to get killed, and GUILT keeps asking me why I didn't insist the hospital keep Cuy overnight. I try summoning Super Suzy, but her cell phone's off.

Suddenly, there's a break in the fog, Super Stu accelerates to an entire six miles per hour, and we nearly drive head-on into a deer. A huge buck, actually, who saunters in front of the Durango like a werewolf emerging from the mist and looks Stu dead in the eye like we're in *his* way.

Now GUILT and PANIC, accompanied by their personal Stones theme song, "This Could Be the Last Time," have made themselves comfortable on Super Stu's side of the car, as well, and he and I keep looking at each other like, *Hmm, maybe we could have learned to live with the traffic in Paramus, the commute to the city, and the lack of parking in our tony hometown. But nah. We chose to come to the country and get killed.*

Forty long minutes later, we pull into Doug's driveway. It's pretty frozen, and I don't want Cuy falling and cracking his head on the ice, lest we wind up back at the hospital, so I carry him to the back door.

It's locked. Not realizing my thoughtful sister-in-law had left the front door open for us, we decide, in our slaphappy state, to go in through the garage. Which means navigating the sloping, ice-covered asphalt that could do double duty as an Olympic bobsled run. And that means I've got front-row seats for the McMen-scapades.

First Super Stu goes sailing, Scott Hamilton–like, down the driveway toward the huge garage door. For a second I'm sure he'll fall, but no! He sticks his landing, and punches in the code. Slowly the door starts to lift, and Cuyler, just this side of delirious and desperate to go to bed, lunges for it.

Unfortunately, but unsurprisingly, his Ninja Turtle sneakers are no substitute for ice skates. His feet fly out from under him and boom, he's on his butt sliding toward Stu. Certain he's split his skull—it's dark, and at this point I'm a little delirious myself—I run toward him, slip on the ice,[50] slide directly into my sick son, and drag us both right into the garage, where we're greeted by those ever-growing Hefty Cinch Saks.

Home, sweet, refuse-filled home. Next stop, the recycling center. Or maybe just rehab.

---

50. Note to file: Sexy black Bandolino boots will not work for the Olympic Ice Skating Team trials.

Country road, take me home. . . .
In one piece, please!

In the short time I've lived here, I've come to one major conclusion: driving in the country is a lot more dangerous than in the suburbs or the city. I hate dodging yellow cabs as much as the next commuter, but at least you expect their abuse. Here, everyone's laid-back and unhurried. Until they pile into their pickup. Then they unleash their inner cabbie, and there's no question the meter's ticking toward my demise. To keep your rides through the rural countryside safe, heed the tidbits I wish someone had told me. . . .

Speed demons are de rigueur. Country drivers tear along like they're related to Jeff Gordon, so get used to it. In fact, they spend more time on my bumper than my kid does on MySpace.

Passing is practically impossible. Common sense says pull over and let 'em pass. But you can't, because the winding country roads don't have curbs; they have deep, rock-filled ditches. This means you're stuck, and it's like having Cujo on your *culo.* Frankly, if the object in the mirror is closer than it appears, then these folks are in the backseat with my boys.

Beware of tailgating tail waggers. Why do country drivers tailgate so? I think it's because Spot's got the steering wheel.

For starters, it's a scientific fact that dogs like to chase cars. Add to that the slightly less scientific but equally true fact that lots of country folk let their canines sit on their laps and commandeer their vehicles, and you can see how I've come to this conclusion. Road test it yourself: Next time you're cruising the countryside, check your rearview mirror; I'll bet you're greeted by Fido's grinning reflection.

Vanity tags are trouble. Beyond the fact that some Rottweiler has the wheel, there's another reason country drivers are virtually bungee corded to each others' bumpers: they're deciphering the vanity tags. Sure, BUBBASGRL and IBRK4BASS, are easy. But DOMEBABY? I saw that plate, pointed it out to Hemingway, and asked, "What's a dome baby?" Without missing a beat he looked at me leeringly and said, "Do me, baby." I nearly smacked him, because the kids were in the car, and then it dawned on me. Duh. Do. Me. Baby. Sometimes I am so blond.

Watch for stupid speed stunt #1 . . . I call it the Left Arm out the Driver's Side Window Dangle. Maybe you've seen these yahoos cruising along, window wide open, left arm blowing in the breeze? Aren't they cold? Isn't their dog cold? Aren't they afraid of losing a limb? I see them coming, hairy arms and wedding-ringed fingers flapping, and pull so far over, I'm in danger of flipping the car and killing myself. All this just so I don't amputate some idiot's arm at the elbow. Maybe I'll simply reach out, rip it out at the socket, and beat the doofus to death with it.

And #2 . . . Even scarier than exposed appendages or spying Duke in the driver's seat is the "Look, Ma, no hands!" habit so prevalent in these parts. More than once I've pulled alongside some guy in a massive pickup stacked high with hay, doing sixty-five on Route 66, his left hand flicking his Winston into the wind, his right squeezing his cell to his skull. Who's got the wheel? Now, there's an excellent question. I hate to think nuts like this are driving with their knees, but I see no alternative. Unless there are *other* body parts involved, and that prospect I'm not even going to pursue.

Chapter Nine

CAUSE OF DEATH: COUNTRY TIME

I have a confession to make: The sticks are starting to grow on Super Suzy. True, there's still no Banana Republic down the block. There's no J.Crew on the corner. And there's definitely no Starbucks in the center of town, and no plans to put one in, either. The "local" supermarket remains a twenty-five-minute ride, and the closest movie theater is about an hour north. But all this driving means I'm getting a good look around. And frankly, I like what I see.

Each morning at Oakfield[51] I watch the sun come up pink, purple, and orange over the Bull Run Mountains, through bare trees and over winter-green pastures dotted with cows and deer, and you know what? It's one of the most beautiful sights I've ever seen.[52]

At about seven thirty, I walk out to warm up the car and am consistently startled by the heifers mooing their morning hellos. The first time it happened I actually spun

---

51. Because Nate's Place, natch, is still uninhabitable.

52. Not quite as beautiful a sight as the twice-annual Neiman Marcus clearance sale signs I used to be able to see from the bus while sitting in bumper-to-bumper traffic en route to the Lincoln Tunnel, but almost.

around and saw Number Seventy-six and her friend, Fifty-four, looking at me like I had no manners. What I actually lack is brains, as I think I said—out loud—"Oh, hi there. Good morning to you, too," and then I jumped into the Durango and locked the doors before they could charge the car. Some big, tough "New Yawka" I turned out to be.

At ten minutes of eight the boys and I take off for school. The ride, past horse farms, hay bales, and beef cattle operations, is spectacular and calming. This is particularly good for my kids, as I've yet to give in to the urge to pull over and beat them for fighting over which Bowling for Soup, Green Day, or Good Charlotte CD they'll play and how loud. Once they're in school I get back in the car, thank God again that, while it may not have an Abercrombie and Fitch, at least Fauquier County has all-day kindergarten, and cruise off to start my day.

But just what do I do all day? You know, when I'm not wandering lost and unmoored through the veritable four-star hotel we're currently calling home.

I've been giving this some thought, and since I don't have a job to rush to, and I'm not unpacking boxes yet, I feel funny admitting that I really don't know. If that's not bad enough, by three o'clock I'm ready for a nice nap. I can attribute this either to advancing age[53] or being busy. And since I am absolutely not getting older (though a stash of Stri-vectin for my wrinkled forehead would be fabulous), I must be busy. But doing what?

Let's see. I spent one morning (and I really do mean

---

53. I turned twenty-nine again last month and I'll tell you, the ten years between twenty-nine and thirty have been some of the happiest of my life.

one morning) getting my Virginia state license. That was fun. (You know, the way going for an annual physical and finding out you really did gain ten pounds, and no, it's not from a tumor—damn!—is fun.)

Hemingway and I drove to the DMV in Warrenton with grand plans to get our new IDs, do some errands, squeeze in a nice lunch, and make it back in time to pick up the boys. And it was all going according to plan until we presented our New Jersey licenses. Or more accurately, until I presented mine.

"Where's the photo?" demanded a small, stocky woman in a black dress with white pin dots and a badge that read, HI, I'M TESS; I'M HERE TO HELP! She didn't seem to be here to help. She seemed to be here to be unhappy, very unhappy, particularly with me and my pictureless license.

"New Jersey doesn't require one," I replied, smiling. For some reason I always assume that if I keep smiling, whomever I'm dealing with will, too. Eventually.

"His has a photo,"[54] she said, nodding her head in Hemingway's direction and absolutely, positively, not smiling.

"His is newer. Plus I renewed by mail. That's why there's no photo." Still smiling!

"I need something with a photo." Still seriously not smiling.

"I have my old *Family Circle* ID," I reply, rummaging through my wallet. "How's that?"

---

54. Of course it does. He worked at home. He had time to run to our local DMV, stand in line, smile for the camera, and obtain a license that frees him from suspicion of being a terrorist. I, on the other hand, had the big job in the big city where I worried big time about being killed by terrorists, and never once realized that I was carrying an ID that defined me in a big way as being one of them.

"*Family Circle*, as in the magazine?"

Yes! A reader! My worries are over!

"That would be the one." I pause and hand her the ID card, smiling so hard I fear a bicuspid will break. "Do you read it?"

"My mother-in-law does. *The National Enquirer*'s more my style."

Damn, the double kiss of death: the dreaded mother-in-law connection *and* Elvis sightings. Suddenly I foresee a future stuck at Nate's Place. God, I hope we can get high-speed Internet.

"Where does it say *Family Circle*?"

"Umm, it doesn't. It says . . . "

"Are you Susan Gruner T. Jahr? I thought you were married to him." She looks at Hemingway.

"I am. I am married to him,"[55] I reply. "There's my name," I say, pointing to my signature on the card. "Gruner *plus* Jahr is the company I worked for."

"I thought you said you worked for *Family Circle*." Now she's eyeing me and backing away from the counter, like any minute I might go berserk and take out the bottled water machine.

"Gruner and Jahr owns *Family Circle*. It's a corporate ID card."

"Uh-huh," she grumbles. "Marge, you got a minute?"

"When I'm finished with Mrs. Dunlevy," Marge replies in a manner that suggests the Mideast crisis will end before she'll ever be done helping Mrs. D. And of course she's not smiling, either.

---

55. At least until I kill him for snickering to himself. And then I'll be his widow. Won't that be wonderful?

"You'll have to wait," Tess tells me, pushing my inferior paperwork to the side. "Only Marge can make this call."

"Make what call?" I ask, alarmed, and fighting the urge to go all Jersey girl on this gal. "This is me, in this picture, see?" I say, whipping my sunglasses off the top of my head, rearranging my hair, and giving her the most marketing director-ish smile I can muster. "And here's my name, and here it is again on my license." I pause and smile so hard my bottom lip splits.[56] Blood collecting on my kisser, I continue my pitch. "See? It really all makes sense. So you can make the call, right, Tess? I mean, look at poor Marge. She could be all day with sweet Mrs. D."

To my horror, taciturn Tess simply disappears behind a door marked EMPLOYEES ONLY and Hemingway, who until this point had been having a good guffaw at my expense, sidles up and gives me the "No Sopranos Mode, Suzy" stare. I want to kill him. I want to kill Tess. I want to kill darling little Mrs. Dunlevy for having the audacity to hog Sergeant Marge for almost forty minutes.

Ultimately I needed two dozen documents verifying my marriage and status as a natural-born U.S. citizen, while the gentleman behind me, fresh off the boat from Botswana or Guyana or someplace definitely not within the borders of the continental United States, needed a note from his mom.

Another morning (and again, I really do mean a full morning) was spent at the bank opening savings accounts for the boys. My sons have, like, thirty-five cents between them, so I figured, how long could it take? I should've

---

56. Can anyone blame me for wanting to slap Suzy Chapstick at this second?

packed a lunch. I arrived at nine and left at noon. Three hours for two savings accounts. That's ninety minutes each. And for each it was as if they were opening a savings account for the Very First Time.

First, they had to open the special savings account program on the PC. But they couldn't recall what directory it was in. Then they found it, but the computer was "running slow." Finally, mercifully and miraculously before Casey's high school graduation,[57] the program opened and I thought, OK, now we're getting somewhere. And then it dawned on the woman helping me that the Mistress of Savings Accounts Ceremonies was out—on maternity leave, no less—and the only person she'd taught to use this little slice of rocket science was off having shamrocks applied to her manicure in preparation for a big St. Patty's party.

I wasn't sure what to be more appalled by. The thought of having what basically amounts to boogers put on my nails, or the creeping realization that a ceramic piggy bank would be better than this place.

Not to be deterred, Miss Happy—because she was just so happy! And helpful! And positive!—announces to me and the one teller on duty that "It's no problem! No problem at all! We'll simply use the tutorial!" We? Who's we? If I was going to have to sit through Savings Account Software 101, I was doing so as a spectator, not a participant.

This was bad. I kept looking at my watch. I'd been there two hours and we were nowhere near the end of this happy endeavor. My "Be polite; you're the new kid in

---

57. In 2009.

town" composure was beginning to crack. If I wasn't careful, in a moment I'd unleash my New York–perfected impatience (aka Sopranos Mode), complete with condescending tone and clipped, speed-of-light speech, and then I'd have to find another financial institution, maybe even a real one, to babysit my kids' one buck.

While Miss Happy flipped pages in the tutorial, fussed with her glasses, and occasionally punctuated her keyboard pecking with such comforting commentary as "Now, where's that screen? Oh, there it is! Certainly does look different since the last time I did this." Chuckle, chuckle. "Don't worry, we'll figure it out, Mrs. McCorkindale. Won't take but a minute more," I gave some thought to getting up and leaving. I also thought about feigning illness, or suddenly remembering a forgotten appointment for an appendectomy. But instead I sat there and prayed for death to take me, or at least my voice box.

No such luck.

Maybe it was because I had a headache from sitting there *all* morning. Maybe it was because I just couldn't believe I'd get nothing else done but this (if I was lucky) before the day was shot and it was time to get the boys. Or maybe it was my inability to comprehend how I could possibly have selected the one bank out of *two* in this bustling burg where opening a savings account meant descending into the seventh circle of hell, but suddenly my mouth shot out of the starting gate, leaving what's left of my brain far, far behind.

"You know what?" I said really, really nicely, with a big smile and my best "Oh, ha ha, this happens all the time to me" tone, "PCs are so overrated. Really. Forget the PC. And the software. Let's break out some paper and a pen and do this the old-fashioned way. What," I continued, my mouth getting completely away from me as I watched confusion cross Miss Happy's face, "no ballpoint? No problem. I'm sure you've got a quill pen and a piece of parchment that will work just as well. And let's not forget that abacus collecting dust back there. We can use it to divvy up my kids' money. Then I'll just give you their names, dates of birth, Social Security numbers, and such, and you can finish the paperwork whenever Miss St. Patty's Day decides to come back to work. Sound good? Good! Here's our PO box number. You can just mail me the passbooks when they're ready. Or send them via carrier pigeon. Whatever's more your speed. What am I saying? You're certainly not into speed around here. No, no rush. Really. However you want to get them to me is fine. I've taken up too much of YOUR time already. Well, this has been a little slice of heaven. Thanks for all your help. I'll see you soon."

And then I waved, grabbed my bag, and beat it the hell out of there. Surprisingly, it took only a day or two to get the passbooks. And to think I could have spent all that time watching Miss Happy hunt and peck.

When I'm not attempting to bank at Satan's Savings & Loan or being interrogated by the unhappy drones at the DMV, I spend a good bit of time, not to mention money, trying to obtain the perfect blow-out.

Now, please don't think I'm a princess. I'm not.[58] I just cannot blow my own hair dry bone straight. And that's

---

58. OK, I am. Anybody who suggests their bank use a quill pen and parchment paper is more than a bit of a brat.

how I like it: bone straight. Not wavy. Not curly. And definitely not 1980 High School Yearbook Big. Straight.

Naturally, this is the one state I can't get my hair into
on my own. Despite years of purchasing exorbitantly expensive round brushes; professional blow dryers (some of
which I've actually plugged in); and salon-only shampoos,
conditioners, and straightening products as pricey as a
Porsche—not to mention being tutored by my sister-in-
law Nancy and my cousin Lisa, both of whom have the
stick-straight stuff down to a science and who have provided frequent blow-dry coaching sessions while squeezed
into some of the world's smallest the bathrooms with
me—I still look like a blond Ronald McDonald when I do
it myself.

So that means I need to find a salon, or more specifically, a stylist, and frankly, I needed to find her—or him—
yesterday.

You might think that any Francine with a flat iron
would be fine. But you'd be surprised at the ire my poker-
straight preferences arouse in certain hairdressers. At Salon
Demure, a surprisingly chic—for the sticks—salon Nancy
and I decided to try, we encountered a stylist whom I will
forever refer to as the Curl Nazi.

When Nance called to make our appointments, she
told the receptionist specifically that we were coming in for
blow-outs. Stick-, bone-, pin-, poker-straight blow-outs, so
please, allow plenty of time for both of us, and plug that
flat iron in pronto.

On the appointed day and time, Nancy and I stroll into the salon and are immediately ushered to the sinks.
We're shampooed, conditioned, and so wonderfully scalp

massaged I'm certain I can cross *Find new hair salon* off my list of things to do.

And then it happens.

We're sitting side by side, facing a massive mirror, our towel-dried, tousled manes beginning their pre-curl approach, when the stylist (yes, there's just one) spies our rising ringlets and lunges for the diffuser.

Stunned, we protest and demand the attachment's immediate removal, as well as the application of a heaping helping of Straight Stuff straightening balm. This doesn't go over too well, and out of the blue he's berating us for not wanting the lovely curls of the women in "his country." In all my years of weekly blow-outs I've never seen a stylist get so worked up, and for a few moments I actually fear we'll go mano-a-mano over use of the round brush-o.

Ultimately Nancy and I won out, and left (more than two and a half hours later) with our ramrod-straight-haired heads held high. The good news is Mr. Belligerent's oh-so-slow blow-out should last me a week.[59] The bad news is next Saturday I'm trying Shirley's Hair Shack. Why is this bad? When the receptionist has to put you on hold to find out if the salon's *one* flat iron will be back from the repair shop in time for your appointment, and you actually have the good sense to request a stylist who knows how to use that important piece of equipment, it's either time for a crew cut or to see if the Curl Nazi's any more compliant the second time around.

I'm also spending a lot of time in meetings with Nance

---

59. It typically takes a senior stylist forty-five minutes to blow me out. This guy took two hours. "You're not doing it my way so I'm taking my time" time or country time? You make the call.

and the contractor/decorator handling the renovations on Nate's Place. These plodding powwows usually involve Nancy and me walking from room to room, making such pointed observations as "Gee, the closets look great painted! But where's the light fixture and switch? Oh, the electrician is coming *today*, I see. And then the painter will *come back* and do touch-ups. Logical, very logical. And the landscaper with the money trees, I suppose he's due soon, too?"

OK, I didn't make the crack about the money trees. But I wanted to. Especially since, if they actually came across with a couple of those babies, I wouldn't have to use Speed of Flowing Taffy Bank & Trust in town.

Now that I think of it, I'd like to clarify my earlier confession. I'm falling in love with horse and cow country for its looks, its beauty, and its indescribable pastoral perfection. But its pace is going to put me in the ground. I can hear the coroner now. "Cause of Susan McCorkindale's death: country time."

When it finally does happen I've asked Hemingway to please do me a favor and toss my body onto one of the burn piles that are so popular around here. Anything but a local funeral parlor. If they move as fast as the bank, it's a sure bet I'll start to stink long before they locate the coffin catalog or the instruction manual for the new embalming solution they just switched to.

Chapter Ten

TAKE THE "REHAB OR HOUSE" CHALLENGE!

It's six o'clock Sunday morning, and already I'm tempted to add a shot of Baileys to my breakfast coffee. Which leads me to wonder if it isn't time to kick off what I call the "Rehab or House" Challenge. The object is to see where I wind up first: rehab or our remodeled farm house.[60] If things continue to progress at the country time pace of this past week, which is to say not at all, it's a pretty safe bet I'll be happily checked into Hazelden or Betty Ford long before I ever spend a night at Nate's Place.

Herewith, the gory details:

Last Monday, the cleaning lady our combination contractor/decorator[61] supposedly hired cancelled at the last

---

60. We've now been at Oakfield for three months. That's two months and three weeks longer than planned, and the kids are working hard to give my sister-in-law's multimillion-dollar home that frat house feel. They've broken two tables and a DVD player, streaked the wall along the spiral staircase with handprints, and perfected the art of dismantling the window treatments in the dining room and draping them over the table to make an exorbitantly expensive tent. And you wonder why I'm drinking before daybreak.

61. Yeah, our contractor is also our decorator. It's a long, sordid story, one I'm certain to get sued for if I relay it here. Suffice it to say that in the future, I'll keep the two functions separate. And you should, too.

minute. This was a bad thing as, at the time, the movers were coming on Tuesday, and as much as I had dusted and vacuumed and scrubbed and hauled stuff out to the Dumpster on Saturday and Sunday, I'd only finished the upstairs bedrooms and bathroom, and not touched the downstairs.

So I raced over to the house in not-so-joyful anticipation of repeating the process on the first floor, only to discover that my illustrious contractor and crew had not yet cleaned out their crap. Certainly I expect to have to deal with some dust and a few drops of paint, and maybe a couple scraps of sandpaper along with some electrical tape. But can someone please tell me if there's an oath tradesmen take to ensure they make as big a mess as possible in people's homes?

A row of empty green Perrier bottles lined one wall of the living room, cigarettes burned down to their filters sat on the freshly painted but now tar-stained for that lived-in look windowsill in the laundry room, and someone's half-consumed Soup-for-One lay congealing in the corner of the den. In fact the entire first floor, from the front door to the mud porch, was covered in a carpet of crushed Marlboro boxes, half-used books of matches, empty Coke and Mountain Dew cans, dried Dannon yogurt containers, and crumpled Cheetos and Ruffles potato chips packages.[62] And I'm not even going to go into the full complement of contractor-type materials tossed everywhere. Things like dripping caulk guns, tape measures, and still-wet paint pans, strips of lumber, boxes of nails, and swatches of plaster-encrusted sandpaper. Hey, if they didn't care about packing them up,

---

62. Not to mention my personal favorite, a half-eaten peanut butter and jelly sandwich on moldy whole wheat pressed into service as an ashtray. Sort of redefines recycling, doesn't it?

I didn't care about pitching them directly into the aforementioned Dumpster.

Now, I'm no detective and I'm definitely blond, but
standing there surveying the debris, I couldn't help but
wonder, If the house wasn't prepped for the cleaning lady,
was there a cleaning lady coming in the first place?

Hmm. I think not.

And rehab lurches to an early lead!

Cut to early Tuesday morning. The downstairs is as
clean as I can get it, what with no help from the construction crew and my failure to finish maid school, and the
moving people are due sometime between seven o'clock
and noon.

Hemingway gets to the house ahead of me, only to discover a stepladder smack-dab in front of the front door,
a tarp covering the floor, two electricians eyeing the light
fixture above the island in the kitchen, and the painter
doing touch-ups on the baseboard. Not exactly the perfect
scenario for our paid-by-the-hour moving crew to come
upon when they arrive.

Now, we don't occasionally call Hemingway Stu "Marine Drill Instructor" McCorkindale for nothing.[63] He sees
these guys in the kitchen and starts firing off questions
Northerner-fast. What are you doing and why? Who told
you to do it? When did you talk to them? Can you get them
on the phone so I can scream some obscenity-laced common sense at them?

Turns out the electricians have been told to shift the

---

63. I think I've yet to mention that Hemingway was a Marine. He's still got those
finely tuned senses they beat into him. He can read and react to a situation in a
nanosecond, and hear a cricket fart from forty feet. Really, his hearing is amazing.
Though he's deaf to my begging him not to encourage the boys to belch for
company.

light fixture *two inches* to the right. Why? Because some-body screwed up the original measurement and it's off center. Moving it will involve ruining the freshly painted ceiling, which will then need to be repainted (cha-ching!); almost certainly mashing still-damp paint from the ceiling into the surface of the brand new butcher block tabletop below, which will result in its needing to be re-sanded or worse, replaced (major cha-ching!); and the distinct possi-bility that Hemingway will kill someone (for free—finally, a bargain!). So he tells them, "No f-ing way," and the elec-tricians exit, stage left.

Sergeant Mac then turns his attention to Mr. Painter, and determines that no one ever told him about the movers' impending arrival. In fact Mr. Painter was told specifically to come today to touch up the area around the front door, as well as the railing and wall leading upstairs. The very same spots that will most likely be "dinged" as furniture, boxes, and beds are hauled into the house. After a rhetori-cal "Does this make sense to you?" Hemingway dismisses him, too.

Shortly after the departure of Mr. Painter and the two electricians, the phone rings.

Seems the movers, who are coming to deliver two sofas, a chair, and an ottoman that we purchased from our contractor/decorator and move the rest of our furniture from storage into Nate's Place, have a problem. Their truck has broken down, so they have to cancel. Hemingway sug-gests they simply transfer our four measly items onto an-other truck, but they can't. They only have one truck. One truck. Would somebody please tell me what kind of mov-ing company has only one truck?

So the house wasn't prepped and cleaned properly.

The painter was positioned in the entryway, and the movers, with their one truck, called ten minutes prior to their scheduled arrival time to cancel. And so I ask you: Were there movers coming in the first place?

Hmm. I think not.

I also think Betty Ford looks better than Hazelden. Let's hope they take Blue Cross.

Later that same day, while I went to get the kids at school, Hemingway decided to check out our fabulous new refrigerator. Now, what you need to know about the refrigerator is that it is the only appliance, the only amenity, *the only thing* in this entire remodeling endeavor that my honey requested.

Ages ago, when we discussed with my brother-in-law and sister-in-law the benefits of ceiling fans versus central air-conditioning, Hemingway, ever the Scotsman, pushed for the less expensive fans, while I made no attempt to disguise my longing for a Trane AC system powerful enough to cool a hot flash in hell. What can I say? I sweat. And there's no way I can properly primp and perfect my farm chic fabulousness if I'm schvitzing like a field hand. So guess which cooling option you'll find in my cute farmhouse? Right. Not fans.

When talk of freshening up the kitchen with a few new appliances and a little paint escalated into a full-on rip-it-all-out redo, Hemingway was still hollering, "But custom cabinetry is *so* overrated!" when the wrecking crew arrived.

And finally, when my sweet sister-in-law and I were exchanging about a million e-mails and faxes over whether a butter-soft, deep chocolate brown leather sofa or a butter-soft, deep chocolate brown leather sofa with blue and green plaid Ralph Lauren–style fabric insets would look best in the den, Hemingway insisted our old denim couch would do fine. Do I even need to tell you that that cat pee–and-merlot-splattered lounge didn't make the sojourn south? You had to be soused to sit on the smelly thing, so perhaps *that* explains his infatuation with it. I, for one, cannot wait to curl up on our plush, Ralph Lauren–inspired perch, if and when it ever arrives.

My point is that my honey had a hankering for just one thing:[64] a refrigerator with an ice cube and cold water dispenser on the door.

So there he was, enjoying a cold one (a glass of water, not a beer, but it should've been) when he decides to open the fridge to see how much room he'll actually have for his Budweiser. He swings the door open and discovers that it doesn't swing. It opens, but only to about a 45-degree angle. He reaches in and tugs on the crisper drawers, but they open only three inches. Why? Because they hit the door. Why? Because the door is hitting the wall. Why? Because the fridge is too damn big for the space.

One thing that *is* a perfect fit for its space is the phone, which he snatches off the wall and uses to call me.

"Susan, have you seen the new fridge?"

"Please don't tell me it disappeared. It was there when I left!"

"I mean, did you test it?"

"Test it? Oh, my God. The water dispenser doesn't work?"

---

64. OK, two things, but we're talking house stuff here.

"No, it works," he replies. "I'm talking about the fact that the doors don't open all the way."

"What do you mean they don't . . ."

"Susan," he cuts me off, which is highly unusual for Hemingway and simply means he's had it, "the idiots bought a fridge that's too big. The door on the right side"— *BANG*—"hits the"—*BANG*—"wall"—*BANG*—"when you" —*BANG*—"open it!"—*BANG, BANG, BANG.*

"That sound is the door hitting the wall?"

"Uh huh."

Unbelievable. And yet, not unbelievable.

"It's gonna have to be replaced," he sighed. "And the wall's going to need to be repainted."

"Roger that," I replied. "I'll be back with the boys in fifteen minutes. Try not to tear the place apart, OK?"

And so I ask you, if you've got thirty-six inches to work with, should you fill it with a thirty-six-inch fridge?

Hmm. I think not.

Wait! Wait! There's a celeb place called Passages that looks promising. Maybe I can do my rehab in Malibu and room with Kate Moss!

OK, so that was Tuesday. On Wednesday we expected delivery of our living room rug and rug pad. This was perfect, because we figured we could get the rug down and in place prior to the arrival of the sofa, which was now coming on Thursday. Both the rug and the pad were at the decorator's, and we were told her partner would be bringing them over.

So I wait. And wait. And wait. I feel like Martha Stewart under house arrest. Finally the phone rings. Sorry, no rug today. The truck broke down. Of course it did. There are thousands of delivery trucks and pickup trucks barrel-assing all over Fauquier County and I get the two that have barrel-assed their last. Coincidence?

Hmm. I think not.

You know what? Forget Passages and Betty Ford. And forget the Baileys. My rich French roast deserves a double shot of Frangelico. And so do I.

Thursday finally arrives. The movers are due, once again, between seven o'clock and noon.[65] I drop the kids at school and head over to Nate's Place. Hemingway joins me there, as does my sister-in-law. Soon it's ten, eleven, twelve o'clock. No movers. At twelve thirty we call and are told they're just leaving and will arrive shortly. At one fifteen we call again. No one knows where they are. We call at one forty-five, two o'clock, two thirty, and three. We get nowhere. We've been at the house all day. We want our new furniture. We want our old furniture moved. I keep saying silly things like, "Maybe they stopped to get gas," "Maybe they stopped because they *have* gas," and "Let's give them fifteen more minutes."

By three thirty Hemingway is Jake LaMotta mad. Finally, after his fifty-seven-thousandth pace back and forth across the porch he turns to me, snaps his fingers in my face, and says, "Susan, wake up. There's no truck. There may not even be any furniture. They're not coming. We've been waiting *all* day. Do you really think they're coming?"

Hmm. I think not.

Though I do think Hemingway hid the Baileys and the

---

65. Ah, country time.

*Frangelico. So I'm resorting to Kahlúa. Right now. Mmm.
Delish.*

And so we left. And they didn't come. And they haven't
contacted us yet. Despite being contacted by our attorney.
Hemingway aka "Marine DI" McCorkindale may have
been on to something when he suggested that the furniture
doesn't exist. It may not ever have been ordered. And
we may have been BAMBOOZLED COUNTRY STYLE.

Tomorrow should be interesting. I think I heard something about "getting the sheriff and shutting her down." If
we're going to do that, do you think they'll let my kids ride
in the police car?

Hmm. I think not.

*But maybe, just maybe, they'll give me an escort to the rehab
facility I'm so obviously off to.*

A note from the blonde in the boonies: You like chicken? Tastes just like chicken.

So now we come to the meat bird of the matter. A meat bird, for those of you stumped by that sentence, is a chicken raised solely for meat and not eggs. How do I, a city chick lost in the sticks, know that? Because having survived the trauma of wearing two turtlenecks and being called out for my Carmela Soprano sound, among other things, I'm about to enter the fabulous world of fowl. (Not to mention farm equipment, livestock-related fitness faux pas, cow punching—no, it doesn't involve boxing gloves, but it should—and blackout survival, boonies style.)

I'm going to do it all in my spiky stilettos and low-rise Lucky jeans, no matter how many pairs of bib overalls Hemingway brings home. (I swear, if he greets me with "I brought you a little something, Sue!" one more time, I'm going to strangle him with the straps on those damn pants.) And while it may or may not involve a stint in rehab (hey, I'm trying to keep a little mystery in this memoir), it's definitely a trip worth taking.

So what are you waiting for? Turn the page.

First stop, Nate's Place.

Part Three

Five Hundred Acres and a Satellite Dish

Chapter Eleven

I MAY BE A CRAZY RABBIT, BUT I AIN'T
GOIN' TO BETTY FORD

We have finally, unbelievably, miraculously,[66] moved into Nate's Place, which means I've been able to back-burner the whole Hazelden/Betty Ford business. At least for now. Between being surrounded by three hundred boxes, the lack of having anywhere to sit—other than on the three hundred boxes—and the fact that this place gets *Night of the Living Dead* dark as soon as the sun goes down, there's still the distinct possibility I'll be making a trip to rehab somewhere down the road.

In an effort to push that day as far into the future as possible, Hemingway and I have gotten busy turning our 110-year-old farmhouse into a home.

Thanks to my sister-in-law and her spectacular taste, the dated, dreary, 1950s-style wallpaper was ripped down in every room and deep, vivid, French country colors painted in their place. Never have I seen anything so warm, so rich, so ready to crack. As soon as Hemingway drove the one and only nail needed to hang my I LOVE TO COOK WITH

---

66. The miracle being that we did it in under four months.

WINE. SOMETIMES I EVEN PUT IT IN THE FOOD plaque over the door in the kitchen, dozens of tiny fissures raced out and up to the crown molding. This did not make my honey happy.

"Susan," he hissed, nails held tightly between his teeth, "I told you there was a reason the whole place was papered. The walls are plaster."

For a minute I was crushed. What about our family pictures? My dad's paintings? The DOMESTICALLY DISABLED sign I selected specifically for over the stove? It saddened me to think they'd never see the light of day. But then it dawned on me that if my pictures couldn't be hung, then neither could Hemingway's. And since his collection includes an extensive assortment of framed *Playboy* Playmate of the Year magazine covers, I did a quick 180 and immediately embraced the idea of living with a lot less "art."

"You know, hon," I said slowly, so as not to tip him off to the fact that I'd just remembered the pictures of the big-breasted bunny women destined for the den, "I think we'll like leaving the walls bare. It'll feel more open."

"But what about the girls?" he whined, going right to the afore-thought-of but unmentioned band of bleached blond, DD-cup, twenty-somethings who like "strong, sensitive guys who aren't afraid to cry"[67] and having their photo taken buck naked (except for a few strategically placed rose petals).

"I guess you'll simply have to satisfy yourself with the 'ladies' who live out there," I replied, smiling sheepishly

---

67. Take it from me, kids: strong and sensitive pales in comparison to olfactory dysfunctional and fearless when faced with a full diaper.

(that's what we need: sheep!) and pointing out the window to the pasture, where several future filet mignons were munching away on a hay bale.

"You're enjoying this, aren't you?"

"Not at all, sweetheart. I know how you feel about Miss January and Miss February. Not to mention Miss March. What a hottie, huh?"

"Knock it off," he replied, shooting me the McLook, "or the girls are going on the shelves in the bedroom." I immediately McStifled myself. Just the thought of sleeping anywhere near Miss March makes me McSick.

Speaking of sleeping, this is probably a good time to tell you that Nate's Place has four nice-size bedrooms on the second floor. A master bedroom, a bedroom for each of the boys, and a guest room-slash-playroom for the little demons to destroy after they're done doing their Joe Walsh routines in their own rooms.[68]

On the main floor, Hemingway has his *Playboy* Playmate–free den, and I've got my floral-wallpapered living room.[69] There's also a dining room, laundry room, full bath (complete with a gaping hole, courtesy of Miss Contractor/Decorator/Furniture Hostage Taker 2005), and, best of all, the eat-in kitchen that was the deal clincher in the whole Nate's Place negotiation.

I can't cook, but I love my kitchen.

It's mustard yellow with touches of rich, dark red, and

---

68. Of course Joe Walsh tore out the walls in hotels and had accountants pay for it all. My sons prefer to "remodel" their bedrooms and have us bankroll the repairs. Parenthood: It's not just a job. It's a chance to file for Chapter 11.

69. How it escaped painting I don't know, but I'm not complaining. The McMen call it "the little girls' room" and refuse to set foot in it. Thank you, beautiful sister-in-law, for my sweet sanctuary!

rooster accents everywhere. And I mean everywhere: on the window treatments, the area rugs under the sink and by the back door, even on the dinner plates I picked up at a tiny department store down here called Peebles. Hemingway calls it Pebbles, which actually feels appropriate, since living here in the sticks so often smacks of living in the Stone Age.

But I digress.

The floor in the kitchen is particularly fabulous. It's pine painted in a checkerboard pattern. Sure, the kids would like to use it to actually play checkers, but until one of them finds pieces the circumference of a large pasta pot, that just ain't gonna happen. I like it because it camouflages the filth.[70]

Of course the best part of the kitchen is the huge (but incomplete, courtesy once again of Miss Contractor/Decorator/Furniture Hostage Taker 2005) island topped by a massive butcher block table smack in the center of it. Like I said, I can't cook, so I'm unsure I'll use it for serving dinner, but I can think of lots of other things to do on a surface that size. (Take that, Miss March.)

The only problem with our fabulous table is that it didn't come with chairs. We tried stacking several of the three hundred unpacked boxes around it, but when they crumpled, tipped, and collapsed, we decided to hit an unfinished furniture store up in Winchester. There we picked up a few sample stools—or as Hemingway calls them,

---

70. Can you believe the woman who invented the Clean Sweep would prefer not to deal with dirt? I'm really unsure what's happened to me since we've moved. I'd like to think I've gained a new perspective, but I'm pretty sure I'm simply presbyopic.

"stool samples"—and gave them a try. We eventually selected a style and bought four of them. But in the interim it was pretty funny barreling up and down the highway with our stool samples bouncing around the backseat and praying they wouldn't make a mess of the upholstery. Oh, well, at least we had the good sense to leave the windows down. (I know, I know. I'm so immature. But Hemingway started it!)

Anyway, in the back-to-reality, "please, Susan, don't miss any more medication" department, we also picked up a desk, matching chair, two filing cabinets, a media center, side table, and a pantry. As I mentioned, all of these pieces came unfinished, so Hemingway's spent the last several days painting and staining them, and I fear the poor guy's permanently high from the fumes. Sure, the furniture all looks great, but the "I've been tossing back the Jack Daniel's" twinkle in his eye has me troubled.

In addition to Hemingway's new furniture-staining hobby, which I swear must have a sniffing component, because I've never seen him so happy around the kids, my honey seems to have developed a mind-boggling obsession with bib overalls. If I'm not careful, and continue to steer him away from the men's section at Tractor Supply,[71] I'm going to wake up one morning and find myself married to Captain Kangaroo. He's convinced he can carry everything he needs in a pair of those babies, and I worry he'll do just that, and then collapse from the weight of it all

---

71. They have a women's section, too. Complete with Wrangler jeans, Carhartt pullovers, shiny John Deere belt buckles, and sparkly work boot accessories. If I ever launch *Sticks Style Magazine,* Tractor Supply's my source for farm fashion. Now, there's an oxymoron.

among the cow patties in a distant pasture. Can you imagine the headlines?

MISSING: HUMAN EQUIPMENT SHED.
REWARD FOR RETURN OF MAN LAST SEEN
WEARING EVERYTHING IN HIS WORKSHOP.

Of course if the simple life doesn't make me simply insane, putting the finishing touches on Nate's Place should take me over the top.

Our now ex-contractor/decorator is holding several of our new pieces of furniture hostage at a mystery warehouse in Maryland (it's gotten so ridiculous I expect at any moment to see a "recently released videotape of a blindfolded ottoman and cowering couch" on CNN), and, as you may recall, the wrong size refrigerator was ordered for our kitchen. It was beautiful, but it could have garaged a school bus. So it was removed and a replacement was ordered. In the interim we've been using a frat house–size fridge that's got just enough room for ice cream, Coca-Cola, and beer. You know—the three basic food groups.

On Wednesday, after waiting patiently for several weeks, we received a phone call that our perfectly proportioned, brand-new refrigerator would arrive in the morning. Yippee! Even *more* room for beer. More room for ice cream and soda. Plus an "in-the-door" ice and ice-water dispenser! Finally, I thought, something pertaining to this crazy house is going smoothly.

Think again, Suzy, and break out those brochures for Betty Ford.

Thursday morning dawns, and before my coffee is finished brewing, the phone rings. Hemingway answers, and I hear him say, "Uh huh. Uh huh. *Uh huuuuh.* So, can you tell me when you *think* you'll be delivering? Uh huh. Thanks." That expressive sentence completed, he hung up the phone, turned to me, and said, "They can't find our fridge. It's not in the warehouse. It's lost. Or stolen. Or something. They'll call back. You want a shot of Baileys for that?"

Furniture held hostage. Incomplete cabinetry. And the Case of the Missing KitchenAid. You can't make this stuff up. Come visit and we'll take you on the grand tour. See the light that's not aligned! The half-assed island! The cavern where the cabinet should be!

We're open to the public Tuesday through Sunday, 10–4. Closed Mondays for my therapy sessions.

Chapter Twelve

DOG DAZED

It is beyond thrilling to finally have someplace padded to plop my plump behind. Thanks to two terrific detectives who intervened on our behalf and made our ex-contractor/decorator an offer she couldn't refuse—deliver the furniture to our house or get ready for a trip to the big house—our sofas, chairs, and ottoman have at last arrived. Sure, the Barn Door Red–stained pine stools around our kitchen island are nice, and the oak chairs in the dining room are fine for the fancy dinners we never host, but after a long, hard day of rolling out rugs, painting bookshelves, and hanging curtains, it's a pleasure to collapse onto something other than an unpacked packing carton to watch TV.

All this bellyaching about a lack of sofas and chairs probably has you wondering what we sat on in New Jersey. It's simple: other sofas and chairs. We just opted to sell them rather than pay to move them, since we knew we'd be buying replacements as soon as we arrived in Virginia. You can see how well that worked out for us.

In reality, it's not like I have lots of time to sit and lollygag on my brand-new, super comfy, shabby chic–style, red and cream toile-covered couch. If I'm not unpacking boxes, I'm driving around with a muddy, sopping wet and stinking Jack Russell Terrier in my lap, wondering if commuting to New York had really been so bad. I'm beginning to think stay-at-home motherhood is madness, at least on those days when you make the mistake of rescuing stray dogs.

But I'm starting in the middle, so let me go back and explain.

Cuyler and I were on our way home from dropping Casey at school. This had been one of those weeks where the boys alternated sick days. Which means they needed me, and I needed to keep unpacking boxes. Guess who got what they needed? Right. Not me.

Anyway, as we turned onto Rokeby Road, we saw two small balls of fur bounding toward us. They were quite a ways off and I'm quite nearsighted, so at first I couldn't tell if they were cats or dogs or, God forbid, oversize rats, rabid raccoons, groundhogs, or foxes.[72]

But whatever or whomever they were, they were moving fast, and Cuy and I sat riveted as they rushed up. Soon it was clear that they were small dogs; one black and white, the other brown and white. I thought they were going to run straight into the car, so I stopped dead in the center of the street—the lack of traffic, like the lack of a local Starbucks, still stuns me—opened the door, and two tiny Jack Russell Terriers hopped right in.

---

72. This is the country, you'll recall, so the wildlife options, unlike the shopping options, are virtually endless.

As you can imagine, it was quite the scene. The dogs were soaking wet, covered in mud, and manic with exhaustion. They jumped from the front seat to the backseat and back again, flecks of mud-encrusted fur flying everywhere, like someone put uppers in their Puppy Chow. Cuy was giggling and asking if he could keep them. And all I could think was, Please, God, don't let them pee in the car. After the initial shock of suddenly having two small dogs dashing around the Durango, I determined they must belong to someone on a neighboring farm, and Cuy and I took off to find their owners. How hard could it be, right?

So we pull into the first farm, and while I hop out to commence the search-and-return mission, Cuy stays behind with the two hyper hounds. I try the front door. Nothing. I try the back door. Nothing. I'm about to get back in the car when I have the brilliant idea to peek in the windows and look for a dog dish or leash, or some kind of clue to a canine existence. Bad move. These folks may not have dogs, but their kitchen would have made a pack of hogs happy. Too bad we hadn't found a pair of pigs rather than pups running up the road.

Empty cans of tuna, crumpled boxes of macaroni and cheese, dried ice cream containers, yellowed newspapers, moldy dishtowels, half-eaten candy bars, and crushed plastic Dr Pepper bottles lined every inch of the scuffed linoleum. A week's worth of crusted cereal bowls stacked one on top of the other sat surrounded by an assortment of grimy glasses and stained teaspoons on a table glistening with grease. The drawers were pulled out. The cabinets hung open. One chair was flopped over on the floor. I won't even go into what was in the sink (suffice it to say it had something to do with boxer shorts and Brillo pads), and what little countertop space I spied, with its plethora of bread crumbs, browning banana skins, used tea bags, and spilled sugar packets, was a veritable Six Flags amusement park for ants.

And if all that wasn't enough, there was the pièce de résistance: a huge pasta pot filled with *sneakers*, plopped smack in the middle of the mess. Yes, the old sneakers in a saucepan centerpiece trick. Quick, somebody call Martha Stewart! I've seen cleaner cardboard shacks in New York City, and to be honest, if I'd actually seen a dog's dish it would have probably been doing double duty as a soup bowl. As filthy as the two Jacks were, I suspect they would have promptly requested political asylum to stay with us rather than return to this sty.

There was nobody home (or maybe they were buried under the rubble), so I went back to the car, prepared to drive over to the other house on the property. What I wasn't prepared for was for the smaller, black and white Jack to jump right past me as soon as I opened the door. That little beast took off through the fence and into the pens where these folks keep their goats and lambs. You should have heard those poor animals wailing. It was awful, and I was frantic trying to get the dog to come to me.[73]

No matter how I called and cajoled, that terrier terrorist had other plans. It darted back and forth between the goat and lamb pen to a pasture of increasingly agitated cattle, while I ran around trying to find a gate that would

---

73. I just kept thinking, Oh, my God, I'm going to get sued, and not only will they win, but they won't even use the money to hire a maid.

open, or a fence I could climb. The majority of fencing had barbed wire across the top, so it would be tough on my cute new J.Crew khakis[74] if I failed to clear it.

Finally I found a spot and hopped over, just in time to come face to face with six spotted brown cows careening toward me, with that puny pup pounding hot on their heels. For a moment I couldn't move and couldn't think of anything other than that I was about to be trampled to death by a bunch of dimwitted rib roasts so spineless they let themselves be bullied by a dog a housecat could take. This was no way for a former publishing exec to perish. Better to be killed in a scuffle over the last available pedicure appointment at the Avon Spa than in a tick-filled field in Hickville. I mean Upperville.

Terrified, I put my hands up over my face so I couldn't see what was happening and prayed to be beamed somewhere safer, like the New York City subway. I heard their hooves. Felt the breeze on my legs as they blew by. And I screamed. Then Cuyler screamed. And that damn dog never even paused to take a breath.

After my near-death-by-bovine experience—on just one cup of coffee, I'd like to add—I'd really had enough, and while I hated to leave the dog to be someone else's problem, I just couldn't get it to come to me. So I got in the car with Cuy and the other pup, and drove to the neighboring house to inquire whether the dogs belonged to them.

No such luck.

After being informed by a ponytailed, tattooed, John

---

74. Purchased via the miracle of cyberspace, which, despite living in the sticks, I thankfully still have access to.

Deere cap–clad gentleman right out of redneck casting that "this ain't no Jack house, ma'am. Them's sissy dogs," I turned the car around to leave and saw at least thirty head of cattle running for their lives and wailing like they were being chased by a butcher. Of course it was just that manic Jack, barking and yipping and nipping. Suddenly it spotted the car and came running, and again I opened the door and the little brat leaped in.

Whew. Now we had both dogs and could go back to finding their owner, a task that no longer seemed so simple. The brown and white one (a male) was asleep on the seat next to Cuy, but the crazy, wet, muddy, black and white one (a female, big surprise) was in my lap, under my legs, licking my chin, and adding the now too-familiar smell of cow manure to the ambience of the Durango's interior. Despite driving to several other farms off Rokeby Road, during which I daydreamed about clean, dry clothes, piping-hot coffee, and the corporate life I left behind, and calling a few more, we had no luck finding their owners.

Ah yes. Stay-at-home motherhood. It's not just a job. It's also a chance to play Ace Ventura, Pet Detective.

So that's how Jack and Judy (I named them) came to stay with us, at least until the Jack Russell Rescue[75] people showed up. Through the miracle of Invisible Fence collars

---

75. I had no idea the Jack Russell Rescue organization existed, but since we started looking for a dog Hemingway's discovered all this stuff. The Society for the Protection of Saint Bernards. People for the Ethical Treatment of Poodles. (A dangerously fringe group, these folks actually advocate *against* canine couture. Their motto is "Real poodles don't wear Prada." Which I think is fine, because then there's more for me.) Of course the group I'd most like to contact is the Good Samaritan Recovery Society. Maybe they can help me get past the touch of post-traumatic stress disorder I've developed from discovering a kitchen it would take Mr. Clean and a team of bioterrorism experts to tackle. Not that my house is so perfect. But at least I don't store my kids' stinky sneakers in a pasta pot. After all, that's what the freezer is for.

and ID tags, they reunited the pups with their rightful and immensely relieved owners almost immediately.

And then the pressure was really on.

Upon the dogs' departure my heartbroken and crying son Cuyler made me promise to find him a pooch. Pronto. So of course I promised, swore, crossed my heart and hoped to find a hound. This despite the fact that I definitely don't need a dog right now.

Between the hundreds of packing boxes that seemed to reproduce like I'm running a fertility clinic for corrugated cardboard, and the nonstop activity that is the essence of turning a house into a home—moving furniture; moving furniture *again*; arranging crucial collectibles "just so," vacuuming; dusting; running to the dump; hitting the hardware store for hooks, nails, and lightbulbs; trimming rug pads; and picking up groceries because ya gotta eat to stay fueled for the whole endeavor—I really don't need to be scouring all manner of animal shelters in a desperate attempt to give my younger son his own Spot. Or Henry. Or whomever.

But a promise is a promise, and so, on top of everything else, we kicked our quest for a canine into high gear.

We fell in love with Teddy Bear when we saw her picture in an ad for the Middleburg Humane Foundation, but she'd been adopted by the time we called. Shane, an energetic Border collie who played a good game of catch, caught Cuy's eye, but we were five minutes too late; another family had already begun the adoption process. We even spent about two hours with a wonderful, even-tempered Treeing Walker Coonhound named Sandy whom we would have loved to adopt, but doing so would have meant taking his current owner, too. The guy simply wasn't ready to give the dog up, though I think his wife would have happily handed over both of them.

We'd begun to think we'd never find the perfect pup when Hemingway stumbled upon the Web site for the Rappahannock Animal Welfare League. They had a darling little reddish-brown Viszla mix named Wheat available, and since he looked to be the perfect size for Cuy, we went to see him.

Between you and me, I should have known things were not going to proceed as planned as soon as we pulled up at the shelter. Even with the windows closed, we could hear what sounded like a million dogs barking at once. Hemingway got an appropriately hangdog look on his handsome face and said, "I always feel so bad in these places. I just wish we could take all the animals home." Sensing time, and just the right level of enthusiasm, was of the essence, I cheerily replied, "But we already have lots of animals at home. Three hundred cows, two kids, Inky the cat, and Cuy's hamster. All we need now is that *one* perfect dog."

He was leaning in close to hear me over the clamor of what was probably more like *two* million dogs, and his eyes said he wasn't quite sold on my spiel, so I came in for the kill. "Once we've got the whole farming thing down, and the kids are in the groove, then we can get another!"

"You're right," he said after a moment. "We'll take it one at a time."

And that's just how we led both dogs to the car. One at a time.

First came Wheat, who was quickly renamed Pete, and

then came Grundy, a big, sleek, German Shepherd mix originally named Scooby. Grundy/Scooby locked eyes with Hemingway as soon as we walked in, and was, in my dog-loving husband's head, on his way home to Nate's Place long before we'd even met Wheat. I mean Pete. So much for the one step at a time stuff.

At this point, the newest members of the McCorkindale family are getting comfortable. Too comfortable. They love running through the fields, splashing in the streams, and strutting, mud soaked, through the house while one of us tries frantically to towel them off. Grundy enjoys eating the cushions on the kitchen stools, hogging all the dog toys, and burying bones in the houseplants. This afternoon's choice: a formerly lovely but now dead philodendron near the front door. Pete enjoys chasing the cattle, giving Grundy a good nip when he's not looking, and napping.[76]

This business of having dogs has led me to wonder whatever happened to doghouses. Charlie Brown's pal Snoopy lived in a doghouse, and so did my other favorite canine comic, Marmaduke. Hemingway says they're politically incorrect. I think it's equally incorrect for the dogs to deny me even a sliver of my king-size bed, and for my sons to see the pups trying to spoon with their parents. But that's just me.

Speaking of beds, I take pride in changing the kids' sheets and giving them nice fresh covers to curl up in. But I'll be damned if I'll do it for the dog. Leave it to Grundy to commandeer Cuyler's bottom bunk and actually crawl under the blankets to sleep. When I came in to awaken the

---

76. All in all, it's just like having four kids. Five if you count Hemingway. And I do.

small man one morning, I found the furry, burr-covered beast with his head on the pillow and his paws atop the comforter. For a second I thought it was my young son, but his happiness at being told to "come down for breakfast" was a dead giveaway it was the dog.

Like I said, the newest members of the family are getting a little too comfortable.

They're also getting big, and Hemingway has begun training them, and now they sit when you say "Sit," and they just about stay when you say "Stay." Which is a lot more than I can say for the kids. But seriously, they're both rather cute, exceedingly friendly, and maybe just a few Kibbles & Bits short of a full bowl. Complete strangers who just might be homicidal maniacs come to the door, and Grundy and Pete lick them, beg for treats, and roll onto their backs for belly rubs. Clearly they're not attack dogs, but that's what we have Cuyler for.

They're also not like any other dogs I've ever had in my life.

As kids, my brothers and I had our fair share of dogs. There was a little black dog with white paws named Gloves who broke his leg, then took off after the mailman the day his cast came off. I remember my dad searching frantically for my beloved pet, and coming home empty-handed, only to discover the bill from the animal hospital in our mailbox.

We also had a little red dog named Dee Dee, so named because she was supposedly my brother David's dog. (Get it? Dee Dee—David's Dog.) But when Dee Dee, whom my mom not so fondly referred to as Cee Cee, for Carpet Crapper, made a sudden and most mysterious trip to my

Uncle Dan's *Maryland* home one day, I was the only sibling to suspect foul play.

But maybe the pup de resistance of our mutt menagerie was our dumb blond dog with an even dumber name: Good Girl. Again, she was ostensibly David's. But as my younger brother was never around to catch the hell that ensued when his tick-ridden tail wagger snatched a fresh-from-the-oven broiled chicken off the kitchen table, devoured a stick of butter while curled comfortably beneath my mom's desk, and buried my father's boxer shorts out back by the basil and tomatoes, and I was, I blame him to this day for my basic distaste for all things dog.

In short, the mad dogs of my youth definitely did some crazy stuff. But I have no recollection of any of them ever having a confirmed kill. No, that, apparently, is a country thing.

In the past two weeks alone, Grundy's killed six groundhogs. How do I know? He's brought them home. He leaves them by the driver's-side door of the Durango so I can enjoy a send-off the likes of which I've never experienced in suburbia, and lays them at my bare feet on the front porch while I'm deep in an ad-copywriting[77] coma, praying the perfect four-word headline will rush forth from my fingers, and completely oblivious to the fact that the warm, furry muff tickling my toes is *not* the big beast who likes to sleep in my kid's bed.

Hemingway insists Grundy brings the groundhogs to me because "he's not man's best friend; he's Mom's best

---

77. Yes, I'm back to writing a bit of ad copy. It's easy, pays bundles, and helps foot the shoe fetish I suffer from.

friend!" Honestly. How long do we need to be married before that man figures out that this mom's best friend is a hair stylist with a blow dryer, a round brush, and a red-hot flat iron?

I realize I've been going on and on about Grundy, which may mean I'm more traumatized by the whole groundhog gift-giving business than I originally thought, but that doesn't mean there's not plenty to say about Pete.

Petite Pete should have been adopted by a family of means, 'cause that dog means vet bills. He's there almost once a week. He might have mange. His eyes are runny. He could have mites. There's a colony of crud living in his ears. He looks sick. *He* looks sick? Sick is how I look when I open the MasterCard bill. It's gotten so bad the people from Best Friends Animal Clinic call every other day to inquire about their "favorite patient, Pete." I believe there was even talk of adding a new wing in his honor with a plaque that says TO PETE. THANKS FOR MAKING THIS POSSIBLE.[78]

I was indulging my Oreck fixation the other day—vacuuming up the dog hair in my dining room, because Pete's impressive vet bills prohibit my hiring a cleaning lady to do it for me—when I discovered what looked like disgorged cat food on the carpet. I'm pretty sure I've mentioned that, in addition to our two princes and their two new pups, we also have a cat. But if I haven't, well, we do, and most of the time Inky, so named because he's the color of a bottle of black ink, lives in the basement. Except when he ventures upstairs to vomit.

---

78. When we head to the poorhouse we'll be thanking Pete for making that possible, too.

As you can imagine, discovering that the cat had hurled on the housewarming gift my mom gave me when we finally moved into Nate's Place really sent me reeling. I was stomping around, swearing in Italian, and doing my little "*Morte al gatto!*"—death to the cat!—dance, when I flipped off the vacuum, crouched down for a closer inspection, and just about passed out. What I had come upon was not that favorite feline delicacy, upchucked tuna chunks, but rather pup-regurgitated potpourri. I'd put some wisteria-scented stuff in the room in the hope of making it a little more *Desperate Housewives* and a little less eau de dog, and my two mongrels ate it and retched it back up onto the rug. It might have been worth it if it helped their breath or turned me into the Gabrielle Solis of the sticks, but alas, it did neither.

Potpourri isn't the only thing the pups have developed a palate for. The other night I was whipping up spaghetti and meatballs and it came time to put the fresh pub bread I'd picked up at the Home Farm Store in Middleburg—where they charge almost as much for a loaf as you'd expect to pay for a Land Rover—in the oven. Only it wasn't where I'd left it. I checked the cabinets, looked in the fridge, and scoured the countertops. I even called upstairs to the kids to see if in their infinite impatience they'd inhaled it. But it was nowhere to be found.

And then I looked down.

There, torn to shreds on the dining room rug, the very same rug upon which I would find the ralphed-up room freshener just a few days later, was its clear, crinkly wrapper. Lying next to the ruins, sated and sleeping, crumbs like freckles sprinkled on his snout, was, you guessed it, Grundy.

Well, I went batshit. In a matter of seconds I was having a major *"Morte al cane!"*—death to the dog!—tantrum, with a little *"Morte al marito!"*—death to the husband!—tossed in for effect. Why? Because it's Hemingway's fault the damn dog is stealing people food. Despite my begging and pleading, my indulgent spouse has been sneaking table scraps to both Grundy and Pete, and now they love grilled salmon, prime rib, sautéed broccoli, and, obviously, expensive fresh bread.

Mark my words. If I ever get those doghouses I'm after, the hounds won't be the only ones calling them home.

Big Bow Wow Bulletin

TO: Friends & Family
FR: Pete & Grundy's Mom (Not!)
Date: Monday, 8 p.m.
Subject: Grundy Takes the Cake ...

And I mean that literally.

Hemingway's been working so hard around here that I thought I'd be a good wife and make him something special. So I whipped up his favorite dinner (macaroni and cheese, and fried fish sticks—we're fighting low cholesterol), and decided to bake him a cake.

Now, I can't bake, but I can read. I grabbed a box of Betty Crocker Supremely Fluffy white cake mix (white cake is Hemingway's favorite, further proof that opposites attract), eggs, oil, and water and went to town.

Thirty-three minutes later, my first ever faux pas–free baked confection was complete and ready to cool. I was so proud. I placed it outside on the table under a small towel, and set the timer for ten minutes.

Big mistake.

Apparently Grundy set his for eight, because when I went to retrieve the cake, there was the dog, standing over my Bundt pan, chowing down on Hemingway's dessert. I just about died. I mean, who knew he and my honey had the same taste in sweets? (Makes me further suspect that my husband and that damn dog were indeed separated at birth. . . .)

Since it would take longer to drive to the store and buy another cake than it would to bake one, I did just that. Only this time Hemingway was stuck with chocolate, and Grundy was stuck waiting till breakfast to eat again.

If that's not bad enough, twice this week I was awakened by the sounds of that mutt scurrying about and barfing. I'm sure you're thinking it has something to do with my questionable baking abilities, but, alas, it does not. In fact it has everything to do with Grundy's superior groundhog-slaughtering skills. First he kills them, then he consumes them. And occasionally they disagree with him.

Which is how the whole thing starts, anyway, isn't it?

Susan

Chapter Thirteen

EVEN FARM BOYS EAT FAST FOOD

Just as I consider it my duty to kvetch[79] about the limited shopping options here in cow country, Casey and Cuyler consider it theirs to celebrate and frequent the myriad fast food places that dot the landscape. To be accurate, they don't dot the landscape where we live,[80] but if we make the million-mile, full-tank-of-gas trek to civilization, there's plenty to pick from.

And pick they do. Unlike Ridgewood, where they still have a "no fast food" law beloved by many parents, here my kids can pick Wendy's one day and McDonald's another. The only criteria for eating the crap these places proffer is what toy they're giving away that day.

Have I ever told you how much I hate toys from fast food franchises?

First, they only come with those darn Happy Meals, which contain three chicken fingers/tenders/nuggets/you

---

79. That's Yiddish for complain, moan, bitch, bellyache. If I have to define one more Yiddish phrase, I'm signing everybody in Fauquier County up for Yeshiva. If I can find one.

80. Hogs and heifers and horses have that honor.

name it, eight French fries, and a small drink. Definitely not enough food for the two human garbage pails I've produced. So I wind up springing for two Happy Meals at nearly six dollars a pop, plus two "real" meals, and suddenly the "free" toys total twenty-four bucks. Who's happy? Not me.

And lots of times my boys aren't too thrilled, either. Why? Because they've already gotten Patrick and thought SpongeBob would be in the bag this week. But no, it's that goofy pink starfish again, and they're freaking.

"Oh, man. Not another Patrick!" Cuyler wails as he slides from his seat to the germ-infested floor. "Get up! Get up!" I hiss. But it's no use. He's spinning on the floor of Burger King/McDonald's/Wendy's/wherever, covering himself in spilled food and filth from head to toe. I gag at the thought of the millions of disease-carrying microbes clinging to his clothes, hair and hands, and lunge for the little lunatic just as he flips onto his belly and breaststrokes away from me. He's nearly to the door when I dive for his hood and connect—of course—with his hair. So now the boy beast I've unleashed on the lunch crowd is crying and flailing wildly to get away from me. Finally,[81] I wrestle him back to our booth, where he discovers Casey playing happily with both Patricks, and promptly explodes all over again.

I just don't understand my sons' attraction to these plastic pieces of flotsam. We've given them five hundred rolling acres on which to play, and still they prefer the three feet in front of the TV and toys that are frankly nothing

---

81. And without the use of an animal tranquilizer, I'm proud to say . . .

more than garage sale fodder. Heck, they have a collection that's so extensive it could form its own garbage barge.[82] I once tried to pare it down, only to be discovered mid-cleanout by Cuyler, who forced me—under threat of pain from the pointy Little Bo Peep top he brandished—to return every Batman, Spider-Man, Garfield, Power Ranger, Hamm, Homer, Marge, Bart, Scully, Plankton, Woody, Buzz, Rex, and toys whose names I don't even know, to the huge plastic container they call home. Of course I obliged. You've no idea what that kid and Little Bo Peep are capable of.

Frankly, I've come to the conclusion that my sons' fondness for such offal is my own fault. If I'd learn to make more than grilled cheese, maybe my boys could pass the golden arches without salivating like starved Saint Bernards. One minute we're cruising along like a nice normal family (with Casey flipping from radio station to radio station, looking for sports scores, and Cuyler screaming, "Enough talking! Music! I said music!"), and the next I'm assaulted by a cacophony of commands ("Mom, McDonald's at one o'clock! Get into the right lane! They've got Teenage Mutant Ninja Turtles!").

All's well if I agree to purchase the cardboard fare that masquerades as food at these places (along with the "free" toy, of course). But God forbid I decide to do so via the drive-through. My boys go berserk. "We're picking up? NO! They give the best stuff to the kids who go INSIDE!" I hit the brakes in front of the order board and turn to my eldest. "Are you telling me there's some kind of vast fast

---

82. And Hemingway and I obviously have several screws loose, as we didn't lose the damn thing on the move from New Jersey to Virginia.

food–collectibles conspiracy?" He nods, while the madman behind me screams and pounds the back of my seat with his feet to punctuate his points. "Mom, stop talking! We're not picking up. We're *[kick]* going *[harder kick]* in *[hardest kick yet]*!"

Oh, really?

Fast as the Flash, yet another collectible my kids had to have, I'm out of the car and ejecting Devil Boy from the backseat. I pop the seat belt, pull him toward me, and plop him on the walkway. "You want to go in? Go in." Now Casey is frantic. "Mom," he hollers, "are you insane?" Horns are honking. And then, over shouts of "Hey, lady, order already!" and "What the heck's the holdup?" I hear, "It's a rumor! Kid, it's a rumor!" A voice over the intercom is yelling to Casey, who responds, "The toy thing?"

"Yeah," replies the voice, "they're all the same. Doesn't matter whether you drive through or come in—everybody gets the same thing!"

Now my kids go wild with joy. So, to my surprise, do the kids in the pickup truck behind us. Cuyler scrambles back into the backseat and slams the door, and the mom in the pickup catches my eye. "I'm sorry!" I yell. "Don't be," she shouts back. "My boys have tried every trick in the book to get me to go into these places. They like the free toy, but I think what they really like is being surrounded by food that smells like feet."

God, I wish that were true of my kids. If it were, I'd simply whip up burgers and serve them in their bedrooms. But no, for my boys, it's all about the free toys. Doesn't matter if it's Jimmy Neutron or Pokemon. They've gotta collect 'em all.

Maybe it wouldn't be so bad if fast food chains had cool stuff for moms, too. Like a series of *Ocean's Eleven* collectibles. They could stick them in "Mommy Meals," and I bet you'd have women jamming the drive-throughs to get a Matt Damon, Brad Pitt, or George Clooney with their Chicken Caesar Salad. And if you wound up with doubles of Damon or a pair of Pitts, you'd be patient. Unless it took forever to collect a Clooney. Then you'd have to speak to the manager. And maybe even eat inside.

Chapter Fourteen

HOUNDED BY HONEY-DOS

You know that feeling you get on vacation, that sense of relaxation and peacefulness combined with anxious impermanence? If you're at all like me (and God willing, you're not), you lie on your lounge chair and think to yourself, Wow, this is great. Too bad I can't stay right here forever, sipping my Sea Breeze and barely watching my kids play with kids they just met, who might be nice but who might also be bullies waiting to drown them the minute my eyelids droop. Too bad all this sun, sand, and cabana-side drink service can't last forever. Too bad I have to go home and figure out how to pay for it.

I have those kinds of feelings and thoughts all the time—minus the ones about the kids drowning, as there's no serious body of water anywhere near here, which, along with the lack of a Starbucks, really costs this place points from my perspective—*and I live here*. I'm not going anywhere. Trust me; Hemingway hates to travel even more than he hates to spend money.

Maybe after I've lived here a little longer Northern Virginia's singular splendor will cease to take my breath

away. But I doubt it. Between the lazy streams and the rolling pastures, the hummingbirds and the stone farm buildings, I feel like I'm living in a vacation paradise. And we all
know what happens when you go on vacation. Eventually
you have to go home, do the laundry, and address the MasterCard bill. And maybe even enclose a check.

But of course, I am home. This is good, and it's bad. It's
good because I get to drink my morning coffee while
watching baby deer lounge on my lawn in the dawn's
silken yellow sunlight. It's bad because my sons usually
interrupt me to demand something silly, like breakfast.

Everywhere I look, I see the Blue Ridge Mountains.
But it seems the closest I'll come to them is the "mountain-
fresh" scent of my fabric softener. All around me, people
are kayaking, rafting, camping, hiking, biking, horseback
riding, and even hang gliding. And what am I doing? I'm
searching for the mates to missing, manure-encrusted
gym socks;[83] vacuuming up potato chip crumbs from the
arcade that does double duty as my son's bedroom; and
filling trash bag after trash bag with half-consumed silver-
and-blue pouches of Capri Sun juice coolers, bags of moldy
seedless red grapes, and sleeves of smashed saltine crackers. I'm beginning to think I should go through my house
like an old-fashioned street cleaner, carrying a long stick
with a spike on the end, stabbing at garbage, maybe a kid
or two, and stuffing it all in a sack on my back. It might
even make me feel like I'm trekking the trails of the Blue
Ridge.

---

83. And finding them, unfortunately, after they've adhered to the dust bunnies beneath the bathroom radiator.

Adding to this feeling of living in "vacation land" is the fact that I actually am on vacation. This is the first summer in more years than I can recall that I haven't worked.

Every morning Hemingway takes off to bush hog, corral escaped cattle, mend fences, and generally tackle a variety of farm tasks too numerous to contemplate, and I sit here making my own grand plans for my day: take the kids to the schoolyard to shoot hoops while I sun myself and read; or take the kids to a movie while I sit in the parking lot, sun myself, and read; or take the kids to pick blueberries while I sun myself, read, and occasionally say helpful things like "Only the purple ones, please," "Here's another bucket to fill," and "You missed that bush over there."[84]

But whatever I select, you can be sure that as soon as I'm sunning myself and reading, my cell will ring and Hemingway will unfurl a list of honey-dos that kill my vacation buzz faster than the kids tear through toys on Christmas morning.

What's an escape-minded mom to do? Recently I've designated one day a week Reality Day. On that day and that day alone I make myself Clean Sweep at warp speed, do the laundry, and change the sheets.[85]

Next, I jump in the car and replenish the kids' supply of cookies, Hemingway's supply of Budweiser, and the dogs' supply of Milk Bones. In fact—if I may digress for just a few moments—I just returned from my weekly foray

---

84. This activity requires paying them day laborer wages, but it lets me flex my atrophying manager muscles a bit, so it's worth it.

85. Casey gets Cuyler's, Cuyler gets Casey's, and Grundy and Pete swap pet beds.

to Food Lion, and have only one question: Why would anyone name a supermarket Food Lion?

Up north we had ShopRite. Now, that I get. It's the "right" place to do your food shopping. And we had Stop & Shop. I get that, too. You stop and shop and you're outta there. But here we have Food Lion, where, it sounds to me, you're supposed to kill your own dinner like the king of the jungle.

I imagine one day I'll walk in and be greeted by Ginger, one of Food Lion's lovelies, with her seventy-five cute cat pins plastered to the front of her perky polo shirt, her hair in a ponytail so tight it's a wonder she doesn't suffer an aneurysm right there in the aisle, and she'll say, "Welcome to Food Lion! Today is Kill Your Own Chicken Day! Kill one, get a dozen eggs and a frying pan FREE!"

That would certainly be a more entertaining way to spend $188, which is what I just coughed over for snacks, vegetables, cereals, soups, and one seriously frozen Perdue broiler. I can hear my mom now. "How did you spend so much and not get any meat?" Maybe because I didn't shop at Giant.

Giant is the other supermarket chain in this neck of the woods, and from what I've read in the local rags, its claim to fame is that it stocks deer.

See what you suburbanites are missing? You've just got poultry and beef, and they're already belly-up, aren't they? You need to do your food shopping in the country, where it's low-key and laid-back, and deer stroll unimpeded through the automatic doors of a grocery store, make their way to the deli counter, and enjoy scraps of marbled ham and Muenster until Animal Control comes to collect them.

This happened just last week at the Giant in Warrenton, when a deer actually entered the store. Was it sick and disoriented, or desperate to redeem some coupons before the expiration date? The story in the paper didn't deal with the doe's motivation, nor did it mention it was all that unusual.

In New Jersey this would be a giant event and would probably give birth to a new ad campaign for the chain: GIANT SELECTION! GIANT SAVINGS! GIANT OPPORTUNITY TO GET UP CLOSE AND PERSONAL WITH WILDLIFE!

Obviously you can take the girl out of marketing, but you can't take the marketer out of the girl.

In addition to my dead chicken I also picked up paper plates. Don't ask me why those weren't in the house already. I think it has something to do with my new stay-at-home-mom status and delusions of making every meal a beautiful dining experience for my family. You know, the three men I live with who wouldn't know if they were eating off china, paper, or plastic, or out of a box, bag, or wrapper. Maybe I should start serving all their meals in brown lunch bags. It'll definitely make cleanup easier.

If you think my "beautiful dining" idea is a doozy, you should have been around a few weeks ago when, in a sudden burst of delirium, I decided to guarantee my guys' sweet dreams by *ironing their sheets*. To prove just how far gone I was, I actually shared my slip into Martha Stewart mania with my good friend Trish, who promptly replied, *"The hell you are!"* And then, like one of those professionally trained suicide hotline specialists, she kept me on the phone until the feeling passed, and made me promise to call her immediately if I should again begin to look longingly at my can of spray starch.

Recent sheet-ironing thoughts and dining dementia

aside, on Reality Day I also hit the bank, mail the bills, return books to the library and the DVDs and video games to the rental store,[86] and either pick up or drop off the dry cleaning while ignoring Hemingway's weekly "We live on a farm; why do we still have dry cleaning?" query. By late afternoon I'm back to fold and put away the clothes, which will be dirty again by the next day, water the plants, make dinner, clean up the kitchen, and force the kids, under penalty of premature death to the PlayStation, to shower, shampoo their hair, trim their nails, and evict the potatoes from their ears. My vegetable garden should be as bountiful as the ones in my boys' heads.

I should also mention that on Reality Day I do whatever Hemingway needs me to do. Pick up the summer-weight bib overalls he special ordered at Tractor Supply. Re-stock the supply of Deep Woods Off he practically drinks before every foray into the fields. Run to the gun shop for extra rounds for the rifle.[87]

The next day is Recuperation Day, which begins with me in my comfy PJ shorts and T-shirt, cradling my coffee on the porch, progresses to iced tea and a nice nap in one of the Adirondack chairs in the backyard, often in the same spiffy outfit—believe me, the cows don't care—and ends with a glass of chardonnay on the sofa while Hemingway mumbles something about which Netflix selection we should watch and the kids howl about not having been fed. (Hey, there's a fridge full of food. Go pick something out!)

---

86. Before the mortgage payment masquerading as a late fee kicks in.

87. Please note: If anything pertaining to weaponry is on his list, nothing pertaining to Budweiser is on mine.

The remaining five days are Relaxation Days, during which I try to act like I'm on vacation.

The system works pretty well when Hemingway sticks to the program. But it completely collapses when he calls with an emergency honey-do and I wind up standing in the local hardware store, slick with coconut oil, surrounded by a bunch of contractor types, awaiting a gallon of primer or a length of PVC pipe he has to have *now*.

"Excuse me, ma'am, but you smell like a margarita," remarks one of my fellow shoppers, a ruggedly good-looking gray-haired Marlboro man–type in his early sixties, with a tape measure attached to one Wrangler-clad hip, a cell phone on the other, and bigger biceps than the guys in *Men's Health*.

"Piña colada," I reply. He looks at me over his gold-rimmed glasses. "I think you mean piña colada." I add, helpfully, "I have on coconut oil."

He furrows his brow and turns to his pal. "Roy, there a beach around here somewhere?" "Nope," Roy replies. He turns back to me. "Little lady, I think you're lost."

He's got that right. But eventually I'll find some down-time, and when I do, I'm going to sun myself till I'm pink as the hogs Hemingway just helped one of our tenants bring home. The ones he wants help with. Now. How do I know? I've just slathered myself in Bain de Soleil (for the St. Tropez via Virginia tan), and of course my cell phone's ringing.

Chapter Fifteen

THE CHICK IS IN THE MAIL

I was at my desk, writing away, when I heard the phone ring, Hemingway's mumbled response, and then the words "Susan, I'm leaving to pick up chicks."

Huh? I had no idea he was unhappy.

Sure, I haven't exercised since the last time I forced my staff at *Family Circle* to take a kickboxing class in my office, but come on, how about a little advance warning? I was about to go off the deep end and demand to know why we had to rehash the whole perimenopause potbelly business again when it dawned on me that he meant *the* chicks: the variety pack of twenty-six tiny pullets coming via mail from McMurray's Hatchery. The phone call was the post office telling him to come retrieve his poultry PDQ.

You see, sometime last month Hemingway and Casey decided they need to raise chickens. Hemingway came to this conclusion because he "needs" to eat farm-fresh eggs; Casey because he "needs" an A in his agri-science class. Where does that leave me? Needing two Tylenol as I stand in Tractor Supply,[88] helping Hemingway prep for the pul-

---

88. See "The Impractical Girl's Guide to Farm Speak" for more about this Saks of the Sticks.

lets' arrival by stocking up on heat lamps, a fifty-gallon tub, and "premier chicken feed,"[89] and wondering how the hell I let my life take this bizarre turn.

Under normal circumstances I'd have sent my husband to retrieve his bantys by himself, but it suddenly dawned on me that my own chick assortment—my Lucky Chick bath assortment—might have arrived, as well.

Like Hemingway, I ordered my chick collection[90] about a month ago. In fact it was the same day I finally had dead bolts installed on the bathroom doors. If it was at the post office, we'd all be happy: Hemingway and Casey with their Rhode Island Reds, and me with everything I could possibly need to languish with my loofah under lock and key.

If I may digress for just a moment, I feel the need to explain why the dead bolt on the bathroom door business is a big deal to me. It stems from the fact that I'm relatively certain I'm the only woman in America who's put up with lock-free bathroom doors for more than a dozen years. Oh, sure, when we lived in a brand-new condo in a town that will remain nameless but to me will always be known as the absolute armpit of New Jersey, the bathroom doors had locks. They had to. They were the only appeal the place had. But ever since then—in Ridgewood and now here in Upperville—I've lived lockless and at the mercy of the McMen who, when they need me, need me *now*.

To be fair, I'm not talking about Hemingway. Having been a Marine, he's got no problem honoring the honor

---

89. Right next to "premier swine feed," in case you're interested.

90. Comprising soothing eye gel mask, microfiber hair turban, suction-cup supporting bath pillow, and Mandarin White Orange bath salts and body scrub. Ooooh. I love Lucky Chick!

system. I'm talking about the Boys Who Know No Bound-
aries to whom I gave birth. It doesn't matter what I'm
doing—brushing my teeth, taking a bath, trimming my
toenails—they're coming in. And so, after passively per-
mitting company for everything from shaving my legs
to, well, you know, for the past thirteen and a half years, I
finally called a handyman to have locks installed. You
might have thought I'd have done this during the whole
Nate's Place Remodeling Project, but creature of bad habits
that I am, I did not. And you definitely would have thought
that someone cancelled Christmas, the way my kids re-
acted to learning they'd no longer have unfettered access
to Sue in the Loo. "You did what? Why?" they cried. Why?
Because it's time you guys learn about privacy and mod-
esty, and because it really demonstrates a lack of breeding
to have your mother breaking up fistfights while she's sitting on the toilet bowl.

In other, less descriptive, bathroom news, I recently
dug out and dusted off our scale. Wonderful to see it again,
as there seemed to be a tad bit less of me to love. I tried to
verify this veritable miracle by stepping on the scale at my
new gynecologist's office, but no luck. According to hers, I
should be on my way to Weight Watchers. According to
mine, a day at Häagen-Dazs wouldn't hurt me. Which
weight do *you* think I'm going with?[91]

Along with a brief discussion of weight loss—because
there's just not a lot to say about something that ain't
happening—and a more lengthy discussion about weight
gain, I shared my belief that meals eaten while in a head-

---

91. Right. Pralines and Cream in a sugar cone, please.

stand should force food to stay in my poor, deprived boobs and not pass Go, collect two hundred pounds, and assign them directly to my ass.

The good doctor responded by giving me the phone number of a psychotherapist three doors down.

I also mentioned the nonstop schvitzing I'm suffering from. She told me not to worry, it's perimenopause and it will pass. In two to five years. Super. I get to spend the next sixty months sweating. And Hemingway gets to spend them in the smokehouse. Which is where he headed directly after hearing the diagnosis. There was something about the prospect of having the air-conditioning on full blast in February that frightened him.

It didn't frighten me, though. Instead it confirmed what I've known all along. That I'm one hot chick. And this hot chick deserves a nice, hot soak.

"Wait for me!" I shouted as Hemingway started our huge silver pickup. He looked at me, smiling with surprise at my sudden decision to flee my desk and join him on his fowl foray. "I knew it. I knew you'd get into it," he said, all pleased as punch with himself and patting me on the knee.

Oh yeah, I'm into it. The tub, that is. Me, my Lucky Chick spa stuff, and the latest issue of *In Style*. It's like having a hen party without the actual hens. Now, that's farming counterfeit farm girl style. And that's just the way I like it.

Suzy's Poultry-Ordering Primer

Let's say you've got a hankering for farm-fresh eggs and paying $20 a dozen at your gourmet grocer really ruffles your feathers. Then don't do it. Simply order your own poultry via the U.S. Postal Service. Here's how:

1. **Banish the idea that you need to live on a farm to have fowl.** If you've got some free space on a rooftop, a patch of lawn, or a spare bedroom (if you can stand the aroma) you can raise your own egg layers.

2. **Pick up a copy of Backyard Poultry or log on to McMurrayHatchery.com.** You can also search on "chicks by mail," but I wouldn't. Unless you really want books on women wearing chain mail or tips for ordering brides from Borneo.

3. **Determine your preferred chicken temperament.** Do you want feisty hens that will peck at your designer heels but produce several eggs a day, or more docile breeds that lay less but will cuddle with your kids?

4. **What color is your capon?** Sure, you can go with white, but maybe you'd like eggs that will match your eyes, purse, or the paint job on your house. Check out browns, blues, and greens (and you thought Dr. Seuss dreamt that stuff up). The options, like Neiman Marcus's designer shoe department, are virtually endless.

5. ***Equip yourself for success.*** You'll need a coop, a water system, feed, scratch, and a few other particulars for your poultry. Hit Tractor Supply or McMurrayHatchery .com for the whole enchilada. Mmmmm. Chicken enchiladas. Bear those in mind for when your birds are past their egg-laying prime.

6. ***Ignore your neighbors' kvetching.*** Sure, they may not like your chicken coop in their gated community, but whip 'em up an omelet and not only will they stop squawking, they'll start showing up with empty egg cartons and cold, hard cash. You'll never turn a Perdue-size profit, but even minimal financial gains will keep you in facials.

Chapter Sixteen

BACKYARD POULTRY VS. PLAYBOY

*L*iving in the country means I never have to watch Hemingway read *Playboy*. I hated when it arrived in the mail in its slick silver-and-black wrapper, and then I'd go all Gloria Steinem on him. But these days I kind of miss that trashy tome, particularly since his new favorite publication is *Backyard Poultry*.

Just like *Playboy*, there's a hot chick on the cover and a multipage feature about this month's feathered fantasy girl inside. Hemingway reads it and starts insisting our hens are hotter. Before I know it, I'm taking digital photos of our twenty-six divas and drafting a pitch letter[92] in a bizarre attempt to support his desire to be the first hen-modeling magnate. I guess I shouldn't complain. If he's successful we'll all be living high on the hog. I mean chick. Though now that I think of it, the hog-modeling business might have some merit.

Thanks to a recent issue of this "*Playboy* for the pullet set," Hemingway's discovered the joys of bathing one's

---

92. Who knew my marketing skills would come in so handy in the hinterland?

birds. And I'm not talking about pulling one of my frozen Perdue fryers from the freezer and spritzing it with Fantastik. I'm talking about his desire to wash our chickens in warm water and shampoo, follow with a little conditioner, and finish off their "exclusive spa experience" with a pedicure, beak trim, and warm towel wrap.

"You know, like people who show chickens do," he says to me. People *show* chickens? Oh, dear God, what have I done to have been beamed so far from my planet? And who is this guy running off with my Paul Mitchell Awapuhi Shampoo and Conditioner and an armful of my fluffy Fieldcrest Cannon towels?

If that's not bad enough, he wants my help. I'm finally paroled from giving the boys baths, and now he thinks I'm going to join him in pampering the poultry. I don't know why. It's not like we're going to enter the birds in a beauty contest. The only things they compete for is to see which one of them can peck my feet to death fastest; snatch the most food from my kids' hands; and destroy more petunias, impatiens, and begonias in the window boxes.

I don't know how many times I need to explain to Hemingway that his job is to experience farm life. Mine is to survive it. And trust me, if I'm forced to sponge bathe even one of those birds I'll be the only one left alive.

In addition to "making the hens happy with a warm bath," he's begun talking about making our own poultry feed "because it's better for the flock." I have barely any interest in shopping for and making our meals, which can only be considered organic if Stouffer's grows its frozen, family-size lasagna out in a field, yet for some reason Hemingway's convinced I'm eager to join him in gathering earthworms, seeds, slugs, and innumerable other slimy dirt dwellers.

Will someone please tell me when Tractor Supply, the Saks of the sticks, fell out of favor for such essentials?

I swear, if I have to hear one more time about bathing the birds, producing our own organic poultry feed, the tricks to deciphering chicken talk, and the joys of making chicken-feather pillows to give as gifts,[93] I'm going to make one and try it out over his face. I'm sure I won't be the first farm wife accused of killing her bird-bathing, feed-making husband. And I'm also sure no jury of my peers will convict me. Particularly if I plead insanity. His.

But I digress.

Besides caring for, bathing, and occasionally being forced to play Francesco Scavullo to our bevy of bantams, I think one of the things about country life that really gives me a kick is that it's kind of like being in one of those old Hertz Rent-a-Car commercials. Will the electrician call you back? Not exactly. Will the power company show up at the agreed-upon time? Not exactly. Will the dozen or so weather outlets make the same or even similar predictions? Not exactly.

To try to stay on top of whatever weather is coming our way, we augment our TV and radio news with several Internet weather-alert services and a weather radio. The weather radio is a small, satanic device that delights in announcing loudly that "FOG WAS REPORTED" during the depths of our REM sleep. It would be one thing if it alerted us to an oncoming tornado or flood or even frogs falling

_____

93. What, Garnet Hill's no good?

from the sky. But to wake me up in a fog to tell me about fog makes me want to beat the fogging thing with a hammer.

In any case, even with the weather radio and the nine other self-proclaimed storm-watch sources at our disposal, including "Grizzly Bob" at our local livestock exchange, who claims to be half man, half barometer, we still wonder . . . will we get three inches of snow? Not exactly. Will we get thirty inches of snow? Not exactly. Will we know before it arrives? Definitely, absolutely, not exactly.

The other thing I love about country living is that we have to go to the post office to get our mail. I mosey on over; shoot the breeze with the postmaster; collect our catalogs, letters, bills, and magazines; and promptly toss two-thirds of it in the huge trash basket tucked in the corner. I'd love to throw out the Amex statement, but I'll have to satisfy myself with something more expendable. Like the new issue of *Backyard Poultry*. It should arrive any day, and there's no way it's coming home to this house. I just don't give a cluck.

Chapter Seventeen

HOLIDAYS ON CHARDONNAY

*Y*esterday I had a local hair salon get rid of the roots running rampant on my head and match my natural color. What a mistake. Who knew Redken made Tree Bark Brown? The real name is something like Medium Blonde, but that's just to cushion the blow. There's nothing medium about it. No matter how I brush it, comb it, or clip it, it's still brown. Quick, somebody pass the peroxide.

Bet you're eager to know how my new bathroom locks are working out, aren't you? Does the fact that I'm writing this from the comfort of my rooster-, pig-, and cow-clad loo answer that question? I thought so.

Don't worry, I haven't been spending all of my time locked away in a long-overdue solo bubble bath. I've actually been Christmas shopping and while doing so—shock of shocks—fending off the advances of amorous strange men. Why in my old age am I suddenly so appealing? Blame it on *The Simpsons*. Seems if I pick up anything to do with the Fox network's stalwart—from Bart-emblazoned boxer shorts to Homer's HAPPY D'OH!LIDAYS ornaments— men materialize out of nowhere. During a recent stroll around Kohl's one asked me to join him for coffee, and a second trailed me through Target and proffered lunch. I admit I had to seriously consider that proposition, as it *was* almost eleven and I had a bad case of the midmorning munchies, but I stopped myself. After all, I'm a married woman and I know what men really want. And nobody, but nobody, is taking off with the set of Moe Sizlak beer mugs I got my hands on for Hemingway.

Speaking of the holidays, our first Halloween here in the hinterland was particularly frightening. Why? Because there's nowhere around here for the kids to trick-or-treat. Sure, we have "neighbors," but it would take the boys half an hour just to get to the entrance of their farm, and a GPS system to find their house. By then they'd deserve way more than a Butterfinger,[94] so trick-or-treating up and down Rokeby Road is not an option.

At first I considered driving them to a neighborhood I don't know (now, that would be scary), or taking them to what's called a truck-or-treating event. From what I've been told, churches set these up in their parking lots for kids who live on farms. Parents come and park their pick-ups in a circle, and the kids simply trick-or-treat from one truck to the next. I was concerned we needed to be a member of the church whose truck-or-treating crush we crashed, but was assured that everyone—even us heathens—is welcome on Halloween.[95]

The other option was to take the boys to my sweet sister-in-law's in McLean, where they could trick, treat,

94. And I'd need a drink.

95. Nothing like getting a little religion with your Baby Ruth.

and torment the spectacularly affluent. Frankly I really wanted to watch them demand sugar-coated confections from the likes of Ethel Kennedy and Alma Powell, but as Hemingway was certain it would get Nancy banned from bunko, we nixed it.

Ultimately we took the boys to what we learned is the Halloween hotspot in this neck of the woods: Mountain-view Avenue in Marshall.

Marshall is a lovely, laid-back country community of pretty homes with wraparound porches; manicured lawns and lush flower beds; brightly colored swing sets; big, happy dogs; and folks wearing Washington Redskins jerseys from August through January. Imagine their joy at seeing our mini version of Michael Strahan, aka Cuyler, decked out in his blue-and-white Giants uniform, demanding a treat the day after the Giants tricked the Redskins 36–0. There were some tense moments, but each time it threatened to get ugly, Hemingway smiled and quipped, "We figured this was the scariest thing we could do to you 'Skins fans," and all was well. But to be honest, I'm still checking the kid's candy.

Ah yes, the candy. The tons of candy. Why do they bring it home and then leave it where poor, defenseless, self-control-free, Dirty Bathwater (I mean Medium) Blonde moms can eat it? I swear, even from the safety of my bed, with my pillow over my ears, I can hear the fun-size Snickers bars and little bags of candy corn crying, "Hey, you with the mousy hair and the hot flashes: You know you want us. . . ."

What I truly want is for my kids to have a full week of school. Right after Halloween the weather snapped, and the five-day school week went out the window. I've never seen anything like it. If snow is predicted for anywhere across the continental United States, the schools in Fauquier County close.[96] And if it actually snows here, be it a blizzard or just a light dusting that melts by midmorning, you can bet school will be scrapped for at least two days. The problem isn't the schools; it's the roads. The straight and level ones are just fine, but those that twist and turn and jump up and down like a cardiogram—the locals call them rolling hills because they can roll your car right onto its roof—present a problem. There's something about a schoolbus full of kids careening down an icy mountain road that makes the locals err on the side of caution.

Now, I know of moms who love snow days. Women who at the sight of the first flake rush to their special cabinet for their box of craft supplies and index cards full of ideas for Popsicle-stick villages and painted sock puppets, macramé pot holders and milk-carton gingerbread houses. But I'm not on a first-name basis with any of these freaks.

No, when I awaken to a "local" weather report predicting snow in Anchorage, and my Board of Ed Web site confirms what I already know in my heart—that my kids will be home with me instead of at school with adults whose college diplomas declare their ability to deal with them—I, too, rush to my special cabinet. My liquor cabinet.

In it, tucked way in the back behind several unopened bottles of Baileys Irish Cream, a fifth of anisette, and a

---

96. It's true: The mere mention of snow sends hordes of hoarders to the supermarket and gas station. No one is about to risk a Donner Pass repeat as long as there are still SpaghettiOs and Ball Park Franks at Food Lion.

gallon container of margarita mix, I keep what I lovingly refer to as Mommy's Snow Day Survival Kit.

Included in this tried-and-true trauma toolbox are industrial-strength earplugs (like the kind jack-hammering construction workers and rock band roadies swear by), several splits of chardonnay (the good stuff; if I'm stuck taking the kids' crap all day, I'm not drinking it, too), a supply of dry ice to keep the good stuff good and cold, paper cups so I can cave in to inebriation when I take a "Mommy needs to look for something in the car/truck/tractor" sanity break, and a vial of Valium.

OK, I'm just kidding about the Valium. I don't really take it. Instead I take two Tylenol PM. In the a.m. It freaks the kids out when I fall asleep while breaking up their fourteenth fistfight. They think I'm dying, flash on the fact that Hemingway never buys cookies when he shops, and immediately begin to behave. So what if they spend their adult years in therapy? I'll save them a corner on the couch.

When we lived in Ridgewood it was usually well into January before I had to break out my Snow Day Survival Kit. I guess I'm a bit surprised at needing it in December, but I'm even more surprised that it *is* December. What happened to August?

If I let him live through the snow day we're currently enduring, in less than a week Cuyler turns seven. And in a little more than two weeks we'd all better have our shopping done, gifts wrapped, cards mailed, houses aglow, trees decorated, and pantries and bars stocked for making merry. Or else. Or else what, I'm not sure. Though I think it has something to do with having our Hanukkah bushes set ablaze, our Christmas trees toppled, and reindeer doo-doo dropped down our chimneys. At least that's what I heard.

I guess fear of having my Christmas tree toppled—or of not having a Christmas tree *to* topple—is what finally motivated me to get with the season.

For starters, I dug out my holiday music cassettes, the very ones Hemingway hates with a passion he usually reserves for green peas and women wearing Capri pants, and popped one into Casey's tape player—the one he hasn't used since the great CD stampede. Then, while grooving to the beat of Bob Seger's "Sock It to Me Santa," I retrieved the outside lights from among the two-dozen crushed and cat hair–covered boxes in the basement labeled CHRISTMAS, and attempted to hang them on the porch.

What a fiasco. I was freezing. The lights were tangled. Two strands lit. Two strands didn't. My fingers went numb. Frostbite started to set in. And I began to wonder: Isn't this what I have a husband for?

I was seriously contemplating skipping the entire holiday season by tapping into my supply of Tylenol PM and sleeping from Christmas Eve through New Year's Day, when suddenly Casey and Cuyler came home, saw the lights, and whooped for joy. It was all worthwhile, despite my bleeding fingertips and the thin rivulets of blood frozen along the porch railing.

Unfortunately things rapidly returned to normal when they pointed out that I'd missed a spot, so I pointed out that Santa would surely miss the house if they weren't careful. When I came in, they wisely made amends by making me a nice snack of hot cocoa and cookies, so I imagine Santa will be stopping here after all. He can just follow the path of blood and broken fingernails I left behind.

Of course if the porch lights were a pain[97] they were nothing compared to getting a tree.

At first we considered buying a live tree and planting it in our front yard after the holidays to commemorate our first Christmas on the farm. This idea lasted a full five minutes during a trip to our local nursery. There we learned that a live tree would cost close to four hundred smackers, require a crane to lift, and survive a total of three days in the living room before needing to be manhandled into a mammoth hole specially prepared for it in the frozen earth (and kept free of any additional snow blowing in from Anchorage). All this, and the fact that there was no guarantee it would grow once it was in the ground, just made it that much more attractive.

Convinced the four hundred bucks would be better spent by burning it, we quickly determined that the traditional seasonal purchase of a dead tree would do just fine. But should we cut one down ourselves and have our pick of the best blue spruce, Fraser fir, or Scotch pine in the forest, or buy one at the local Boy Scout sale?

Still riding the weird wave of "Rah rah, we're country rookies" enthusiasm that led us to want a live tree, we decided to go the cut-your-own route. We quickly drove to the nearest tree farm, and just as quickly realized we didn't know what we were doing, as evidenced by the fact that we didn't bring a chain saw, hand saw, or even a large

---

97. Which might explain why so many people down here leave them up all year . . .

pocket knife. Of course we did bring our own human measuring stick: Casey. We dragged the poor kid to four different tree farms, looking desperately for a tree at least as tall as our six-foot son, but never found one.[98]

As it turns out, folks around here hit the tree farms in droves the day after Thanksgiving. They snatch up the ten-footers and leave the Charlie Brown pickings for those who refuse to rush the holiday season, and others who are seriously considering Rip Van Winkling their way through it. How they keep the trees green and fresh for a full month is still a mystery to me. I mean, is there some way to pickle a pine?

Ultimately we gave the Boy Scouts our business. For fifty-five dollars we got a perfectly proportioned, six-foot-tall Fraser fir. The fact that it shed so many needles during decoration that it was like trying to put Christmas lights on a leper doesn't make it any less lovely.

Right this instant, we're all managing to get through another snow day. Hemingway's glued to a German film called *The Tunnel*, which he's watching with English subtitles, so why the kids have to "keep it down!" I have no idea. Casey and Cuyler have consumed every sugar and carbohydrate in the house and are attempting to put snow pants on our small dog, Pete. And I'm sitting at my laptop, sipping a cup of the new green tea I'm writing an ad for and realizing the stress-relieving qualities it claims pale in comparison to its ability to produce indigestion. Like I can't get enough of that from my family.

---

98. We did, however, see several that would be perfect in the cat condos PetSmart sells.

I think what I despise most about snow days is that, without fail, they happen when I have plans. Plans to meet my sister-in-law for a civilized lunch. Plans to do a little shopping. Plans to have my tree-bark-brown hair color replaced with something in the blond family. I swear Mother Nature looks down at my Day Runner and says, "Susan's Tuesday is booked solid. Let it snow!"

The other thing that drives me nuts about snow days is that frankly, I can predict them. Forget the discombobulated television divas, the weather radio, and the online storm-watch services. When I discover at ten o'clock at night that we're completely and utterly out of milk, bread, J. Lohr and La Crema,[99] it's pretty much a done deal that the kids will be home the next day. Really. I'd issue my own alert, but I don't want to step on any toes at the school board.

With any luck, the kids will soon return to school and life will return to normal. The ice will melt, the snow will take a walk until next winter, and I'll get to keep my appointment for a full highlight. Good-bye, Medium Blonde abomination. Hello, Porn Star Platinum. I can't wait, and nothing is going to keep me from the salon. Not even a snow day. If I have to, I'll bring the kids. Or maybe they'll nap. I've got a couple of extra Tylenol PM they can take.

---

99. My two favorite brands of chardonnay.

Hemingway's Christmas List

Hemingway has two kids. I have three. How else can I explain the fact that every year he writes a Christmas wish list and leaves it for me in the kitchen? At least Casey and Cuyler are smart enough to put their lists in my makeup case or near my moisturizers. *That* stuff I use. (Let's face it: The only reason we have a kitchen is because it came with the house.) Anyway, this year's requests and last year's are as different as night and day, black and white, sticks and suburbia. I'd show you mine (last year I asked for Manolos; this year I'd need them with mud flaps) or even the kids' (last year they asked for *Call of Duty*; this year the brats wanted *Booty Call*), but they're not nearly as entertaining as Farm Boy's. Check it out and chortle.

In the Suburbs	*In the Sticks*
Books on history	Books on making snakes history
Rubik's Cube	Range cubes
Carving knives	Hunting knives
Case of steak	Side of beef
Dear John on DVD	John Deere logo on belt buckle
Giants gear, like jerseys and helmets	Giant gear, like wood chippers and batwing bush hogs
Fencing lessons	Tensile fencing
State-of-the-art egg timer	State-of-the-art egg turner
NFL-OPOLY	FARM-OPOLY

In the Suburbs	In the Sticks
Sports Illustrated Swimsuit Calendar	Whitetail Super Bucks Calendar
Snow shovel	Plow
Swim club membership	Pond
Barbecue	Burn pile
Bathrobe	Rain poncho
Alarm clock	Rooster
Sport jacket	Shooting jacket
Shot glass	Hip flask
Briefcase	Cargo pants
Cell phone	Walkie-talkie
Golf lessons	Shooting lessons
Trip to the Caribbean	Trip to Cabela's

Chapter Eighteen

DAME JOAN MAKES HER FARM DEBUT

I hate polishing silver, but it sure beats the hell out of scrubbing chicken poop off the soles of the kids' sneakers. It was actually my mom (aka Dame Joan in deference to her fondness for all things British: the BBC; mysteries set in Lancashire, the Cotswolds, and along the Thames; vicarages; scones; Merchant Ivory Productions—you get the picture) who noticed how tarnished the pieces were and offered to clean them up. Of course there was no way I was letting her do *that* during her vacation. At least not while there was laundry to be folded and a fridge to be cleaned.

But really, it was great having her here during her winter break. Dame Joan[100] is the principal of a large elementary school in Fort Lee, New Jersey.[101] There are about six hundred students in the school and fifty teachers. She gets a week off in February, which is a damn good thing, as she

---

100. Aka Joan, Joanie, Joanie Poo, JP, and The Joan of the House.

101. Where they refer to her, respectfully, as Mrs. C. My dad was a teacher, too, and everyone called him Mr. C. I attended the school where he taught, and was christened "Little C." I still "c" a therapist over the whole thing.

really needs the time to recover from those rascals. And getting a respite from the kids is crucial, too.

Her break usually coincides with my birthday, which is fun because then we get to spend it reminiscing about the night I was born (a Sunday night, *after* the *Ed Sullivan Show*, thank you very much; my selflessness and consideration made me my dad's favorite from the start[102]), my first words (*handbag* and *shoes* and *Chablis, please*), and how old I was when I took my first steps (nine months, wearing a pair of winter white, trapdoor footsie pajamas slipped into Dame Joan's sleek black pumps, and carrying her black patent leather clutch, her midnight-black muff perched on my head like a hat).

We strolled down memory lane during this visit, too, only this time I managed not to crawl into her lap and demand to be regaled with tales of my birth and trendsetting toddlerhood. Instead, and only because I've put on a few and not because I've achieved any modicum of maturity, I forced myself to stay on my side of the "sofa that started it all."[103]

Dame Joan had her nose in a copy of *Missing Joseph*, a British murder mystery[104] by Elizabeth George she's read a million times and was only re-reading because she fin-

---

102. Take that, David, Nick, and Dan!

103. I've shared that story, haven't I? My spectacular toile-covered living room sofa (aka "the sofa that started it all") is the reason we met Miss Contractor/Decorator/Furniture Hostage Taker 2005. I saw the sofa in some home magazine, Googled its manufacturer to find out where I could purchase it locally, and wound up in Miss Contractor/Decorator/Furniture Hostage Taker 2005's shop. We got to chatting, I ordered the sofa, and before the ink was dry on my check she signed on to helm the Nate's Place Remodeling Project. The rest, as they say, is history. And so is my relationship with her.

104. Told you!

ished the dozen or so books she brought with her within five minutes of her arrival, and I was sitting next to her, Indian style, on my sweet couch, clutching one of its red and cream toile-covered pillows to my freakishly flat chest.[105]

I didn't say anything. I just sat there hugging my pillow, smiling like Nurse Ratched missed me on her rounds, and staring a hole in the side of Dame Joan's beautiful blond head. For Pete's sake, how long would it be before she tore herself away from the adventures of the dashing Detective Inspector Thomas Lynley and brilliant but sensitive forensic scientist Simon St. James? I mean, she knew the whole damn book by heart, and besides, my face was starting to freeze.

Finally she turned and looked at me. "Susan, I know it's your birthday," she began, peering at me over the top of her tortoiseshell glasses. I nodded. Come on, come on, I thought. Tell me! "And we've been doing this every year since you were what, six?" I know! I know! Tell me! "Don't you think it's time for a new tradition?"

You mean like lunching someplace other than Neimans after hitting the annual shoe sale? Was Dame Joan delirious?

"But I like hearing about the night I was born," I pleaded, trying not to sound like my once six-year-old self but feeling the same kind of knot in the pit of my stomach as I did the day I discovered H.R. Pufnstuf (starring the

---

105. My unique A-cup condition is the one thing I inherited from my mom; my brothers got her square jaw, high cheekbones, and wide-set eyes. I got my dad's teeny, tiny, pimple-size face and pointy chin. I'd cry, but it comes in handy for opening canned goods.

mega-cute Jack Wild[106]) missing from my Saturday morning selection of cartoons. "You know, how you and Dad were watching the *Ed Sullivan Show* and the Beatles were on and they sang 'I Want to Hold Your Hand,' which is so cool because to this day that's my absolute favorite Beatles song. You know?"

"I know, but . . . "

"And how your water broke, and Dad raced you to the hospital, and I was born, like, a split second after you got there (making me the most considerate newborn in the Northern Hemisphere, I'm sure), and how the nurses said I was the most beautiful baby they'd ever seen."

Silence.

"I *was* the most beautiful baby they'd ever seen? Right?"

"Yes, sweetheart. They thought you were the most beautiful baby *boy* they'd ever seen."

Huh?

"You bore an uncanny resemblance to John Glenn."

"John Glenn the astronaut?"

"Correct."

"He had, like, a whole Yoda thing happening."

"Maybe later. But as a younger man he was quite the looker."

We sat in silence for a second. Me, absorbing the fact that I was born with the mug of a four-thousand-year-old Jedi Master. Dame Joan reading the back of the *Missing Joseph* book jacket. Again.

---

106. Obviously I've got a Brit thing, too. The figgy pudding didn't fall far from the tree.

"So you've been lying to me."

"Honey, I never told you because I didn't want to hurt your feelings. You're very sensitive sometimes. But what does it matter now? You're a beautiful, successful woman."

"Who started life looking like a man."

"Don't you think for a minute we let people presume you were a boy. Absolutely not, dear daughter. Your dad ran right out and bought a huge pink bow, which we Scotch-taped to the top of your sweet bald head."

"I was *bald*?"

"Just like John Glenn."

She was right. It was time to start lunching at Neimans *before* hitting the shoe sale. Reduced-price designer footwear on a full stomach. If I didn't have to stop midshop to eat, who knows what I'd walk away with. And in.[107]

So we didn't spend the entire time talking about what a fabulous, firstborn, only girl I was. But we did do lots of other neat mother-daughter things.

For instance, we watched the Winter Olympics, and decided it's much more fun to watch Hemingway nearly be crushed by two dozen cows in hot pursuit of a bucket of range cubes. We also went to lunch and did some shopping, and of course she cooked. That's what moms do when they visit, right? They cook. I mean, it's that or she gets the $365 a night room rate.

The shopping was a riot, because of course I dragged

---

107. Welcome to the Suzy School for Living Your Life with Your Head in the Sand. For just $99 you, too, can learn how to never face reality again! Discover the tricks to mentally checking out of conversations and situations that pain you. Classes meet once a week over margaritas. Guest speakers do not include Elizabeth Gilbert, Pema Chodron, or the Dalai Lama.

her to Middleburg, where a T-shirt can cost upwards of $125. I say "of course" because Dame Joan is one of those women who can outfit herself for a year on fifteen, twenty bucks, tops. And yes, that includes shoes.

"But it's a Three Dots, Mom," I exclaimed at the massive T-shirt table in Tully Rector, the trendiest clothing boutique the Big Apple's never seen. "Feel how soft it is." "It's soft all right," she said, touching the baby pink V-neck I proffered. "And you're soft in the head if you pay that price."

Like I said, Dame Joan's never been one to wear her paycheck on her back, so how she raised me—Princess Suzy—I swear I couldn't tell you. She's also one of those people who likes salespeople to know she's put off by the cost of something. How does she accomplish this? By doing what I call her "Dame Judi Dench Fake Brit Business."

Her shtick starts with a stage whisper the whole county can hear ("Susan, *please* don't tell me you're going to be *foolish* enough to spend *that* on *that*!"), and escalates into a monologue old Billy couldn't have written better.

"Five hundred dollars for that coat? Is it at least cashmere?"

"No, Mom. It's a Milly."

"So I should pay more for the honor of wearing Miss Milly's name on my back? Why do you young people insist on being somebody's billboard? You know, I had an Aunt Milly and she was quite the fashion plate. She didn't shop foolishly, though. Oh no, she taught me the value of a pound. I mean dollar. And the importance of not squandering it. Just look at the jacket I'm wearing." She pauses to remove her coat. While she's folding it oh, so neatly and laying it on one of those chairs women's shops keep handy for bored husbands, the woman next to me grabs six Three Dots and my arm. "Chardonnay," she whispers before running to the register. "It's the universal cure for shopping with one's mother. If you don't have some, get some!"

Luckily Dame Joan doesn't hear her and turns to me like I've had her attention the whole time. I smile. (Correction: I continue to smile. What, she shouldn't get to enjoy the grin she footed the orthodontist's bill for?) She looks gorgeous in her red-and-black plaid jacket, her blond hair tucked behind her ears, her oversize gold clip-ons[108] bringing out the chunky gold buttons on her blazer. It kills me that this woman who won't spend a dime on herself looks like a million bucks in this chichi boutique. Of course you can't tell her that. Try, and she'll tell you what a troll she is. Self-effacing, maybe. Body dysmorphic, definitely.[109]

"Susan," she starts, "look. Look at the lining. There's not a single spot where it's worn, and I've had this piece for years. Check out the buttons and the buttonholes. A finish like that is the mark of fine workmanship. Those"— she flicks at the flat, pearlized buttons on the Three Dots I'm still drooling over—"are a machine wash away from disappearing down the drain." She pauses for dramatic effect. "And check the fit. Like it was made for me." She

---

108. My mom had four kids without as much as an aspirin to take the edge off. But pierce her ears? And endure *that* kind of pain? She'd much rather cope with the swelling, itching, and occasional "What is that in the Petri dish?" discoloration that comes with clip-ons.

109. My brother Nick and I share custody of a photo of my mom taken when she was in her early thirties. In it she looks just like Jessica Lange. When I was a kid, I used to worry she'd one day wake up and realize she had the whole package— beauty, brains, talent—and hightail it outta there. She never did, and to this day I love her most for her total lack of self-esteem. Thanks, Mom!

gives me a little twirl. "Fabulous, right? Guess how much? Guess."

"I can't. Tell me."

"Don't be a killjoy, dear daughter."

"Two hundred dollars," I respond knowing full well that if she paid more than twenty-five bucks there was a "buy one, get one" going on.

"*Really,* Susan," she says in her imperious, just this side of condescending trademark Dame Joan tone, the one she's been using to keep me in line since I was little. "Don't be ridiculous."

"OK, OK. Fifty dollars."

"Nineteen dollars and ninety-nine cents."

What did I tell you?

The woman may not spend a lot on clothing, but when she gets her "I'm appalled" act going it's a performance worth paying for.

When we weren't shopping we were discussing several of my half-baked, out-of-the-blue desires. Like my plan to add to our assortment of farm animals by getting some pigs. Think about it. We have 500 acres, 350 head of cattle, 26 chickens, and more groundhogs than Grundy can ever hope to consume, but no pigs. A farm without pigs is like a kitchen without a cookbook from the Pork Council. And since that tome's tucked neatly next to my Perdue "Poultry Basics" guide, I'd say I've practically put the cart before the horse.[110] As I told Dame Joan, Hemingway has the cows. Casey has the hens. And I'll have the hogs. After

---

110. Now that I think of it, horses might be nice, too. It's the riding pants portion of that program that gives me pause.

all, I'm already used to the mess. I'm a mom. Dame Joan disagreed, and decreed it might just be time for me to find a job. . . .

It was fun not only having Dame Joan here, but getting her here. For the first time ever, I drove from Virginia to New Jersey alone and picked her up. Just me, my mix CDs, and several large bottles of Poland Spring water, which I consumed with reckless abandon and then made as many rest stops as I needed, thank you very much. It was a wonderful six-hour vacation during which I howled shamelessly along with Annie Lennox (whose rendition of "Walking on Broken Glass" pales in comparison to mine, for the simple reason that I actually *sound* like I'm walking on broken glass), whizzed through West Virginia and Pennsylvania at seventy-five miles per hour (the speed limit is seventy; what's another five among friends?), and took in such thought-provoking roadside signage as MY BABY WAS BORN AT HOME (which featured a photo of a tiny tot who looked like his dad popped him out with a calf puller[111]).

I should also confess that the scenery was so spectacular it brought on a full-blown blond moment. While I was enjoying the landscape and rather loudly accompanying Gretchen Wilson on "Redneck Woman," it occurred to me a) that America really is beautiful, and b) that this must have been the inspiration for the song "America the Beautiful." Brilliant, I know, and deduced *without* drugs. Can you imagine if I indulged in an illegal substance or six? Clearly I need to stop obsessing about the fact that my

---

111. The forceps of the bovine OB-GYN.

forehead has more lines than a sheet of loose leaf paper, and schedule a lobotomy before I hurt somebody.

Anyway, I arrived in New Jersey without incident, squeezed in coffee, lunch, a little shopping, and dinner with several dear friends on Saturday, then returned on Sunday with Dame Joan in tow.

The ride back was a riot. We gossiped about who in the family *really* belongs at Betty Ford, where the cows go when it snows (Dame Joan: "You mean you don't bring them indoors?" Me: "What?" Dame Joan: "Well, it just seems cruel to leave them outside, Susan." Me: "They're five minutes away from being London broils, and you'd have me keep them in the living room?"), and mangled more than our fair share of country music. (I'll tell you, Dame Joan does a damn good Shania Twain impression.) Then we strolled into the house, appetites primed for the roast Hemingway promised for dinner, and discovered Grundy cowering in the corner, my growling and snarling husband wielding a broom, and a billion pieces of Pyrex all over the kitchen floor. Where was the aforementioned roast? Marinating in a mixture of glass and dog saliva on the rooster rug in front of the sink.

Getting all that mess shipshape took some time, but when she was done, we all went out for dinner. Our treat, of course. Either that or pay Dame Joan's ninety-five-dollar cash-only cleaning fee.[112]

But really, thank God for my mom. I don't think she'd even unpacked before she was down on her hands and knees with some steel wool, a rag, and a value-size bottle

---

112. And she didn't even dust!

of Old English Oil painstakingly removing the millions of paint splotches that formed a poor man's Pollock in the hallway. (Ms. Contractor/Decorator/Furniture Hostage Taker 2005's painter never did clean up properly.) I tell you, I was moved to tears. And then I got her bill and really started to bawl.

Even the dogs were delighted to see her. Grundy and His Expensive Highness Pete (the pup who never met an ailment he couldn't contract or a vet he wouldn't visit) have developed a special rapport with my mother. They give her the sad-eyes stare, followed by a little ankle-lick action, and before you can say, "Roll over and act you like you haven't eaten," she's whipping them up a second dinner. But I'm not really surprised. She spoils the boys, too. And watching them eat from the dogs' dishes is pretty funny.

To the kids, Grandma's coming was like a surprise visit from Santa, and her "workshop" was the Radio Shack in Marshall. She strolled in, credit card locked and loaded, and made the manager's day. Not to mention the boys', who, upon racking up close to five hundred dollars' worth of remote-controlled submarines, helicopters, portable CD players, and model race-car kits, declared her "SO much better than Mom and Dad." Just remember, kids: The gravy train will eventually leave the station and you'll be stuck with the chuck wagon.

Speaking of trains and other modes of transportation, Dame Joan truly cannot believe how many hours of each day I spend in the Durango.

As she and I drove the kids to school (fifteen minutes away), took a "quick" trip to the supermarket (twenty minutes door-to-door), and ran Cuy down to the pediatric dentist (a thirty-five-minute foray he makes almost as frequently as Pete sees the vet), the look on Dame Joan's face alternated between "My daughter gave up a huge career to spend all day in the car?" and "I paid for four years of college for this?" I tried to tell her that it's OK; I don't mind all the driving. I actually like it because it lets me think. But she wasn't hearing a word of it.

"You poor thing, dear daughter. Don't you miss the convenience of mass transportation?"

For a moment my mouth almost got away from me. "Absolutely," I wanted to say. "I used to love stepping into a cab fresh from the shower and coming out covered in some slob's body odor. And let's not forget the unmitigated joy of squeezing onto a crowded, crosstown bus and having my foot run over by a lazy bike messenger pulling a Rosie Ruiz.[113] Or better yet, the fun of waiting for the A train, and glancing down to discover Ben[114] and several of his rodent pals sniffing at my pumps."

But instead I simply said, "Nope."

"Well, you must miss having things closer," she continued. "Everything's so far away. I like knowing I can walk to the post office or to buy a loaf of bread. All this driving would drive me nuts."

Maybe it already was. When she finished *Missing Joseph*—again—she wouldn't let me take her to our local

---

113. The woman who tried to steal the 1980 Boston Marathon. Rumor has it she skipped half the route by hopping on a bus, then jumped in from the crowd and made for the finish.

114. Ben the rat. You know, from that old Michael Jackson song. I realize it's not the most recent social reference, but believe me, Ben was big in his day.

library ("Local? You call a fifteen-minute drive local?"), nor would she agree to a trip to our brand new Borders ("It's twenty-five minutes away? No way!"). In fact she acted as if we're as close to fresh reading material as Porky Pig is to wearing pants.

True, things are different here in the hinterland. But it's nothing you can't get used to. Like the long distances between places. The pace. Even the price of T-shirts in Middleburg.

Of course one thing I may never come to grips with is the fact that I was born John Glenn's doppelganger, or worse, a young Yoda. And Dame Joan thinks driving's a royal pain in the ass.

Chapter Nineteen

SWIMSUITS IN THE STICKS

I have a confession to make. It doesn't matter if "cruise season"[115] finds me in the city, the suburbs, or the sticks; buying a bathing suit makes me feel bovine.

That's right; despite all evidence to the contrary—the white stuff falling from the sky, the frigid wind literally lifting the chickens off their frightening feet, the frozen ponds, flake-flecked hay bales, frost-covered cows, and the kids home for yet another snow day[116]—it's time to commence my annual quest for a little something in Lycra.

Correction: a big something in Lycra.

I have no intention of wearing a bathing suit in the balmy twenty-degree weather we're currently enjoying here in the hinterland, and I may not even wear it this summer.[117] But I need to buy one while there's still a decent selection.

---

115. That arctic time of year when normal women want toasty, soft sweaters, but magazines and catalogs converge to torture us with the latest in near nakedness, i.e., stuff only starving (but warm on the beaches of Bali) models can wear.

116. My kids love living in the sticks. Why? Because come winter there's simply no school. If it snows, there's no school. And if it just looks like snow—in another state—there's no school.

117. It's more comfortable to go naked in the nine-hundred-degree heat we get down here. Granted, my clothes-free form is not pretty, but what's more important? My comfort or scars on my sons' psyches? That's right, Dr. Freud. Now come here and hold my socks.

Because gone are the days when I could run into the store, grab whatever bikini I thought would give my current boyfriend heart palpitations,[118] and hit the beach.

In fact these days I don't even go to the store. The closest one is an hour away, so why bother to waste the time and the gas when I've got bad lighting and mirrors that morph into magic magnifying glasses right here? Instead, these days I log on (via a satellite connection so slow I'm certain turtles and snails head up HughesNet) and order 135 bathing suits from Lands' End, L.L. Bean, and Eddie Bauer; Macy's, Target, and Gap; Victoria's Secret, Nordstrom, and Neiman Marcus; Old Navy, J.Crew, and Venus .com,[119] and try them on in the private hell of my own home.

I call it Bathing Suit Day or B. Day for short; the day when all the bikinis, tankinis, boy shorts, and built-in bra tops, swim skirts, and one-piece wonders I've ordered arrive and it's time to try them on. Hemingway calls it time to load the boys into the Durango and drive to New Jersey to visit family, friends, and, frankly, anyone who'll take them in and delay their return trip for as long as humanly possible.

In preparation for B. Day, I shave my legs, exfoliate, and slather on self-tanner. I have palm trees applied to my finger- and toenails. I break out my favorite beach jewelry (huge silver hoops, bangles, and ankle bracelets, blimp-

---

118. And the overwhelming urge to buy me a Mercedes . . .

119. Yes, my UPS man loves me. I tip him not just for bringing the millions of boxes to my door but for putting up with my manic response. "Oh, my *gawd*, I hope one of these fit! The stuff you delivered yesterday? Complete crap! Why doesn't somebody give those kids in the Chinese sweatshops a size chart?"

sized baubles for my fingers, and several tiny, shiny toe rings for my feet). I do my hair and makeup. (Hey, let's not forget that I grew up in New Jersey; it's unnatural for me *not* to hit the shore like a showgirl.) And I limit salt, except for what's on the rim of the frozen margaritas I consume to make the whole process more palatable.

Then I close my eyes, pull the first suit from the top of the pile, squeeze into it, and let the games begin.

I dash from the bedroom to the bathroom, stomach sucked into my spine, screaming as I steal quick peeks of my fleshy self as I fly past the mirror. I cry, pluck at my flab, and fantasize aloud about do-it-yourself tummy tuck kits, which I imagine being sold on late-night television by that guy with the Ginsu steak knives. He can have my $29.99 as long as I'll look less gruesome in one of these Gottex numbers.

Nixing self-mutilation in favor of self-flagellation, I run to the TV in the Pucci-print tankini I appear to be trapped in and grab the remote. Suzanne Somers will save me! I flip to the Home Shopping Network, and nothing. No Suzanne Somers ThighMaster. No Chuck Norris Total Gym. No Bill Phillips *Body for Life* weight-training tape or Winsor Pilates Sculpting Circle set. Not even a Denise Austin "Deniseiol-ogy" personal training DVD. I'm on my own. Just me, my jiggle, and the $200 designer swimsuit I may have to learn to live with. And in.

The horrified squealing and fat poking, pushing, and pulling goes on for about forty-five minutes. And then my margarita kicks in. Suddenly I'm looking at my lumps in a whole new light. And I feel good. Piña colada in Key West good. Sex on the Beach in Bermuda good. Mango mojito in

Malibu good. There's a one-piece that works wonders, thanks to built-in steel girders, metal panels, and a packet of ibuprofren attached to the tag. A tankini I could also wear to a costume party for my debut as a Double Stuf Oreo. And a bikini that's perfect if I ever vacation at a resort for the vision impaired.

I feel like James Earl Jones in one of those old Yellow Pages commercials: I've got choices! In fact, I've hit the trifecta of B. Days: three barely wearable bathing suits is a windfall.

For a moment I consider keeping the discards, as well: the midnight blue cover-up that makes me look like a monk, the white crocheted bikini that bears a striking resemblance to the backs of my thighs, the chocolate brown tankini that brings out my age spots, the paisley-print one-piece that oh, so subtly accentuates my aircraft-carrier width, even the coral pink pin-dot halter and matching boy shorts that delicately play up the birthmarks on my décolleté and derriere. Maybe someday they'll look good. You know, about the same time some big pharmaceutical company makes Paris Hilton's hips available by prescription.

In the interim, I've at least found a few suits. I may not really like how they look, but it doesn't matter. They'll probably never see the light of day. Unless, of course, it's a snow day.

Chapter Twenty

HISTO-WHO?

I have a confession to make: I'm really unclear as to our address. I know that sounds ridiculous; even kindergarteners know their address. But back in Ridgewood we had one address. Here we have two. And each has a different zip code. We have a P.O. box because, according to Hemingway, real farmers go get their bills at the post office in order to shoot the breeze with the boys, and we also have a street address. I know this because it's glued to the fence adjacent to our walkway. What I don't know is which one to use and when. You'd think someone might have clarified this for me before my budding farmer had a heart attack, but no. I was clueless when I called 911.

Emergency operator: "Nine-one-one. What's your emergency?"

Maybe it was the sudden realization that by calling for help I was admitting Hemingway might truly be in trouble, or perhaps I thought the police who'd accompany the ambulance would discover that I mix department store and supermarket cosmetics and haul me in on a makeup misdemeanor, but suddenly I began speaking with the speed of someone on, well, speed.

"Oh, hello! You really do answer on the first ring, don't you? OK. Well, then. My name is Susan McCorkindale and my address is one-ninety-three Franklin Road in Ridgewood and . . ."

Emergency operator: "Ma'am . . ."

Me, barreling forward: "Oh, wait. Sorry. That's our old address. Our new address is actually, well, we use a P.O. box. It's P.O. box four-seventy-six, in Upperville and . . ."

Emergency operator: "*Ma'am* . . ."

Me, hurtling into maximum Alvin and the Chipmunks mode: "Oh, wait! I'm sorry! I'm sure you want our *physical* address, which is eight-oh-one-one Quaint Road in Upperville, only we never use it because we have everything sent to our P.O. box since we live in the sticks and it gives my husband a chance to get out of the house and see people when he goes to the post office to pick up our mail, so I always forget that we actually have a street address and that's probably what you need to send an ambulance and . . ."

Emergency operator: "*Ma'am!*"

Me: "Yes?"

Emergency operator: "We *have* your address. What is the nature of your emergency?"

Me: "My husband thinks he's having a heart attack."

Emergency operator: "Now we're getting somewhere."

It wasn't long before several good-size emergency rescue workers were squeezed into our small hallway. They checked Hemingway's vitals, gave him oxygen, and took a history. "So you say the pain started in your forearms and moved into your biceps, and that you got both your dogs from the Rappahannock Animal Welfare League, right?"

The lack of histrionics is one of the things I'm learning to love about the country (although I've yet to incorporate it into my own personal approach to things). Even if you think you're having a heart attack, there's always time to talk about what really matters. Like our two mutts begging for a belly rub while Hemingway's being strapped to a stretcher, and whether they're good for hunting, herding cattle, or just plain playing with the kids. The calm, country way helps keep things in perspective, something I'll have to bear in mind when I'm having a stroke and the medical personnel ask me if I'm experiencing any sensitivity to light, and if Grundy and Pete prefer Purina or Science Diet.

The long and short of it is, after spending just over four hours in the emergency room while they examined Hemingway and conducted a variety of tests that involved scans and electrodes and monitors with colorful, blinking lights that attracted the boys like a mating call from Nintendo's mother ship, the doctor determined he should be admitted for observation.

Personally, I think the poor man was concerned that if my honey wasn't already having a heart attack, Casey and Cuyler—who'd consumed every stale piece of candy in the vending machine, blown up and popped half a box of latex gloves, and helped themselves to a couple of hospital gowns and slippers from the supply closet and put on an impromptu freak fashion show in the hallway—would drive him to one before daybreak.

The boys were pretty upset when we had to leave

without their dad and the unfinished package of Twizzlers I wouldn't let them take, but it was nothing compared to Hemingway's distress when, as we were saying our good-byes, he reached up, grabbed my hand, and said, "Sue, you did give them all the insurance information, right?" And I stopped, looked down at him lovingly, and replied, "Nope. I told them you're indigent. And incontinent. Should make for an interesting evening. Have fun!" and walked out the door.

Of course I gave them the insurance information. What did he think I was giving the gal in the Santa cap with the clipboard, his Christmas wish list? "Let's see. He'd like a brand-new brush cutter, a pair of flannel-lined overalls, and for this little trip to the hospital, the sixteen stethoscopes the kids ruined in rigging them into a jump rope and the damage they did to the mobile chest X-ray machine to be completely covered by Blue Cross!"

My actual conversation with little Miss Santa Cap wasn't nearly as convivial and light, and in fact reminded me more than a little of that fateful day at the DMV.

Miss Santa Cap: "I need to make a copy of your insurance card."

Me, smiling and searching my bag for my wallet and finding everything but: "Of course. It's right—holy cow, Casey! Here's the homework you owed Mr. Mulvey." I flip a crumpled piece of loose leaf at my lunatic firstborn and cast a quick "Ah kids—can't live with 'em, can't kill 'em" glance at Miss Santa Cap. I figure she'll give me some sort of "You got it, sister" signal, but no. She just looks at me like I'm trying her patience, my kids are trying her patience, even the patients are trying her patience. So I keep smiling (what is it with me and smiling?), and return to my rummaging.

Casey: "Why'd you take it?"

Me: "I didn't. You must've put it there."

Casey: "Why would I put it there?"

Me: "Maybe for the same reason you think latex gloves look good dangling from your ears." No kidding. He had the open end tucked over the top of each ear with the fingers flopping around his chin. He looked like a *Star Wars* character George Lucas left on the cutting room floor.

Miss Santa Cap: "Mrs. McCorkindale . . ."

Me, ducking my head back into my bag: "Yeah. Sorry." Where the hell's my wallet? I'm getting nervous now, so I start to talk. Fast. And from inside my spectacular Prada purse—which at this point I may have to barter to help cover the bill (yes, it was that expensive)—so of course I sound like I'm in a wind tunnel. If that's not bad enough, Miss Santa Cap's begun tapping her clipboard, and the kids are playing a quick game of mummy with the gauze bandages they found beneath the sink. (Quick because it's quickly escalating from mummy to hostage, from what I can hear. Casey: "Wrap my feet first." Cuyler: "No way. Eyes first. I'm a terrorist and I'm going to take you out." He can, too. I just pulled a plastic pistol out of my bag. Wonderful. Fake weaponry, I've got. Wallet, not so much.)

"We have Anthem," I stammer, literally nosing aside my day planner, makeup mirror, sunglasses, and six tubes of the same shade of lip gloss. (Apparently I have a fondness for ULTA's Ginger Fizz.) "The premium's paid up. You know the drill; I give them a thousand dollars a month, they give us a newsletter filled with tips on fighting the common cold, staving off depression, and performing do-it-yourself tonsillectomies on the kitchen table. You know, anything not to cover a claim."

Miss Santa Cap: "Why don't I get somebody from patient services. They can work out a payment plan. . . ."

In one second I'm going to slap Miss Santa Cap. I'm not a welch. I just can't find my wallet. So I do what I should've done from the start: I dump my bag by my feet, bend over to search the ruins, and suddenly, out of the corner of my eye, catch a glimpse of my wallet sticking out from behind my right butt cheek. I'd tucked it there for easy access to the change compartment. The boys had been so busy plowing through both vending machines on my dime (make that about fifty of my dimes) that at some point I decided just to leave it out.

How little Miss Santa Cap, who was sitting directly across from me, didn't see it, I don't know. But I hope she gets coal.

So they kept Hemingway overnight, during which they monitored every flutter, twitch, and tremor. In the morning they announced there was something amiss with his cardiogram, and told him to come back for a stress test on Monday. I asked if a visit to Chuck E. Cheese on Sunday (don't ask: We promised the kids, so we were committed; or maybe we *should be* committed) counted as a stress test and they said yes, actually, and promptly offered me a battery-operated defibrillator. I took it, bundled my man into the car, and hustled him home.

OK, I'm just kidding about the defibrillator. The truth is they didn't want Hemingway anywhere near noisy, germy Chuck E. Cheese. But I figured if we packed a Stoli-filled flask and his new nitroglycerin tablets, gave him a piece of pizza, a cup of Chuck E. Cheese tokens, and exclusive access to the sharp-shooter game he'd be fine. And he was.

Hemingway went for the stress test today, and even though we've yet to hear from the doctor, we're pretty sure it went well. For one thing he didn't drop dead on the treadmill, so that's a good sign. It's possible that the twitching in his arms and pressure in his chest were brought on by histoplasmosis, a condition contracted from chickens. After the doctor rules out heart issues, Farm Boy will be paying a visit to a pulmonary specialist to check on this possibility.

If his beloved birds have made him sick, I'll feel bad. But not so bad that I won't butcher the little beasts and put up a nice pot of chicken soup.

Happy Health News from the Hinterland!

TO: Friends & Family
FR: Suzy Nightingale
Date: Wednesday, 7:25 p.m.
Subject: Hemingway's "Heart Attack"

Hey all,

Thank you so much for your concern about the health of my dear, sweet Hemingway. His condition is indeed dire.

In fact not only will he live, but he'll be forced to spend the rest of his days with his "till-death-do-us-part," black-rooted, blond-tipped beauty, me (as opposed to the sexy sportscaster he was going gaga over during Sunday night's Giants game), and his two surly sons.

He's a lucky boy, that Big Mac of mine.

Early this afternoon we received word that his nuclear stress test was completely normal, which is more than any of us can usually say for Hemingway, so, gang, he's going to be fine.

Now all I need to do is watch him for signs of a cold. If he starts sniffling, coughing, or complaining of body aches, it could be histoplasmosis. And that would spell the end of his foray into chicken farming. A tragic loss to the organic egg community, for sure, but a necessary one for the sake of my honey's health and my peace of mind.

After all, I've waited sixteen years to kill him. No damn birds are going to beat me to it.

Love,

Susan

Chapter Twenty-one

BURN CALORIES: RUN FROM COWS

*Y*ou haven't lived until you've nearly been killed by an angry cow.

I made this exhilarating discovery recently while zipping around the farm on Casey's military green Honda Recon. With Hemingway on his red Rancher ES ahead of me, Grundy galloping a football field length ahead of us, and Pete darting dangerously in and out of my path,[120] we zoomed over to the field where the "ladies" are currently living.

When it's just me and my favorite farm boy, I simply wave to the gals as we go by, and silently agree to keep my distance until we meet in the butcher section of the supermarket. But with the dogs in tow, there's no such thing as a civilized social call.

The crazy mutts bark and nip at the 1,500-pound beefcakes until a chase ensues. And of course one did. Before we knew it, Grundy was chasing a cow. Then several cows

---

120. And tempting the great Canine Commando in the sky to secure him a spot on Road Kill Hill.

started chasing Grundy chasing the cow. Desperate to save the dog from being trampled to death, we took off in pursuit of the cows chasing the dog chasing the cow, completely unaware that we'd angered a trio of future flank steaks who were now chasing us as we chased the cows chasing the dog chasing a cow.[121]

Suddenly, over the roar of the ATV engine, I heard heavy breathing. I turned and there were Carmela, Denise, and Angeline[122] coming up fast. They were so close I could almost feel the breath billowing hard and fast from their flared nostrils, and, had I been brave enough, I could have easily reached out to touch the muscles rippling under their skin.

I have always thought of cows as slow, lumbering animals. I thought wrong. These mamas can move. They were closing in on my right leg when I let out a holler. Hemingway flew off his four-wheeler, strode right up to the barreling beasts, and—wagging his finger in their fly-swathed faces—yelled, "Back away from my wife or you can forget about the range cubes I promised for dessert!"

Carmela and Denise[123] stopped dead in their tracks. But Angeline, who obviously didn't care about tonight's post-dinner confections, continued inching toward me, baring teeth that had clearly never seen a Waterpik or a Crest White Strip. I was fixated on this fact, and lost in wondering when I'd last done a little whitening, when I heard Hemingway yelling at me to drive up the hill.

---

121. I know. You need a drink. I needed one, too.

122. Also known as numbers 19, 27, and 93.

123. Numbers 19 and 27, in case you're keeping track.

"Go! Go!" he shouted, and I would have gone. Except that at that very second a massive Black Angus bull with a gold hoop the width of my wrist through its nose took the opportunity to rise up and mount one of the ladies Hemingway was lecturing. And I thought for sure I'd be checking the "widow" box on my income tax returns this year.

In a flash, the cow quickie came to a conclusion. I came to my senses and literally headed for the hills. And my cattle-whispering husband walked away from the becalmed bovines, hopped back on his ATV, and joined me on the rise, where I proceeded to make a plethora of questionable pronouncements including "THAT WAS AWESOME!" and "WE COULD HAVE BEEN KILLED!" and "CAN WE DO IT AGAIN?"

Nothing like a little adrenaline rush to make you say things you'll regret in a big way. Because I did regret it. Every word of it. And sooner than I ever thought possible.

About a week later I went for a run. I didn't mean to. I meant to walk. But as I strode purposefully across the pasture, my goal being the fifty acres of woods behind the old grain silo and ultimately a wonderful, flat, green-gray rock upon which I typically sit and ponder this country turn my life has taken, the cattle took note of my presence and began to approach. They do this all the time to Hemingway, and, as I've explained, he's comfortable with it. But my husband is six feet tall,[124] weighs a bit more than I, and is usually carrying range cubes—the dog biscuits of the bovine world—which the ladies eat *out of his hand.* Yeesh.

---

124. I'm five-five on a good day; five-three when my kids have been crushing me with their many needs.

Anyway, there I was, sans snacks, and wearing leather gloves most likely fashioned from one of the gals' moms. No wonder they were ticked. One of them, number 93 (aka Angeline, *again*), was mooing loudly, frequently, and, I might add, frighteningly, as she trotted toward me. Within seconds she was in a full run, and this signaled the rest of her pals to also pick up the pace.

Now, I know what to do in these situations. I'm supposed to stop, face the barreling beasts, and say, "KNOCK IT OFF" in my loudest, most confident "Don't pee in the bushes, boys!" voice. And I did that, but cows listen about as well as kids, so I repeated myself—another technique that's never worked with my sons, so why I thought it would save my hide I have no idea—and nothing. No matter what I said, how loud I said it, or whichever way I flailed my arms, they were coming.

So I decided to get going.

Stupidly, I turned and ran. Sweat pouring down the back of my neck and butchering a perfectly good blow-out, I ran as fast as my flabby, muscle-atrophied little legs would carry me and was immediately reminded of why I quit high school track: running sucks. Even with death in the form of heated heifers hot on my heels, it's a heinous form of exercise.

Luckily I didn't have to do it for long.

If I'd been looking where I was going—instead of alternately down at the ground to dodge meadow muffins and behind me to gauge my rapidly decreasing distance from the girls—I'd have seen our tenant driving toward me. As it was, the ladies saw him first and, as cows instantly respect things that are taller than they are (and his Ford F-150 pickup probably looked like the Great Bovine Buddha), they slammed on their hooved brakes and bowed their matted heads in homage. I, of course, had no idea they'd stopped pursuing me, and nearly plowed directly into the guy's grille.

Freaked out but determined to continue my pursuit of better health and slimmer hips, because after all, I've got the cutest new pair of cropped cargo pants and *Desperate Housewives*–style heels I can't strut around in unless I lose six pounds, I asked my hero if he wouldn't mind holding the beasts at bay until I reached the gate to the woods. He said no problem, so I took off again. Running. Have I mentioned how I hate to run?

You'd think that after an animal adventure like I'd just had Mother Nature would move on to torturing somebody else, but you'd be wrong. First of all, as I sprinted past the grain silo the cattle in that corner of the farm caught sight of me and decided, like their girlfriends in the adjacent field, to join me for a group jog. It was nip and tuck for a few seconds as I panted my way to the gate, hopped it, and landed with a spastic plop on the other side, where I found myself face-to-face with not one, but two, foxes.

Wonderful. I'd eluded death by trampling only to meet my maker by being mauled. And all because a pair of pants are a little snug.[125]

Anyway, for a moment, nobody moved. And then, unable to hold my tongue a minute more, because frankly we all know that even in the face of my own mortality I have to

---

125. OK, I admit it, they're tight. Really tight. I tried them on and looked like a bunny stuffed into a Glad sandwich-size Baggie. Particularly unappetizing, trust me.

make a comment, I said, "Is that your real fur color, or is it Clairol?" Maybe I offended them. Maybe they were repulsed by my New Yawk regionalism. But whatever it was, it did the trick. They charged off faster than Casey and Cuyler flee their chores, leaving me to stroll unimpeded to my favorite rock, where I meditated on my near-death experiences and the merits of simple starvation over exercise.

In the end, I decided to cut out carbs. Sure, I miss rice and pasta and bread. But I get to eat lots of beef. And that really doesn't bode well for number 93, now, does it?

Fresh Fowl News!

TO: Friends & Family
FR: Hemingway's Better Half
Date: Saturday, 11:00 a.m.
Subject: Omelets, anyone?

We have eggs! Or at least we had eggs. No sooner did Hemingway discover the first of the big, brown farm-fresh beauties the hens have begun to lay than he was in the kitchen, hollering, "Who wants omelets?" For all my belly-aching about those birds, I just couldn't join him. I felt like I was eating family.

In other fowl news, I learned an important lesson this week: Always turn off the power before hopping an electric fence. The electric fence protects the chickens from predators like foxes, dogs, and me with my Perdue "Poultry Basics" cookbook.

Anyway, I went out to give the girls some scratch, and thought, Why shut the power off? The fence is low; I'll just hop it. Despite a running start, I didn't clear it, pulled my right hip flexor, and wound up once again fleeing the feathered fiends as they tried to attack my ankles. It's this kind of stupidity that wins people Darwin Awards, so somebody better nominate me.

As much as the hens hate me is as much as they love Hemingway. And damn if he isn't fond of them, too. Right now he and Casey are building the crotchety beasts a *traveling* chicken coop. Talk about girls who get around. Known in farming circles as a chicken tractor, the damn thing has a specially constructed laying box with *curtains* so the gals can lay eggs in private (you'll recall that *I* had to fight for locks on the bathroom doors), a heavy-duty perch (the chicken equivalent of a Sealy Posturpedic mattress), and wheels so it can be pulled by an ATV from one patch of fresh green grass to the next. I get to go nowhere, but the friggin' hens are living the high life.

On second thought, maybe I'll have those eggs. A few sunny-side-up might brighten my day.

Love,

Susan

P.S. This just in! Maybe the pullets are in cahoots with Hemingway's pulmonary specialist, but we just received word that Farm Boy does not, I repeat, does not have histoplasmosis. Pastured poultry proponents from sea to shining sea are celebrating. And down here at Nate's Place we're pretty damn happy, too!

Chapter Twenty-two

YOU GOT A REFERENCE FOR THAT ROOSTER?

Some days I miss my big job. Why? Because I enjoyed making big decisions. Things like, "Yes, you may spend forty-five thousand dollars on the new presentation the sales staff has been begging for, but in reality will use just once, decide they hate, and then stuff in a desk drawer. And no, you may not take a week's vacation the week before the crucial, all-the-corporate-bigwigs-will-be-there national sales meeting. That's when I'll be away." Those were the days.

These days I take rooster references. The phone rings; I answer, and am treated to the curriculum vitae of any number of cocks. "Hi, this is Bob at Grass Up to Our Ass Farm. Your husband called and spoke to my wife's aunt's stepmother, Myrtle, regarding a rooster. We've got one for ya of mixed stock and good temperament. Had him with us awhile and he ain't never hurt but one hen, and she had it coming."

Sounds great, Bob. Can you hold while I get a pencil and stick it in my eye?

When I'm not fielding fowl calls I'm pursuing escaped poultry across the pasture. Unfortunately, I usually find myself in this predicament while wearing my low-rise Gap jeans and Via Spiga stilettos. Not a pretty picture, I assure you, and probably the reason the hens are doing their chicken-run routine in the first place. Just today, twelve of them literally flew their electrified coop. Hemingway kept yelling, "Head 'em off at the hog pen," and "I'm too old for this!" And I kept shouting back, "I'm improperly attired! I'm improperly attired!" Together we chased and cajoled and even tackled a few of the future fryers—one of whom air-kissed my honey so fervently on the face it redefined the phrase *peck on the cheek*—but we didn't have any real success until Cuyler came to our rescue. He raced out to us, announced we were "retarded," and then kicked some serious pullet posterior. When he was finished he simply said, "You call yourselves farmers?" and then returned to his spot in front of the PlayStation.

Of course my life isn't just about chasing chickens or finding the perfect rooster to ride herd on them. Sometimes I'm also in sales. That's right, the phone rings, and suddenly I'm the chief rainmaker at the McCorkindale Used Farm Equipment Company. "Morning, ma'am. I'm calling about your ad in the *Valley Trader*. The one for a trailer. I need to replace mine on account of my kids. Damn high schoolers and their naked hay rides. You got high schoolers, ma'am?"

No, and at this rate my kids are never going.

To be honest, phone sales is just not my forte. I seem to do better in person. Why do I think this? Because thanks to my fabulous personality, astonishing powers of description, and enthusiastic *The Price Is Right* approach, I helped unload several thousand dollars' worth of hay equipment. Allow me to explain.

One morning I was playing the piano and howling just below the maximum noise level allowed in Fauquier County when there was a knock at the door. I answered, and there was this man who reeked of, how shall I put this? Money. Lots of money.[126]

Mr. Money said he was here about the hay equipment, and I said, "Oh, darn! My husband's not here to show it to you." And he said, "Well, why don't you show it to me?" And I thought, Well, Daddy Warbucks, you're assuming I know where he keeps the stuff. Which I don't, as there are only fourteen buildings on the farm to choose from, and I'm really unsure which he's chosen, but instead I said, "Sure!" and then teetered off in the direction of the Butler building. I figured the hay equipment, being big, would need a big place to be stored, and nothing's bigger than the Butler building (so named for the company that built it: Butler. Ingenious!). In fact it's so huge, it could house a J.Crew, Gap, and Banana Republic, something I beg for frequently, with a little Starbucks Express on the side. Oh, Lord, for how much longer will I be forced to go without my morning mocha?

Anyway, I take Well-Heeled Harry, who's real name is Kent, or Trent, or some other moneyed-sounding moniker, into our Yankee Stadium–size equipment shed, and there it all is: massive machinery I know absolutely nothing about. Wonderful. Where the hell is Hemingway when I need him? Repairing fence boards the bulls broke through in a desperate quest for a booty call with the cows? No, that

---

126. For a minute I actually thought the prize van had finally arrived, and then I remembered I'm married.

was yesterday. Moving hay bales from one snake-infested storage spot to another? I don't think so; even over the roar of the skid loader, I'd hear him hollering. Maybe he's plowing a field, or planting one. I can't recall. Jeez. What if he's out on the tractor and he's had an accident, and I don't know and he can't call 'cause cell phones don't work here in the sixth circle of hell, and he's slowly bleeding to death while I'm standing here with Daddy Warbucks, wondering, If I help sell this stuff can I get the Gucci mules I've had my eye on? Hmm. It's times like this when I think it might be wise to start tuning in when he's telling me what he'll be doing all day.

And I will. Tomorrow.

Right now it's time to get back to Tad, or maybe it's Chad, who's taken the lead. "Ah, there's the Discbine mower your husband was telling me about!" "Yes, the Discbine mower," I reply, like I've been speaking farm forever, "a fabulous piece of machinery made by"—(quick glance at the logo)—"New Holland. Can't even believe we're parting with that baby."

It went on like this for about ten minutes with Biff, or maybe it was Brad, walking from one hunk of metal to the next, and me following along, doing my best game-show-hostess-meets-used-car-salesperson patter: "Look at that fabulous shade of green!" and "You know what they say: Nothing runs like a Deere." I must have done something right, because shortly after Hemingway showed up[127] and relieved me of my sales duties, I learned that, thanks to me, Randolph would be taking almost everything.

---

127. He'd been at the bank, post office, and hardware store. Who knew it was farm errand day? "You did, Sue. I told you this morning." Note to self: When Hemingway speaks, take nose out of *Vogue* and listen. At least a little.

And all I wanted to know was who the hell is Randolph?

In any case, about a week ago I was promoted, and my sales rep responsibilities expanded to include cow puncher.[128] I was awarded this advancement because twice in one day I helped round up and return several escaped cows to their rightful pastures. Not an easy thing to do in peep-toe platforms, but I managed.

Cow punching, for the uninitiated, is done in pairs. One person positions himself near the renegade ruminants to block them from going any farther astray. This is Hemingway's job: he's big; they're big. It all works out. The other person stands about fifty yards away from the gate through which the cattle need to go, in an effort to force them in that direction and prevent them from coming closer to the house and possibly copping a squat on the porch. This is my job: the cattle are scared; I'm scared. It all works out.

Once both people are in position, the person near the cattle yells, claps his hands, and threatens the beasts with a trip to the butcher until they take off toward the open gate. For about a minute, it looks as if the cattle will parade into the pasture without any further fuss, and then it happens. They veer away from the gate and straight toward you. Or in this case, me.

Instantly I assumed the crucial basketball shuffle position so key to cow punching. Such instinct! Such an innate knack for the job! Why I spent so many years in magazine marketing when I was born to hurl Italian invectives at future hangar steaks, I'll never know. But there I went, arms and legs stretched wide, feet shuffling first to the

---

128. Who knew I'd have such professional success here in the sticks?

right, then to the left, silently praying I wouldn't snap an ankle.[129]

With the beasts trotting toward me, I darted from side to side, swearing like a Soprano until they stopped dead in their tracks. Were they offended by my foul mouth? Frightened by my resemblance to a psychotic scarecrow? Who knows what goes on in the head of a head of cattle. Then they cocked their fly-ridden craniums, exhaled breath so rank it could remove wallpaper, turned, and headed straight back to Hemingway.

It took a while to re-secure our prison-breaking bovines, but eventually we did it. Twice. Hemingway offered to pay me, but since the ten bucks he proffered won't keep me in Keds, I told him forget it. Just put it toward the Visa bill for the leather JLo pumps I picked up. It's not an even exchange, but to me (as I'm sure you can tell) nothing celebrates a job well done like designer footwear.

Despite my affection for impractical attire, a fact that frustrates my work-boot-wearing better half, I demonstrate my willingness to be a helpful farm wife in other ways. For example, I read the rural magazines we get every month.

Right this instant I'm perusing an issue of *Hobby Farms*, and I'm shocked to find myself wondering what the "Six Strategies for Fighting Flies This Summer" include. Showering daily? Using deodorant? Walking softly and brandishing a big fly swatter? There's even a feature on "The Secret Life of Farm Dogs," but I plan to skip it. One whiff of our manure-befouled bowwows and it's no secret what they do all day.

---

129. Or, horrors, a heel!

I'm also doing my best to get through the latest copy of *Grass Farmer* and a feature entitled "Train Your Cows to Be Weed Managers." Can they really be encouraging cattle to climb the corporate ladder? And if so, how long before there are several in places like my BB&T, wearing buttons that say, "Beef up your savings. Ask me about our moo-velous opportunities!"?

When that day comes, and I'm standing there with my checking deposit, desperate to cover my latest foray into couture footwear, I really hope they won't recognize me. And if they do, I pray they'll recall I was the cow puncher who didn't use a cattle prod. After all, they'll be in a position to hire. And since I'm pretty sure bank pay tops the whopping wage I can earn around here, I hope they'll consider me. Particularly if I promise to leave my leather pumps at home.

Chapter Twenty-three

WELCOME TO STUBURG

After making me take about a dozen references for roosters, Hemingway finally bought one from a farmer in Hume. Mr. Rooster was promptly christened Hefner, so I suspect my better half still has a soft spot for the old "I read it for the articles" rag, *Playboy*, and let loose on the hens. Hef's a handsome devil, a purebred, black-and-white Cuckoo Maran with a French lineage, a red plume, and a swinging strut.

And the chicks dig him.

Or maybe it's just that he digs the chicks. After all, that's his job, and he pursues it with the zeal of a Scientologist soundproofing a delivery room. The hens, on the other hand, don't seem to share his passion for pullet procreation, preferring to continue pecking the ground for grubs while Hef does his stuff. In fact the hens seem so bored, I expect at any moment during "the act" to hear them suggest new paint colors for the ceiling of the chicken coop.[130]

But back to Hef. We had houseguests last weekend, and

---

130. And they say hens and female humans have little in common.

our cuckoo Cuckoo Maran proved particularly entertaining. He provided ample chicken fornication demonstrations (a big hit with the teenagers in attendance) and free wake-up calls at three o'clock, four o'clock, and five o'clock every morning (not a big hit with anybody, believe me).

If you're thinking that roosters are supposed to crow only at daybreak because that's what some guide told you and the rest of the first-graders during a field trip to the zoo, you'd be wrong. But don't feel bad. The guide told Hemingway the same thing.[131]

The fact is, roosters crow every fifty-eight minutes, or whenever their authority is threatened. And since the hens like to cluck in the laying box, a direct violation of Hef's silent–birthing room rule, it's no wonder he hollers constantly.

In addition to being awakened before dawn and subjected to the sight of innumerable bantam booty calls, we treated our guests to many of the unique forms of fun found on the farm.

For starters, we walked them through our Power Outage Response Procedure.[132]

I was helping my friend Kim unpack her and her husband, Pete's, stuff when I suddenly blurted out a fact that's become as important to me as locating the nearest Nordstrom. "As soon as the power goes out, you fill the tub."

Now, my friend Kim is a senior executive at ESPN. She has a brilliant, strategic, marketing mind. She's been

---

131. I myself skipped that excursion, though I did see several former residents of the snake house at the handbag trunk show I attended instead.

132. This isn't something we ever had to do in suburbia; in fact we didn't even have such an animal. But here in the hinterland it's a must.

profiled in magazines and awarded all kinds of honors. She's logical, a born leader, and beautiful to boot. She's also got a couple of loose screws and that's what makes me love her.

"Why would you take a bath during a blackout?" came her reply. An excellent question, and one I just so happened to ask myself the first time I was told this important tidbit. Is it any wonder we're friends?

"No, no. You don't bathe in it," I responded, laughing and fussing with the huge guest basket next to the bed. "You use it to flush the toilet. When the power goes out, the pump goes out, and then that's that for flushing. Unless you've filled the tub."

"Got it." She paused a moment. "When does the power usually go out?"

"Whenever it damn well pleases."

"OK, then." She smiled and glanced at the massive goody collection I was trying to corral. "What *is* all that?"

Back in Ridgewood, I had the sweetest little basket of snacks on the nightstand next to the bed in our guest room. In it were such essentials as extra toothbrushes and tooth-paste; travel-size bottles of shampoo, conditioner, and body lotion (every bit of it from Bath & Body Works, natch); all manner of mouthwatering gourmet goodies—Dale and Thomas popcorn, Godiva chocolate, Toblerone bars, Kettle Chips, Peanut Shop peanuts, splits of Pinot Grigio, bottles of Perrier; and the latest issue of *People*. (Nothing like a little mind candy with some real candy before going to sleep, I always say.) Here at Nate's Place I've still got a guest basket, but it's a lot less luxurious.

"It's your sticks survival kit." I barely get the words

out before we both start cracking up. "Two flashlights, extra batteries, candles, matches, a pair of walkie-talkies, and a couple bottles of Poland Spring. Even some peanut butter crackers, in case you need a nosh in the dark. I'm telling you, Kim, this is a four-star farm we're running here."

To prove it, we dragged our pals and their sweet daughter Noelle (whom I started calling NoliCannoli when dinner discussion turned to talk of my favorite Italian pastry, which, like Passover cards, you simply cannot get in these parts) out into the pasture for a rousing game of Name That Snake. Within ten minutes Hemingway saw three huge black snakes and assumed he had us all beat. But when Cuy tripped and connected with a nest of baby copperheads, we knew who the real winner was, not to mention how fast he could run.

Sometime later that day we took the kids on a hay ride. Sure, you can do that in suburbia. But once your charges are bored and tired of bouncing up and down and being stuck in the butt and the back of the legs with hay stalks, all you suburbanites can do is send them pumpkin picking. Here in the sticks, we hand them BB guns and send them pigeon popping.

"Casey, you use Dad's four-hundred-dollar Panther Air Rifle, and let Noelle use your less expensive, but equally effective, Walther Air Pistol." We were standing in the Butler building, home to more pigeons than Central Park's ever seen. The kids were tricked out like terrorists in masks, pads, all kinds of protective gear. And of course guns. "Cuyler, if I catch you, or any of you, without your goggles it's 'Game over,' got it?" They looked at me and nodded. "Now, remember: aim for the rafters, and the kid with the most confirmed kills wins. You hear me?" Three goggled, eye-blacked, helmeted heads nod in unison. "You've got twenty minutes. Bring back dinner."

Of course I'm kidding about dinner. We don't eat pigeon. But the groundhogs Grundy brings home are another matter entirely. . . .

In addition to busting a cap on the birds, we also flew kites, hiked, and navigated massive mounds of cow poop. We barbecued, collected eggs, played with the dogs, and played the piano. The only thing we didn't do is sing, which is a shame, as we let a perfectly good noise-volume waiver go to waste. Oh, well. There's always next time.

One of the more entertaining ways we spent our time was coming up with alternate uses for the farm. The fact that we can sunbathe naked in our own backyard prompted plans for turning the place into a nudist colony. Lots of trees, bushes, and strategically placed cows for shy nudies who'd like a little natural coverage make this a viable option. Then we tossed around the idea of going condo with the old grain silo, the Butler building, and the barn, but I nixed it in favor of making the whole thing a mall or maybe just a mammoth DSW. And finally it was decided that with a little effort, and some folks dressed in Colonial garb who don't mind spending the day dipping candles, shoeing horses, and churning butter, we could kick Colonial Williamsburg's butt with our very own Stuburg.[133] For some reason, maybe it was the beer, we all liked this idea best.

133. Although I'm partial to my honey's literary nickname, his pals prefer to call him Stu.

Just goes to show you: Drinking and marketing don't mix.[134]

One thing we didn't consider doing to the farm was burning it to the ground. No, that we left to Mother Nature, who appeared to have it in mind a few days after our friends' departure when lightning zapped several round hay bales and set them ablaze. I quickly jumped into Suzy, the Fabulous Farm Wife, mode and dialed 911, only to have Hemingway grab the phone from my hand, slam it down, and say, "Sue, we put out field fires ourselves."

To which I replied, "But muck boots look lousy with these jeans." Obviously I didn't help fight the fire, but I was intrigued to see the cattle munching the burned hay bales the next day.

Hmmm. Maybe cows are whom I should be cooking for.

Of course there's no question about *what* I should be cooking. If that meaty Cuckoo Maran doesn't knock off the pre-dawn cock-a-doodle-doing he's going to find himself deep fried and served with a side of slaw. Unless there's a better recipe in L. Ron Hubbard's *Scientologists Serve It Up Home Style Cookbook*. As you'd expect, Hubbard's a big fan of eating in silence. But since I'm an even bigger fan of eating the silenced, we should be able to work something out.[135]

---

134. No matter how I felt in my *Family Circle* days.

135. I confess this cookbook's a complete fabrication. But I really believe there's a market for it, so why don't they make one?

Have You Heard the Moos?

TO: Friends & Family
FR: Your Favorite Fake Farm Chick
Date: Wednesday, 2:15 p.m.
Subject: Starbucks is coming to the sticks!

Hold on to your hay bales, friends and loved ones; there's a Starbucks coming to the country.

According to today's *Fauquier Times-Democrat*, the Arby's in Warrenton (aka civilization, compared to where we live), decided not to renew its lease. While I do feel bad for all the honest, hard-working country folk that'll have to forgo their curly fries and Big Montana Roast Beef sandwiches, I'm thrilled Starbucks swooped in to keep the community caffeinated.

Because it has been tough staying hyper around here.

In fact, up until now the only way I could get my Venti Half-Caffe Soy Mocha with Whip Latte was at the mini Starbucks stand tucked inside the Safeway (also in Warrenton). Sure, it was better than nothing, but the local high school kids running it never could get the big, bad condescending barista act down. And if I don't get a heaping helping of abuse with my coffee, or at least a really good eye roll and a belittling "You want *whip* on your *soy* latte?" crack, it's just not worth the twelve bucks.

Speaking of abuse, I made the mistake of visiting the chickens this week. After hearing for days how docile they are, how they like to be petted, and how "they'll perch on your arm if you hold still!" I let myself be cajoled into paying them a social call. Never again. Those girls came at me with a furor never before seen outside of a designer handbag sale at Saks. Maybe it was the fact that I didn't come bearing feed—I brought chocolate; I thought *all* chicks liked chocolate— or that my footwear was more fashionable than the wrinkled, three-pronged, ET-type concoctions they're cursed with, but they attacked my ankles with the zeal of a vendor at an ear-piercing pavilion. Five cotton balls, eight Band-Aids, and a tube of Neosporin later, I nestled onto the couch with my copy of *Family Circle's All-Time Favorite Family Recipes* book. I'm no chef, but I plan to become pretty adept with poultry dishes.

I vowed from that point forward to limit my visits to human guests only. On Saturday Hemingway and I entertained a ninety-five-year-old gentleman who lived for forty of those years in our house. Spry, and sharp as the beaks of the pullets that'll soon be chicken Parmesan, Mr. White regaled us with tales of farm life in the good old days of child labor, locusts, and plows pulled by prized oxen (but only when the kids were too busy to do it themselves).

In the course of conversation we learned lots, including the fact that our house was built in 1890, to replace a house that was home to murder. Sometime in the late 1880s, a farmer murdered his wife and two children on this very spot. He then tried to set fire to the house. It didn't completely catch, which he or may not have known, as he was off in the woods putting a bullet in his brain. When new owners bought the property, they tore down the original, half-burned house, and built this one.

In hindsight, maybe I would be better off hanging out with the hens.

Anyway, I'm awaiting the grand opening of the new Starbucks with bated breath, which, to my way of thinking, is a lot better than bad breath, but not as good as coffee breath. I intend to be first in line, armed with a credit card cleared just for the occasion.

Of course if I discover more high school girls behind the counter, blowing kisses to their boyfriends over the steamed milk machine, I'm going to urge the management to consider poultry for all future positions. After all, a designer coffee is only as good as the diva who doesn't want to serve it to you.

Love,

Susan

Chapter Twenty-four

LIFE IN THE FARM LANE

So there I was, rushing the kids to day camp, desperate to make the nine o'clock drop-off time lest they miss a pre-paid minute of *Wide World of Sports* (Cuyler) and paintball (Casey), or I miss a precious moment of peace. We were cruising Rectortown Road at a good clip when we zipped past a slow-moving John Deere tractor headed in the other direction and holding up four cars that were bumper-to-bumper behind it when Casey says, "Wow, you don't see that every day."

Huh? Is he kidding? That's all we *do* see around here.

There should be a Starbucks for every tractor I've been trapped behind. An Ann Taylor for every pickup truck piled high with hay doing 15 where the speed limit is 50. A Cole Haan for every horse trailer with the horses' heads hanging out the windows, the breeze flinging their drool directly onto my windshield. And a Neiman Marcus for every equestrian type straddling the middle of the road and flaunting that "horseback riders have the right of way" silliness we've quite literally saddled ourselves with down here.

Maybe what he meant to say is, "Wow, you don't see that every day *in Ridgewood*," and he'd be right.

Not once in all the years we lived in New Jersey did I have to stop my car and wait while a group of men forced an escaped bull back into a field. Nor did I ever see anyone making hay on their property or taking a stroll with their pet alpaca. No, suburbia has its wonders, and frankly I still wonder how I live without them, but the country has its fair share of sights to see, too.

Like the six-foot-long black snakes that surround our springhouse and dine alfresco on the frogs and fish in the stream. Occasionally they attempt to slither their way into our cellar, and sometimes they even come creeping up on the chicken coop in search of eggs when a seafood diet no longer satisfies their forked-tongue taste buds.

This happened recently, in an event that will forever be known as the Day of the Great Reptilian Attack, and it was Casey who came to the rescue. While Cuyler and I locked ourselves on the mud porch to watch out the windows, and Hemingway tried in vain to call in an air strike on his cell, our gentle giant calmly grabbed a shovel and killed two of the king-size kielbasas with more passion and force than he ever exhibited on the football field.[136]

Of course the wildlife we live with isn't the only thing that keeps me feeling like a fish out of water. For that refreshing, "Boy, Sue, you're really lost at sea" sensation, I simply need to attend a local social event.

Take, for example, the annual Upperville Colt and Horse Show. We attended this last year with Doug and

---

136. Could it be that my sweet son has finally found his sport?

Nancy, and I thoroughly enjoyed strutting my stuff in my cute "horse race" straw hat and doggie-bedecked skirt. I guess I thought I was so Jackie O., but looking back I'm sure Jackie Oh No! was more like it. Well, we went again this year, and while it was a hoot hanging out with all the movers, shakers, and big money makers, I finally saw the event for what it really is: Halloween for the horsey set.

The women wore more makeup than I've ever seen this side of a Clinique counter[137] and their preferred costume was anything Lilly Pulitzer, a line that, let's be honest, looks a whole lot better on fourth-graders than forty-year-olds.

Maybe it's because I'm a big man fan, but the guys looked much more normal, not to mention age appropriate, in their blue blazers and khaki pants. There was, however, a rather rowdy contingent in pastel sweaters and coordinating plaid trousers that had me worried, as they appeared poised to grab the women's oversize Prada purses and take off trick-or-treating from tent to tent.

As if watching my fellow spectators wasn't enough to make me feel like I'd suddenly been plunked down on another planet, there was the little matter of the show itself. And I'm not talking about the jockeys and the jumping competition.

I'm talking about the pre-show entertainment. This consisted of the hound pups from the Piedmont Hunt scampering around the ring to more oohs and aahs than any *human* baby has ever heard, followed by a nineteenth-century horse-drawn carriage parade led by the Master of

---

137. And please don't forget, I grew up going to the Jersey shore, where we girls hit the beach "faces on" and big hair high, so I know what I'm talking about.

the Hunt, whom I can only hope handles his horse a whole lot better than he controlled that coach.[138]

As he careened around the ring with his top hat ready to fly off and his tails flapping in the wind, I was positive he'd flip the contraption and kill himself, along with several members of the horsey set who were sitting inside the coach, alternately waving and trying desperately not to spill their Bloody Marys and mimosas. Had he done so, it would have been quite the tragedy, not only in the number of human lives lost but in the destruction of what looked to be the remainder of the wardrobe from *Gone with the Wind*.

Of course there aren't always social events to attend and poke fun at, so often I amuse myself by perusing the local paper.

Not unlike the local newspaper in NJ, my new paper typically contains a full complement of features about suspicious fires and traffic accidents, store openings, and chamber of commerce meetings. There's even an entire section dedicated to school sports, and a pull-out that's primarily real estate ads, just like in my paper back home.

But that's where the similarities cease.

Down here, any feature on education will most likely revisit the ongoing debate on where to locate the new high school and whether building it next to a firing range, which happens to be the case with one of the locations under serious consideration, is a minus or a plus.[139]

---

138. Even a novice could deduce this guy was more comfortable at the wheel of his Porsche than at the helm of a four-horse phaeton.

139. A plus? There's even the slightest possibility it could be a *plus*?

And while the business section bursts with stories on cattle auctions, livestock sales, and tips on how to buy the right brush cutter, the home section offers ideas for decorating with ladybugs and new ways to prevent snake infestation. More *House Practical* than *House Beautiful*, but believe me, I cut it out.

Even the "Things to Do" calendar features, to my way of thinking, some pretty questionable things to do. An "Appreciating Venomous Snakes" seminar? I'd appreciate not knowing such an event is even taking place. An evening "Bat Walk" to be "properly introduced to these flying mammals as they wake and begin their nightly bug hunt"? How's about an evening trunk show to be properly introduced to a new designer whose fashions I'd be happy to go batty about?

Yes, despite my eldest son's latent observation, for things you don't see every day, there's no place like the country. In fact on Friday, Casey discovered a big box turtle relaxing on our front porch. It had been pouring frogs and hogs for days, and maybe Mr. Turtle got lost looking for a little cover. But there he was, minding his own business, when Casey, the family snake smasher, ever so gently picked him up and carried him all the way to the pond in the corner of our property. Then he put him down in the grass and watched as he took off into the water—all without the background accompaniment of an iPod or PSP soundtrack to punctuate the moment.

Now, that's something you don't see every day. And the box turtle's pretty rare too.

Chapter Twenty-five

URINE MY HOUSE NOW

If I wanted to spend my life surrounded by the scent of urine, I would have erected a tent in the bowels of the New York City subway system.

But no. I chose to move to Nate's Place to (among other things) escape the spectacularly acrid aroma of the Big Apple's mass transit system. To be free of the animals that relieved themselves in the cars, behind the ticket counters, next to the magazine stands, inside the little stand-alone security booths (which, trust me, stood alone, as no police officer could stand the pungent scent), and onto the tracks in full view of all of us commuters, because they knew they could. (I mean, who was going to stop them? Certainly not me in my four-hundred-dollar Prada pumps, that's for sure.)

Well, the pee may not have been on me, but the joke sure is. True, I'm free of the sight and smell of the pigs that whizzed wherever they pleased during my morning and evening commutes, but they've been replaced by bulls. And cows.[140] And deer. And dogs. And groundhogs. And foxes. And horses. And hens.

---

140. Yes, there's a difference. See the Impractical Girl's Guide to Farm Speak for clarification.

At any given moment I can look out my living room window and catch some member of the animal kingdom piddling in my front pasture. I can't tell you how this pisses me off (pardon the pun). Why can't they find a nice private spot, like by a tree, behind the springhouse, or near the side of the barn, to do their business? Why do they need to treat me to it? Do they think I'm some sort of weird fan of wildlife bodily functions?

And if that's not bad enough, my sons have gotten the impression that they too can tinkle wherever they please. Where did they get this great "act like a guy" idea? From their dear old dad, Hemingway, who now has them using the farm like a mall-size men's room.

He thinks I should be happy about this, and maybe he has a point. After all, it's nearly impossible to get them to pee into the toilet bowl.

As I see it, it's a three-step, failsafe formula. One, stand in front of the toilet. Two, aim. And three, fire—pee, urinate, tinkle, twinkle, whiz—into the water. It's step three that my kids skip, and I'm almost positive it's on purpose.

I think Cuyler fancies himself a little "pee-pee Picasso."[141] For starters, he takes forever in the john. Then when he comes out he leaves the light on, knowing I'll go in to turn it off and discover the intricate tinkle designs that bedeck the rim of the bowl. What's a mother to do? Well, this one's been known to drag her little guy by the ear back to his "easel," hand him some paper towels and a bottle of Fantastik, and say, "Scrub!" Sound harsh? Try heartbreaking, particularly when my mischievous Monet wails, "But,

---

141. In his yellow period, I might add. I know, I know. It's a bad joke. But I couldn't resist.

Mom, it looks so pretty, and I made it just for you!" You made more work for me, you little bugger. But OK, you win. Let's grab the camera, capture this precious moment, and do what all good moms do for their budding artists, no matter what their preferred medium: find a spot on the fridge for their work.

Casey skips step three also. OK, I'll be honest. He doesn't even remember there *is* a step three. His adolescent brain is everywhere *but* the bathroom. While he's standing over the toilet, he's intent only on his image in the full-length mirror in front of him.

This might be a good time to tell you that, in Nate's Place, the toilet faces away from a mirror that runs the length of the wall in the bathroom. So if you're standing and you've got the toilet seat up[142] you've got an excellent view of your upper body and ninety percent of your lower body.[143]

So there's my handsome kid, relieving himself and taking in the view. Suddenly he sees a facial hair—his first—and leans in with the speed of a running back barreling downfield with the ball for a closer look. Urine flies everywhere, soaking the back of the bowl and dribbling down to the floor. By his feet. On his feet. Does he notice? Don't kid yourself, people. All he cares about is the wisp of a whisker he's sprouted and how fast he can get to the phone to tell his friends. Which would be fine except that, as he's running from the bathroom to his backpack to get his cell, *he's still peeing*. Aim for the water in the toilet? I'd be happy if my son would be in the *room* with the toilet.

---

142. With no intention of putting it down, I'm sure.

143. Of course, if you're sitting, as I always am, being the lone female in the family, this interesting positioning means I can peek around to see how badly my butt belongs back at the gym. Not something I do frequently, I assure you, but I digress.

Of course both Casey and Cuyler's lack of peeing precision pales in comparison with that of their father—known lovingly as the Titan of Urinary Untidiness.

I've seen Hemingway take a freshly cleaned toilet bowl and soil it almost beyond saving in under thirty seconds. Honestly, to follow my lover in the loo requires either a very strong stomach or a penchant for public toilets. That's the kind of mess the man can make. Urine everywhere but the bowl, with a pinch of pubic hair thrown in for good measure. And of course the seat is up, always up, and sprayed to the point of streaking.

Sounds disgusting, right? Disgusting doesn't even begin to describe it. You need to experience it firsthand, or should I say tush first, as I did one night late in my pregnancy with Casey.

There I went, waddling silently into our bathroom,[144] desperate to relieve my bursting bladder, and keeping the place pitch-black so as not to wake my better half. What did I get for being little Miss Considerate? Urine-soaked slippers and the shock of my life as I lowered myself down, down, down to a toilet seat that was nowhere to be found. Before I knew it, I lost my balance and plunged into the toilet-seatless toilet bowl below. I tried to stand but I was stuck, really stuck—hips wedged, feet and legs flailing in the air stuck.[145]

---

144. In our brand-new condo in a town that will remain nameless but to me will always be known as the absolute armpit of New Jersey . . . sorry. I know I already said that. I seem to have some sort of post-traumatic condo disorder from our days in (shhhh) Little Ferry.

145. If you're having trouble envisioning my predicament, picture one of our 350 cows stuffed by its hindquarters into a Kohler. Now add to this vision a pretty pink flowered nightdress the size of Disney World draped over said cow, and you've got one scary sight indeed. Agreed?

You'd think that after two kids, two dogs, one cat, seventeen chickens, three-hundred-plus head of cattle, one husband, and sixteen years of marriage I'd have made peace with the fact that the toilet was never going to be tidy. After all I'd had plenty of advance warning, particularly while using the Cheerios trick to train Cuyler.[146] You toss some Cheerios in the toilet bowl and tell the kid to aim for them. My son loved it, his aim was incredible, and for one brief moment I was certain I'd raise a man who wouldn't leave a mess for *his* wife one day.

And then it happened.

My little guy stopped peeing midstream, plucked the urine-soaked Cheerio from the bowl, slapped it on the rim of the toilet, took aim, and then sent that baby soaring across the room and into the tub. I was stunned. He was hysterical. Before I knew it, Casey and Hemingway were crowding into the room to get in on the game.

So I should have known ages ago that, while other women would have fresh flowers in their bathroom, I would always have a family-size bottle of Fantastik in mine. It's not sophisticated, but it's practical.

And since I'll do practically anything to stay one drip ahead of my men, it makes sense. Even if their bathroom behavior—indoors and on the five-hundred-acre urinal on which we reside—doesn't.

---

146. I'm sure the folks at General Mills *love* this unique use of their product.

Chapter Twenty-six

WHO YOU CALLIN' A LOULOU?

$\mathcal{S}$ometimes, despite the excitement of corralling escaped cows and the thrill of selling used farm equipment to mega millionaires, I really miss the stimulation of New York City and my staff at *Family Circle*. If I'm honest with myself, I have to admit that this is the reason for my recent, over-in-a-flash-fast foray into the retail arena.

In an effort to save my sanity and make a positive contribution to the community (i.e., use my marketing skills to convince the women of this county to trade their riding pants for something roomier in the rear), I sought employment at a lovely little shop called LouLou. Why they hired me, when I have about as much style as our chickens have social skills, I don't know, but suddenly, for the first time in forty-plus years, I was in fashion. Literally.

I loved being at LouLou. It was so much fun to spend the day among clothing and jewelry and handbags and boots. I got to dress and accessorize the mannequins,[147]

---

147. Which kind of frightened me, as there are days I can barely dress and accessorize myself.

and I got to help people pick out the perfect outfit for work, dates, and parties, and to give as presents. Helping others shop all day was almost as good as shopping all day myself, which is what I did when things were slow. In fact, I don't think I ever brought home a paycheck from LouLou. Instead I simply signed it over to my manager to cover the Matt & Nat bags, Free People tops, Tribal cords, and Lucchese cowboy boots I had to have. After all, I got everything at a discount, so it was like constantly being at a terrific sale.[148]

The joy of being surrounded by clothing quickly faded when I learned that part of my job was to steam each article as it came out of the box. For a true fashionista, such an assignment would have been a snap. But for me, the original *Glamour* "don't," it was a disaster.

It goes without saying that I scalded myself, but I also suggested to a customer that she try on a "hot little number" we'd just received and that I'd just steamed. Lucky for me the garment's toastiness tickled her pink—which is about the shade it left her back—and she didn't sue me for stupidity. After that I demoted myself to hair accessory straightening duty, feigning a sudden, psychotic fear of the steamer.

Steamer aside, the only thing I found really scary was being slow. It's not in my nature to do nothing, and without a minibar to manage or a team to coerce into taking a kickboxing class, I had to find other ways to entertain myself.

One particularly quiet morning,[149] I curled up in the

---

148. And who can resist a sale?

149. I'm talking no-customers-in-ninety-minutes quiet. . . .

comfy wing chair in the corner and lost myself in a day-dream I only wish I'd had the guts to indulge. In my "fash-ion savior" fantasy, I tugged, stretched, and practically split a size-two pair of riding pants by pulling them over the posterior of a size-ten mannequin. Then I placed the mannequin butt-front in the window with a sign that said NOT A GOOD LOOK. Next I dressed another size-ten dummy in a pair of beautifully proportioned Tribal trousers, stuck it fanny-front in the window, and slapped a sign that read LOULOU TO THE RESCUE! right below its rear.

In my mind, this was a perfect marketing ploy: It ad-dressed a consumer problem and positioned LouLou as the solution. The more I thought about it, the more excited I became. In seconds I was out of that chair and dancing to Green Day's *American Idiot* CD.[150] It could work! The store would make a mint! My boss would be beside herself!

The thought of my manager stopped me midshimmy. I loved Barb, but she was built way more like Wonder Woman than like Angelina Jolie. Plus she rode. (Horses, not the sub-way.) What if she was put off by my approach? It wouldn't matter if we sold out our entire inventory of Tribal slacks in six seconds. If she was offended, she might fire me. Or, worse, make me wear a pair of supersnug jodhpurs with a placard around my neck: "Try our Tribal pants," it would say. "See my butt for the biggest reason why!"

Clearly, it's best if I stay really busy. Although had it been a little slower the day the Contessa strolled in, I wouldn't have complained.

It was a Tuesday and the store was hopping. I was helping people find the right size pants and a shirt that

---

150. How appropriate.

goes just so and ringing up sales and answering the phone. In the midst of the mayhem, in walked this little old lady who decided she wanted to try on this swinging, chic skirt. It was a good thing she was tiny, because the skirt was cut for a toddler. I grabbed her size and said, "Here you go! Let me get you into a dressing room!"

But no. She didn't want a dressing room. She wanted to "Slippa the skirta on, over mya jeansa." (Did I mention she's Italian?[151]) So she stood at the counter with the hordes of women I was trying to ring up, tugging this tiny, slim-cut skirt up over her jeans. Did it get stuck? Of course it did. And of course as she stepped out of it, she stepped on it and nearly careened into a metal belt display. I made a mad dash around the counter to catch her midfall, the word *lawsuit* flashing across my mind, and again suggested she use the fitting room.

But no. Now she decided to slip it on over her head. Did I mention she was wearing two shirts? She was. Did it get stuck again? Of course it did. And now I had hordes of women desperate to pay and depart with their purchases, and one older woman, her arms flailing wildly in the air, a $225 Basil & Maude skirt stuck between her eyeglasses and her armpits, crying, "Helpa, helpa, I tinka I'ma stucka!" Unbelievable.

Finally she wriggled it down to her waist and then decided she really should take off her jeans[152] to check the fit. So she hiked up the skirt, unzipped her jeans, and took them off. Right there at the register. In a store full of people.

---

151. I am too, but unfortunately my accent is a bit more Brooklyn than Bologna.

152. Something I'd been suggesting she do all along, IN THE DRESSING ROOM.

They're looking at me. I'm looking at them. And we're all doing our best to look anywhere but at this elderly lady's tiny stocking-covered tush.

Ultimately she bought the skirt and the matching sweater, and I was sold on the idea that it just might be safer for me to stay on the farm. Sure, I miss LouLou. But at least here the only heinies I have to look at are the hens'.

Chapter Twenty-seven

HEMINGWAY, AND ALL THAT JAZZ...

Since I no longer have a staff to cajole into taking a kick-boxing class, and since I can't speed walk around here without being chased by a clutch of cattle, I've been forced to find other ways to exercise.

For starters, I Rollerblade. I race up and down our private road, which, while paved, is still an obstacle course of pebbles, chunks of gravel, and leftover deer bones Grundy managed not to digest. (Nothing like getting one of those suckers caught in a wheel for an airborne experience unlike any the Wright brothers ever imagined.)

I'm sure it doesn't help that as I'm 'blading along, I've got my iPod blaring dance music so loud I'm lost in a fantasy of strutting my stuff at Studio 54. To my way of thinking the farm and that disco are not so different. I'm surrounded by animals here, and I was surrounded by animals there. Of course those animals were doused in Obsession,[153] so maybe I should buy a gross for the gals.

The fact that I'm pretty tuned out while charging

---

153. Which made them a tad more tolerable.

around is fine in flat spots. But twice while lost in dance land I've gone hurtling downhill only to be greeted—suddenly—by the cattle guard that cuts across the road.

In case I haven't already explained, a cattle guard[154] is a series of metal slats designed to catch the hooves of an escaped cow and prevent it from charging out into the street and becoming chop meat. I've never actually seen a cow get caught in one of these contraptions, though Hemingway tells me it isn't pretty, but I've definitely had firsthand—or should I say headfirst—experience with the device.

If memory serves (and it may not, considering the smack I took to the skull), I was "Last Dance"ing with Donna Summer when I connected with the cattle guard at light speed. My right Rollerblade wedged between the first two slats and my body sailed forward until the anchor that used to be my ankle caught and catapulted me down to the ground.

A minor concussion, badly scraped jaw, and large "egg" over my left eye later, I came to the conclusion that this is the reason people wear pads.

Sure, I still Rollerblade, but not outside. These days I practice my figure eights in the Butler building (our Yankee Stadium–size equipment shed). There's no cattle guard or gravel to fear, and dodging the hens[155] as they scamper by and ducking the pigeon poop as it rains down from the rafters are really helping perfect my form.

---

154. For a complete definition, see The Impractical Girl's Guide to Farm Speak.

155. Hemingway lets the chickens free range, which means they go (and I do mean that literally) wherever they want. The Butler building, the window boxes, the backseat of the Mustang. Yeah, that went over well.

This is fine, to a point. But being an exercise freak, social butterfly, and longtime dance music lover (as well as someone who really doesn't relish pain in conjunction with her fitness program), the bottom line is that I've had to find some other way to fight fat and make friends.

So I joined Jazzercise.

I know. I know. Jazzercise has been around since the '70s. It smacks of striped leg warmers and matching leotards. It brings back memories of headbands and Olivia Newton John belting out "Physical" in one of the earliest music videos known to man. It was done by fat ladies who loved Cher and the Bee Gees but wouldn't be caught dead in a disco. Your mom did it. Your grandma did it. Your aunt Gladys did it before she got the gout.

Cool kids did not do it, right? Wrong.

Cool kids definitely did it. I did it. So admit it: You did it too. You just didn't tell anybody.

The woman who invented Jazzercise was—and still is—brilliant.[156] She took Bob Fosse's and John Travolta's best moves and melded them with aerobics. Then she tossed in a heaping helping of thumping, driving dance music, and gave women what they craved: a safe place to let their hair down while they brought their weight down. To me, Jazzercise is the world's best disco—but without the cocktails and the come-ons. Which is of course what makes it the world's best disco.

Hello, my name is Susan and I'm a Jazzercise addict.

Six days a week I drive down to Warrenton and dance,

---

156. Not to mention gorgeous and in the most amazing, inspiring shape. She's not just one hot mama; she's one hot *grand*mama.

as my instructor Nancy says, like no one's watching. Because unless you count my pals Toni and Lisa, Kim, Karen, Jenn, and Marina, no one is. And even they're not really watching. They're flat out laughing at my fabulous (and I use the word, like the muscles that once were my triceps, loosely) form.

The twenty-five-minute commute doesn't bother me, but lately I've begun to consider converting one of the barns or the aforementioned Butler building from its current use as roller rink/oversize pigeon coop and henhouse into a Jazzercise studio. Then I could have my own facility and all my friends could come here. Every day. Several times a day in fact. And then I'd no longer feel isolated because I'd import my own people!

I got so high on the idea I took it to Hemingway, who just happened to be working in my future Jazzercise center at the time. "You know what we should do with all this space?" I practically shouted, stepping through the twenty-two-foot-high sliding (if you're Arnold Schwarzenegger–strong) metal doors and surprising my busy farm boy.

He looked up from the length of gutter he was preparing to cut and eyed me suspiciously. "If I've told you once Suz, I've told you a million times. We're not making it a mini mall."

"No, no. Forget that . . ."

"Or a Panera Bread . . ."

"No, no. Listen . . ."

"Or a Banana Republic or a martini bar or a jewelry store."

"Not a real jewelry store," I replied, exasperated. How many times did I have to explain my grand plan? "A fake-diamond store. Really good cubics and stuff. I'd call it Just Faux Fun. Isn't that a great name? Someday I gotta open a store like that just to use that name."

"Yeah, yeah. Great name. Come here and hold this."

"I don't want to get cut."

"You won't get cut. I will if I try to hold and slice at the same time."

So I held and he sliced, and soon we were both side by side on ladders, working a brand-new patch of gutter into place along the front of the bank barn.[157] I'm not big into manual labor (my feeling is they have people for that, so let's get some), but I love watching Hemingway work. In fact I love watching Hemingway read and write and flip burgers on the barbecue. I love watching him play catch with Cuyler, and patiently explain to Casey why porn sites are inappropriate (and how, if we find him surfing one again, we're tossing his PC on the burn pile). I love watching him nap, with his reading glasses on his nose, the cat nestled right under his neck, and a book flopped open on his belly.

I love watching him stroll through Tractor Supply, smiling as he picks up specialty chicken feed or a stone-washed pair of "Look, Sue! John Deere flannel-lined jeans!" I love how saleswomen fall all over themselves to help him, and how waitresses rush to save him from starving to death.[158]

The cutest are the ladies at our favorite lunch spot who

---

157. It's literally a barn built into an embankment. We use it to store hay and other stuff that attracts creepy-crawlies.

158. Oh yes, at six feet tall and 210 pounds, my man's obviously malnourished.

scramble to serve my honey his sweet tea before he's even seated. The kids and I can be parched to the point of expiration, literally licking the table in a desperate search for some leftover condensation to quench our thirst, and all these gals can see is Hemingway.

> *Waitress,* looking directly at my husband: "What'll it be to drink, hon?"
>
> *Hemingway:* "Iced tea, please. Sue, you too?"
>
> *Me:* "No. I think I'd like . . ."
>
> *Waitress,* completely unaware anyone else is at the table: "Sweetened or unsweetened?"
>
> *Hemingway:* "Sweetened's great. Sue?"
>
> *Waitress,* inspecting Hemingway's sweat-stained, grass-flecked thirty-year-old Marine Corps sweatshirt with the intensity of a garment worker: "Been bush hogging?"
>
> *Hemingway,* who thinks he's always dressed for success with his collection of clothes from the 1970s: "Um, a bit this morning." Pause. "Kids, what'll it be?"
>
> *Cuyler:* "Can I have chocolate milk?"
>
> *Waitress:* "Try the meatloaf; it'll fill you up."
>
> *Hemingway:* "I was thinking about a burger. Case, you want a . . ."
>
> *Casey:* "Coke, please."
>
> *Waitress:* "Burger'll work. Medium, right? With fries?"
>
> *Hemingway:* "Sure. And I think we'll also need . . ."
>
> *Me:* "Could I just have an ice water with a slice of lemon?"

Waitress: "I'll be right back with your sweet tea."

Me: "Ask her if she can bring four straws."

I'm unsure I need to state this at this point, but just in case it's unclear: My husband is truly one of the handsomest men I've ever seen. In fact he's one of the best-looking men any woman has ever seen—in a diner in Marshall or on a movie screen, for that matter.

Blue eyes, salt-and-pepper hair (it was chocolate brown when I met him; I'm unsure who's given him more grays, me and my insane ideas or the kids), high cheekbones, and a chiseled, model-perfect jaw us regular folk would kill for. (I, on the other hand, have a chin so pointy it could function as a hole puncher, but I believe I've mentioned that fact. Guess whose jaw both boys got? You got it. Not Hemingway's.) Sure, George Clooney and Brad Pitt are hunks. But they've got nothing on Hemingway.

And now back to me, my cute guy, and the gutter.

"You're right,"[159] I continue. "The Banana Republic and Panera Bread ideas were ridiculous. But now I've got a much better one."

"Lift your end higher." In case you've forgotten, we're on ladders. I hate ladders.

"I can't. I'm afraid I'm going to fall."

"Stop looking down."

"I feel unbalanced."

He shoots me a look. "Do you really want to give me an opening like that?"

---

159. I always lead with "You're right" when I want my own way. It usually works. Usually.

"I'm not kidding," I whine.

"Neither am I." He's laughing at me. What a cutie. How is it I want to kiss him and kill him at the same time? Ah, the mysteries of marriage. "I want to make it a Jazzercise center."

"Make what a Jazzercise center?"

"The Butler building."

"You're definitely unbalanced."

"I'm serious. My friends and I would have a blast! We'd dance to all my favorite disco tunes, like 'Night Fever' and 'Staying Alive.' You know how much I love Barry Gibb and the Bee Gees, right, hon? Right?"

"Uh huh."

"And 'It's Raining Men,'" I continue, warming to my mission and sorta, kinda forgetting I could plunge to my death at any moment. "Such a cool song. But of course if it *were* raining men it would just be one more thing you guys would leave for me to clean up, right?" I pause, smirking, and wait to see if he'll take the bait. He doesn't.

He simply shoots me the McLook.

Undaunted, I plow forward. "I mean, how much could it cost to convert it into a Jazzercise studio? A little heat, air-conditioning for the summertime, new flooring, mirrors, a stage, sound system. The hens will have to find someplace else to hang out, but really, it can't be that much. Can it?"

He stops hammering and surveys the gutter. "OK." He looks back and forth along the length of it. "OK, then. Good."

For some reason I think he's talking to me. "So I can do it?" I yell at the top of his head, because suddenly he's climbing down the ladder, leaving me alone up in the stratosphere. I hate being alone up in the stratosphere.

He stops mid-descent and looks up at me. "You want to turn the Butler building into a Jazzercise center?"

I nod.

"And I suppose we'll put the tractor and the boys' ATVs in our bedroom?" he replies, looking at me with those blue eyes that still, after all these years, make me weak in the knees (which is not a good condition for *anybody* on a ladder), and then says, "I don't think so, Sue."

He's on the ground now, walking away. I skip the remainder of the rungs, leap down, and dash after him. "That stuff can go in the barn, can't it?" No reply. He's either ignoring me or he's gone conveniently deaf, so I resort to a trick I picked up from an old Kibbles & Bits commercial:[160] I sort of hop up and down next to him while we're walking. It's my way of making sure the sound of my voice actually reaches his ears. Or at least the ear of the side I'm on. "I'd get certified to teach, too," I say, jumping up and aiming for his right ear. "Then I won't need to hire an instructor. That's smart, right?" Hop. "I mean, remember how"—hop—"I used to love teaching kickboxing? And don't forget"—hop—"I got my personal trainer certification[161] too. I know I never did anything with it"—hop—"but this would be different. *This* I'd actually use."

---

160. You know, the one where the little dog keeps hopping back and forth over the big dog, trying to get its attention. At five-five, I'm the little dog; at his afore-alluded-to six feet, Hemingway's the big dog.

161. I don't think I've mentioned that. I am, or I was, a certified personal trainer. It was one of the ways I passed the workday at *Family Circle.* I got certified to beat other people's butts into shape. I never actually pursued it, and eventually I let the whole thing lapse. It just didn't seem smart to give up a six-figure salary to earn sixty bucks a session.

He stops, puts his hands on my shoulders (stopping my further impersonating a pogo stick), and looks at me. "You're nuts, you know that? It would cost fifteen or twenty grand to refurbish the Butler building. It's a shed, Suz. It's meant for farm equipment, not fitness."

Notice he didn't actually say no.

And that means just one thing. If I take it slow and play my cards right, the Butler building will be a Jazzercise center in no time. The fact is it's already my personal roller rink. From there, it's just a few short steps (and some well-placed strobe lights, a fog machine, and my iPod in a speaker dock) to disco.

And once I teach the hens to Hustle, I'm home free.

Jazzercise, anyone?

A note from the blonde in the boonies:
"But more, much more than this,
I did farm life my way. . . ."

I'm a Jersey Girl; you had to know I was going to invoke Sinatra at some point. To be frank, or at least to paraphrase him, I think I'm finally getting this farm stuff under my Dolce & Gabbana belt and doing it my way.

Not that my way always makes Hemingway happy. I'm pretty sure he thought that once the girl left the city, the city would leave the girl, but I'm simply incapable of making that kind of metamorphosis. In fact the reverse is true; I'm doing my best to Park Avenue this place up. You might say I'm on a mission to cosmopolitanize the country. Or at least my little corner of it.

I call it farming, counterfeit farm girl style, and am seriously considering patenting a program based on its principles. My mission? To teach other city chicks how to survive and thrive in the sticks. I've provided a brief primer over the next several chapters, so check it out. Together we'll discover ways to escape fowl fashion choices, ferret out a hairstylist who actually subscribes to *In Style*, and most importantly, find other fish out of water to befriend.

As the song sort of says, I'm living a life that's full and traveling each Virginia byway. But more, much more than this, I'm faking this farm stuff my way. . . .

Part Four

FARMING, COUNTERFEIT FARM GIRL STYLE

Chapter Twenty-eight

HAWKING EGGS IN ESCADA

*H*ave I told you about Hemingway's vegetable garden? Whereas I can't grow weeds,[162] my husband's produced enough produce to run a salad bar seven days a week.

One day recently I walked into the kitchen and discovered about twenty pounds of lettuce soaking in the sink, a massive mound of carrots dimpled like the worst case of cellulite the world's ever seen sitting on my counter, several Tupperware containers packed with tomatoes I'm pretty sure Progresso would pass on, and a colander full of lumpy green beans awaiting their turn for a bath. All we needed were some French, Italian, and blue cheese dressings, plastic containers and cutlery, and an Asian woman screaming, "Who nex?" and I would have been positive I was back on Forty-second and Lex at lunchtime.

To be clear, Hemingway's bounty goes way beyond the

---

162. It doesn't matter if I prepare the soil. And fertilize. And follow the nursery's instructions down to the last detail. I can kill all manner of vegetables and fruits faster than moviegoers can flee a Pauly Shore film. I swear, the plants and shrubs mock me when they see me approach. "Here comes black-thumbed Thusie!" they whisper. Yes, they lisp. It makes it even more painful.

aforementioned fresh foods[163] to include corn, which he'll probably harvest soon, so pray for me, and pumpkins, which really shouldn't make their debut until October unless the high-society horsey set we're surrounded by decides to host another pre-Halloween party. And of course eggs.

Truth be told, I am sick of eggs.

Twice a day Casey checks for eggs, and twice a day he leaves the basket full of the light brown orbs, often sticky with the yolk of an egg that broke or that the chickens ate, on the island in the kitchen. This makes me crazy for two reasons. One, because that damn basket is covered in chicken cooties and shouldn't be touching my kitchen table. And two, because he leaves them for me to wash, dry, plop in an egg carton, and cart the carton down to the refrigerator in the basement.

And that's when the fun really begins.

Our basement fridge, like the kitchen fridge, is full. Not of fabulous foods and lip-smacking libations, decadent desserts and connoisseur-class condiments, but of eggs. Dozens and dozens of eggs. It doesn't matter how many I load in the car and deliver to friends, the kids' teachers, our family doctor, his office staff, our dentist, his office staff, the postmaster at our post office, the local librarians, the bank teller at the drive-through window,[164] even the lady who runs the recycling center, there are always more eggs.

---

163. So why he wanted me to have my own garden, I have no idea. But he did. You should have seen me plant the tomatoes, lettuce, cucumbers, and carrots he insisted I start from seeds. My back ached. The wind whipped my hair. And Hemingway stood there smiling and saying, "Look at you! You're getting the gardening bug!" (Just between us, *he's* getting the gardening bug. I put the biggest one I found beneath his pillow.)

164. Bet you didn't know you could fit a dozen eggs in one of those narrow deposit drawers, did you?

It also doesn't matter how many I poach, hard boil or scramble, let the kids color,[165] or use for cutlets, soufflés, brownies, quiches, or cakes. There are always more eggs.

So when I'm standing in our basement, trying to work the twenty-fifth carton of eggs into the fridge and the only spot left is the back corner of the bottom shelf where Hemingway's Budweiser is cooling, you can count on one thing: He'll be pouring himself a warm one.

It has occurred to me that the hundreds of pounds of produce and unceasing production of eggs are an opportunity to make money. Specifically by selling our all-natural, home-grown goods at a farmer's market. But that would mean I'd have to admit to being a farmer, or at least being married to one.

And what's left of my formerly sophisticated marketing director self is just not ready for that.

Of course if I were to market our eggs I'd need to call them something.[166] I'm partial to Nate's All-Naturals as an overall brand name, because when I'm ultimately forced by the organic farming militant I married to expand the line from Nate's All-Natural Eggs to Nate's All-Natural Green Beans, Lettuce, Carrots, Corn, Tomatoes, Broccoli, Cucumbers, Spinach, Zucchini, Asparagus, and Ativan (hey, the least he can do is grow something to soothe my anxiety), it'll make each launch a whole lot easier.

Oh, my God. Can you even believe I just used the word *launch* in relation to a line of produce? Magazines, sure. I've helped introduce at least a dozen of those in my

---

165. Who cares if it's not Easter? We have too many eggs!

166. Notice I said *market* and not *sell*; if I'm even going to contemplate this lowly undertaking, I've got to spin it so I can stand it.

day.[167] But fresh veggies? What does a canned, low-sodium, frozen, chopped chick like me know about promoting newly picked produce?

And if I embark on this endeavor, will the natural-food fashion police force me to trade my Manolo Blahniks for a pair of Birkenstocks?

I won't do it, you know. I'll market Nate's All-Naturals, and I'll pop those Ativan all the way to the bank in my Balenciaga boots. I may be the only vendor at the Farmer's Market hawking crops in couture, but if I play my cards and my arugula right, my tent will be the talk of the Range Rover, Hummer, and Escalade crowd.

In fact I won't have just one tent. I'll have several in order to accommodate all of Nate's All-Natural foodstuffs. Which means I'll need staff. And my staff will need a uniform. I could go with something Eddie Bauer–bland like khakis, polo shirts, and deck shoes (shoot me), or I could go with something along the lines of the Robert Palmer girls: little black cocktail dress, fishnets, and heels. Not the usual look for pushing overpriced eggs and artichokes on the affluent, but can you imagine the news coverage?

———

BORED, FAKE FARM GIRL AND FORMER
MARKETING PRO LAUNCHES ORGANIC
PRODUCE LINE. EMERSON, LAKE &
PALMER LEND SUPPORT WITH
GROCERY STORE TOUR.

———

167. Years ago, I helped launch several new magazines. There were two titles: *Country Living Gardener* and *Country Living Country Cooking*, which I thought were the height of hilarity. I distinctly recall poking fun at the yellow-clogged people profiled in each. Now I think they're getting the last laugh.

That's right. Before long, Nate's All-Naturals will enjoy prime real estate in the produce departments of the nation's swankiest supermarkets. And my little black cocktail dress–clad team will top their ensembles with a sexy wrap to stay warm, of course.

Speaking of warm, I think I'm actually starting to warm to these wacky ideas. Now if I can just persuade my former *Family Circle* cohorts to kiss off publishing for produce and join me in the sticks, I'll have the perfect staff. I realize they've all moved on to big new jobs making nice big bucks, but this is a big opportunity too.

Together we can put an end to the old "bib overalls and pitchfork" perception of all things organic, and usher in a new era of fashionable fresh food, of bounty and beauty, of high yield in high heels. This is important work we embark upon, people!

And if it sucks, we'll open a salad bar.

Who nex?

Red Haute and Green: Suzy's Tips for Looking the Part When Killing Your Plants

Unlike Hemingway, I'm no one to ask for gardening tips, "green" or otherwise. But I take great pride in looking the part and protecting the earth when I set out to unintentionally kill my plants. Here's how you can, too:

1. **Starting in February,** I scour eco-couture-minded magazines, catalogs, and Web sites for the latest earth-friendly fashions. I pick up soy-based track pants and hoodies, and the occasional pair of posh hemp boots that are perfect for early spring when it's still cold and Hemingway's riding me to help plant some Savoy cabbage seeds he's got to get in the ground *now*.

2. **Next, I move on** to organic cotton Capris and T-shirts, shorts, and vegan-approved earth shoe–type slides that look cute whether I'm lunching at a chic café or being forced to harvest corn. In fact one of my favorite green gardening accessories is an organic cotton tote bag I bought awhile back. It's flamingo pink and it looks fabulous with my 90 percent organic cotton floral Capris. (The other 10 percent is some Mother Nature no-no like Lycra or spandex; bad for the earth, but good for my girth.) The tote's got ten pockets and a spacious interior, so it can hold gardening gloves, a wide-brimmed hat, sunblock, bandana, hand fork and trowel, shears, and

clippers. And maybe someday, when its compartments aren't crammed with the contents of an entire Clinique counter, it will.

3. *I'm also a sucker for stylish,* cool-sounding eyewear. I'd been a fan of the Uvex Tomcat because frankly, any goggles that appear to be named for Tom and Katie Cruise are too funny not to buy. But as they're about as good for the environment as Mr. Cruise's soft shoe was for Oprah's sofa, I've switched to sunglasses made of sustainable wood. The bad news is that they're pricey as Prada's. The worse news is that they make me look like The Fly.

Poor eco-couture eyewear selections aside, I'm proud to have fashioned a wardrobe of unrefined fabrics. I'll never be one of those people with an organic knack for gardening, but if you need help in the designer green dressing department, let me know. I'm a natural.

Chapter Twenty-nine

BROKEN BY SPRING BREAK

*B*eing on a five-hundred-acre farm, you'd think I might like to know the answers to such questions as, What the hell is a skid loader? Do you spell *bush hog* as one word or two? And how should I respond to someone who calls about buying the hay elevator and asks what kind of shape it's in? My reply: "It has its ups and downs." No sale; big surprise. But no. Answers to all those questions can wait while I solve a much more crucial query: Who the hell invented spring break?

Really. Whose idea was this brief educational breather? And have they ever had to endure the ten-day severance of scholastic structure with a seven-year-old and a fourteen-year-old? I'll grant you, the first two days are fine. But the next eight are a nightmare of nonstop movie rentals, snack foods, sugar highs, muddy clothes, trips to the mall, music videos, and screaming matches at the PlayStation.

And that's just how I survived my sons' academic abyss.

Of course we did our best to keep our two chicken-chasing, manure-tossing madmen busy during their instructional interlude. They cleaned out the old chicken coop, gathered eggs, pulled weeds, and chopped wood. They straightened the smokehouse, bathed the dogs, watered the tulips, and washed the truck. By Tuesday, both boys figured out that if they simply went outside like we're always asking them to do, their chores dwindled considerably. By Wednesday, Hemingway and I figured out that their foray onto the farm extended only as far as the Butler building, where our two connivers hid crouched over their Game Boys, completely oblivious to the dollops of pigeon poop hurtling onto their heads. Clearly, I'm raising brain surgeons.

On Wednesday night it poured cats, dogs, and deer, and Cuy and I played an aggravating game of Aggravation by candlelight.[168] He was winning, and ultimately won, so I was aggravated. Every time I came close to bringing a man home, he landed on it and I had to start over. I got so incensed, I started noshing and, before I knew it, had consumed almost an entire bag of sour cream and onion potato chips. Sodium count: 2,400 milligrams. In the morning the bags under my eyes were as big as breasts. But it was nice to finally have a pair.

To be fair, I have breasts. But the fact that they're about as voluptuous as the Gerber Baby's really bothers me. In order to combat my despair at having seen deer better endowed than I,[169] I'm constantly on the lookout for all the latest padded, cup-size-boosting bras I can get my mitts on.

---

168. A brief note about rain in rural America: If it looks like rain, the power goes out. If it rains in the next county, the power goes out. And of course if it actually rains on our house, on our farm, on our kids and pullets and pups, the power goes out.

169. Yet another benefit of living in the boonies!

And you know what that means. Even out here in the hinterland—no, especially out here in the hinterland—I've got to have my Victoria's Secret catalog.

I've also got to have electrical power in order to make my phone or online purchases. And since, as I mentioned, we frequently forgo that modern convenience, getting the latest fuel-injected, cleavage-enhancing miracle of mammary maximization from the leading manufacturer of such is not always possible. I guess I could drive the ninety minutes to the closest Victoria's Secret store, but I really hate to do this, particularly since I already spend too much time carting around the two boobs I gave birth to. But I'll get into that shortly.

No, when it's time for a little padded push-up pick-me-up, I do what I did that fateful day: throw both boys in the car and drive thirty minutes to the "local" Old Navy. Not because Old Navy sells bras, mind you, but because I needed a ruse to get the kids to accompany me to the Kohl's next door. And nothing elicits cooperation like the lure of camouflage-print cargo pants, anoraks, T-shirts, backpacks, boxers, and belts.

Ten minutes and two hundred dollars on bogus military attire later, my boys were ready for buzz cuts and boot camp. But not before I found a bra.

I should've made a beeline for Kohl's lingerie department, but I made the mistake of first hitting home furnishings. Like most women, I could spend hours shopping for picture frames and pillows, scented candles and duvet covers, wreathes and wind chimes. But like most kids, my sons have a fifteen-minute department store best behavior maximum before the threat of losing all their video games and several vital organs wears off and they go back to being themselves.

I'd wasted at least that amount of time mooning over some rooster-shaped oven mitts when I heard scuffling, shouting, and the general mayhem of unsupervised young men.

My young men.

To my horror, my sons were engaged in a full-blown SpongeBob Squarepants vs. Washington Redskins pillow fight in the main aisle of the store. To make matters worse, several other children had chosen sides and were cheering them on. I flashed on *Lord of the Flies* just as fluff began to fly out of SpongeBob's yellow head. One of the sales clerks noticed, too, and, although I made a big show of how the boys were going pay for the pillow themselves, in the back of my mind I kept thinking that if I didn't find the perfect bra I could simply tape the cotton cascading out of Sponge-Bob's cranium to my chest and call it cleavage.[170]

So while Casey sulked and moaned about the mortification of waiting for his mom to find a bra, I finally began scouring the lingerie aisles, hunting high and low for my size: 34M, for *marble*. I was so intent on this endeavor that I didn't see what Cuyler was doing. I did, however, hear about it. As in, "Can you believe that boy's behavior?" I knew without even looking that the silver-haired seniors shopping two rows to my right were referring to my little rascal. And I just knew what he was doing, too.

Slowly and sneakily, my puny pervert was walking up

---

170. Talk about making lemonade from lemons. Oh, who am I kidding? My breasts aren't even *that* big.

and down the aisles, "tweaking" the Maidenforms and Balis and beaming like, well, like a little boy in a bra department. He must have felt me watching him, because he stopped, put his hands on his hips, and, glaring at me for daring to derail his meteoric rise to juvenile delinquency, shouted loud enough for all the little old ladies to hear, "*What?* What's the problem? It's not like there's *breasts* in them."

Ultimately I found a hot little number that promised to boost my booty to a 34GB, as in *golf ball*, and would have liked to get the matching panties, despite the fact that they possessed no butt-reducing attributes. But when Cuy donned a bra so big each cup could've contained a football, and came running up to me, shouting, "Hey, Mom, this is better than a ball bag!" it was one incident in intimates too many for the sales clerks at Kohl's. And so, rather than wait for security to escort us, we departed the department store sans skivvies.

If our adventures in underwear land weren't enough to make me wonder why I ever pitched my birth control pills, the next day the kids and I helped Hemingway replace the perch in the movable chicken tractor.[171] I was busy howling away at the piano with no idea this task had commenced when Cuy came running in, screaming, "Dad needs you! Dad needs you!" I took off after the free world's fastest child, losing my sexy and oh-so-farm-inappropriate Chinese Laundry sandals somewhere between the kitchen and the white-trash tire planters that grace my otherwise gorgeous backyard.

---

171. The original perch snapped under our fat fowls' burgeoning heft. For everything you ever wanted to know about chicken tractors—including what they hell they are—see The Impractical Girl's Guide to Farm Speak.

(Have I told you about the tire planters? Ages ago, some creative soul took two huge tractor tires and cemented them into the ground in my backyard. Then he, or she, filled the center of each tire with dirt and planted them with lilies. They're lovely, really. If you like landscaping that can do double duty as a punch line in a Jeff Foxworthy joke. But back to the tale of the chicken tractor.)

Barefoot and frantic because all I could see was the tractor tilted precariously downhill and Casey holding on to the hitch for dear life, I raced up, shouting, "Where's Dad?" to which he replied in that churlish, teen-trademarked tone, "It's about time you showed up."

Drawing a deep breath and, miraculously, refraining from decking the little doo-doo head, I paused and then flipped a heaping helping of the cow manure and chicken scratch concoction squishing between my toes at my insufferable firstborn. It wasn't pretty, but it had to be done. And then I began looking for Hemingway.

After a quick peek under the wheeled mini mausoleum, I discovered the poor guy stuck in a squat inside. In searing pain and unable to escape the accelerating pullet palace, he'd flown into High Thesaurus Mode, shouting to Casey to "Grab the thing! Grab the thing!" And our big guy complied, responding to such specific instructions by first grabbing a hammer, then a cordless drill, and finally a post to the electric fence, which fortunately was off at the time but which managed to shock Hemingway into saying, "The hitch! Grab the hitch!"

And that, of course, is how I found them. I quickly freed the Bob Vila of Bird Land and relieved Mr. Happy of hitch-holding duty. Together we replaced the perch, and I went back to the piano, but only after carefully—wearing a bright yellow pair of plastic gloves and using a heavy-duty scrub brush soaked in bleach—digging out the live-stock detritus packed between my piggies.

For me, though, the highlight of the week was the hike I took with Cuyler. He wanted to hunt for treasure in the woods, and I didn't want him anywhere near the forest primeval without a parent, so I dug out some relatively appropriate footwear and went with him.

I imagine we were a pretty funny sight, Cuy in his tiny Timberlands and me in my midcalf Naughty Monkey cable-knit wedge-bottom boots, clomping past the cattle, both of us wearing binoculars around our necks and carry-ing walking sticks we found by the barn. Cuy also had his military-style backpack, which he'd filled with a magnify-ing glass, a book on insects, two bottles of Poland Spring water, and several Oreo Mini snack packs in case we got peckish. I love a second-grader who can pack a picnic.

We spent about two hours following old horse trails, playing on a decomposing wooden wagon we found hid-den beneath an overgrowth of bushes, and poking at aban-doned snake skins with our walking sticks. Cuy stuffed a couple in the Ziploc bag he brought along and was pretty happy with his loot, when suddenly he made the discovery of the day: a buck skull, antlers and all.

"Mom, look," he hollered. "It's Stevie the Skull!"

The damn thing had a name before I even knew what hit me. And then I thought Hemingway was going to hit us when he saw us carry it into the house. I believe his exact words were, "Do you know what kind of germs are on that thing?" Anyway, he made us (me) boil it in water and bleach on my brand new Jenn-Air range (trust me; I'm not using *that* pot again), and I felt like Glenn Close in *Fatal*

Attraction. What a stink. Makes me wonder if that bunny smelled as bad as our buck.

Now that the kids are back in school and my bout of Post-Traumatic Spring Break Disorder (complete with freaking my family out by jokingly suggesting we enjoy a bowl of the Stevie the Skull soup I whipped up[172]) has begun to abate, I'm starting to look forward to spending the summer with my two crotchety kids. Of course it won't be the whole summer. What with basketball, lacrosse, football, baseball, paintball, and shooting[173] camp on their calendars, we'll get about a day together at the end of August. Just enough time to hit Old Navy again; drop a bundle on stuff they'll outgrow, shred, and lose in as little as a week; and then stick their butts on the school bus. Ah yes. Nothing quite warms my heart like family time. All five minutes of it.

Which is about how long spring break should be. Unless it involves a trip to Miami Beach. Then I'll just see the boys when I get back.

---

172. If you think the eating's gotten a little funny around here, you ought to join us for the drinkin'. To quench his thirst while tackling his farm tasks, Casey scoops water from the fresh, flowing streams on the property. This is fine, until he tires of drinking alone and decides to join the cows for a cold one in a stream they're using. Not a good idea, particularly since cows shit where they eat (and drink), and city slickers gone cuckoo for country can catch E. coli. Case of course didn't know this, and was just bringing the water to his lips when Hemingway stopped him. (Perhaps you heard his scream?) Whew. It's really too soon to be on a first-name basis with Fauquier Hospital.

173. Yes, the nice folks at 4-H are going to teach my eldest to use a rifle and shotgun. This should improve his social standing and allow him to attend his buddies' birthday parties without embarrassing himself. See, the invitations to several have said things like, *Join us in bagging a buck for Billy's birthday! Wear your camo and bring your ammo!* But my kid can't bag anything but groceries. I don't want to turn him into a sharpshooter, but if he wants to attend one of these parties where "There'll be lots of pizza and cake, but no gift bags. The kids can just keep what they kill!" it's time for some target practice.

Chapter Thirty

ME AND BOBBY D.

$\mathcal{I}$ hope they have chocolate in hell. Why? Because that's where I'm headed. It's not my fault of course, and I blame *Esquire* magazine for the whole mess.

You see, several Fridays ago, which just happened to be Good Friday, I did what I do every Friday and raced into my favorite hair salon[174] to get my hair blown out. (Yes, I get my hair done once a week, just like your grandma did. As I've previously explained, I absolutely, positively cannot wield a round brush and a blow dryer without ultimately bearing a striking resemblance to a thatched hut, a blond Ronald McDonald, or a square bale. And yes, the twenty-five big ones it costs me is nothing in comparison to the therapy bills I'd rack up without my weekly appointment with Ashley.)

I mention that it was Good Friday because, out of deference to that high holy day, I typically try to think only pure, irreproachable thoughts about things like pastels,

---

174. Salon Emage in Warrenton; ask for Ashley. When I go home, I hit my other favorite salon, Panico in Ridgewood. Ask for Christine. Tell them both that Susan sent you.

white rabbits, and Easter eggs.[175] This isn't easy, since I like to daydream about finding Johnny Depp at my front door (Oooh, look what the bunny brought!), but I try.

Anyway, I sprint into the salon from my Jazzersize class[176] and collapse onto the sofa. I'm sweaty, spent, and in no mood for the extra work demanded by the women's magazines cluttering the coffee table before me. *Better Homes & Gardens* wants to help make my meat and potatoes "pop!" (Fine. They can start by cooking them for me.) *Vogue* has "630+ pages of fabulous fashions!" (Which I'd look at if I had the strength to lift it.) And Oprah believes "the time is now!" for me to live my best life. (Hmm . . . how does she know I'm not? Has she been following me? Maybe there's some truth to the theory that Ms. Winfrey is really Big Brother.) The thought of digesting all this drivel exhausts me. And then I see it. Or to be specific, him. Robert Downey Jr. on the cover of *Esquire* magazine.

Have you any idea how much I love Robert Downey Jr.?

Like lots of women, I have a secret place in my heart for a hot bad boy. Sure, my brain says the clean-cut Brooks Brother in the shiny Beemer is the way to go. But my weak knees and racing pulse want the scruffy, ripped hunk on the hog. The one who looks like he's been around the block a time or two. Or three.

---

175. Would somebody please tell me the trick to dyeing organic eggs? The boys and I tried for an hour to color our homegrown pale brown orbs with a Cray-Pas kit before giving up and breaking out the big guns. Sure, Hemingway's Panther Air Rifle and blue paintball pellets were probably a bit of overkill, but the four pretty eggs we netted are nice.

176. Hemingway, the hens, and the pigeons have yet to depart the Butler building, but don't worry; I'm turning it into a disco/Jazzercise center. . . . Soon.

I'm not going to explore the psychological underpinnings of this covert preference. First of all I'm not that bright, and second of all it's not that complex. If given a choice between Josh Hartnett (cute as he is) and Leonardo DiCaprio, I firmly believe most women would leave with Leo.

I, on the other hand, would depart with Mr. Downey.

To me, he's the baddest of the bunch. Handsome, hot, and always in a whole lot of trouble, he was the man who made *Ally McBeal* worth watching. And I did. Up until he was busted for something, hauled off to the clink, and all David E. Kelley could think of was to replace him with a note pinned to a snowman.[177]

I flip frantically to the article, bad girl thoughts kicking those snowy white bunnies in the butt, and there he is. Badder and more beautiful than ever. I'm not three words into the story when I'm told to go back to have my hair washed. How lovely; an opportunity to recline with Roberto.

Clutching *my Esquire* (because there's no way I'm leaving without it), I flop back in the sink and say, "Jamie, who's your favorite bad boy?" "Tommy Lee," she replies. Instantly. Without hesitation. Like she knew I was going to ask. I love that the world's best shampoo girl has bad boys on the brain.

In seconds we're carrying on like a couple of high school sophomores. "He's so hot." "That hair." "Those eyes." "His shoulders." "Nice butt!" We're giggling and making so much noise the other patrons and stylists want

---

177. On behalf of the millions of women who put up with Ally's absurdly short suit skirts each week for a few minutes with Bad Boy Bobby, all I can say is, gee, thanks, Dave.

to know what we're talking about. "Bad boys," I announce, popping up out of the sink and spraying shampoo and warm water everywhere. "Who's your favorite bad boy?"

Mark Wahlberg. Viggo Mortensen. Taylor Kitsch. Leonardo DiCaprio. Jamie Foxx. Charlie Sheen. Adrian Grenier. Taye Diggs. Patrick Dempsey. James Franco. Aaron Eckhart. Clive Owen. Denzel Washington. The names are flying fast and furious. I rip out my notepad and start scribbling. And then it dawns on me: I've written Colin Farrell's name at least fifteen times.

"Ladies! Ladies!" I yell over the near riot that's erupted. "Colin Farrell? He looks like he needs a bath."

"And don't you wish you could run the water for him?" cracks my pal Ashley.[178]

It couldn't have been more fun if there were margaritas involved. I doubt they'll have those in hell, but I'm holding out hope for something sweet. You know, like a Hershey bar. And a spot next to my boy Bobby.

---

178. Obviously, all those concerns I had about being "too Suzy for the sticks" were unfounded. I've been blessed with a whole slew of new Southern girlfriends who love me for the lunatic I am. And they don't even mind that I sound like Carmela Soprano!

Chapter Thirty-one

STYLE SMACKDOWN

It doesn't happen often, but sometimes I find the farm incredibly boring. I mean, how many bulls can you watch mate with cows before you start to go cuckoo? When it happens, I do my best to entertain myself. I go through my collection of *Family Circle* cookbooks and come up with new ways to make poultry,[179] and I ponder—and occasionally attempt to implement—unique uses for the ticks I pull off Grundy and Pete.[180] But sometimes nothing works. Nothing distracts me or stimulates me. And I find myself lost in flights of fancy.

Like the other day. I suddenly started thinking about launching a new game show.[181] I call it Style Smackdown. It came to me when, for the one million and twelfth time, I opened my closet, sweater chest, and T-shirt drawer, and it hit me: I have absolutely nothing to wear. Sure, I have a few decrepit pairs of cords, some decomposing black suit

---

179. Though leaving the feathers on didn't go over big with the family.

180. My plan for having them suck the pimentos out of green olives went really awry.

181. This from a woman who hardly watches TV. Unless of course it's *The Sopranos*.

pants, and a pair of bib overalls Hemingway brought home one day when he'd obviously missed whatever medication he typically takes to prevent such spending sprees at Tractor Supply, but other than that I've got nothing. Nothing stylish. Nothing "now." Nothing I can't wait to wear.

In an effort to smack back and fill my drawers and closet with cool stuff I'd actually look forward to putting on, I ran to my "local"[182] Borders, staked out a spot in the magazine section, and grabbed a fistful of fashion bibles. Ten minutes into *Harper's Bazaar, Vogue, In Style, Glamour, Marie Claire,* and *Cosmo,* it dawned on me that I didn't have a prayer of finding something "now." But if I want something "then," that could be arranged.

Before I get to where I'm going, and I promise I am going somewhere with this, I'd like to take a quick poll. How many of you are reading this while wearing a pair of skinny jeans? Come on, be honest. And if you've succumbed to the attraction of these sausage-skin sheaths, I simply must know, oh, fashion-savvy sisters, what do you wear on your feet? Nice, safe flats or sexy stilettos? Slouchy boots or a pair of over-the-knee leather bad boys that should come with a whip for a really wild date night?

And please don't tell me you've got them tucked into a pair of Timberlands.

I may be going out on a limb here, but I'm betting that, like me, most of you don't clad your limbs in skinny jeans. Sure, you have friends who do, and some of them look darn good. But I'm equally certain you have others in your

---

182. If I do sixty-five where it's fifty-five, I can get there in twenty-five. Minutes, that is. And to me that makes it local. Hmm. I may be getting the hang of living in the hinterland after all.

social circle that look less like Kate Hudson and more like upholstered pears in their Rock and Republics. But not you. You're not slipping into a pair of those suckers. Why? Because you're not blind. And because years ago you made that most important of fashion purchases: a mirror.

I credit my mirror, my eyesight, and my common sense for keeping me away from the '80s-inspired styles making a comeback. It's tough, though.

Page after page of magazines like *Vogue*, where you'd expect to see such silliness, to more traditional, middle-of-the-road reads like *Redbook*, where you'd expect to be spared it, are showing fringed boots, one-shoulder shirts, blousy bubble-hemmed miniskirts layered over leggings for a look that may have come from the catwalk but belongs on the court jester.

Of course that's just my opinion, but it's one based on firsthand experience, in-depth research, and painfully personal trial-and-error product testing. After all, I went to college in the '80s and, unfortunately, I've got the pictures[183] to prove it.

In one I'm suffocating beneath a cowl-neck sweater with so many folds it could double as a BabyBjörn. In another I'm wearing a pair of lavender corduroy gauchos with purple suede cowboy boots and a shimmery (and very sheer) pale violet poet's blouse. I recall buying the entire ensemble at Henri Bendel, which proves you can drop a bundle and still look like Barney.

In a third photo, I'm posing in a white faux-fur jacket

---

183. Like my kids' fast food toy collection, this is another box I can't believe I paid to move. Every book Hemingway and I read on relocating said, "Pare down, pare down, pare down." Did we? My under-bed storage box of Kodak moments from my Duran Duran days says, "I don't think so."

worn atop a long-sleeve, skintight, silver turtleneck mini-dress, with matching sparkly leggings and Valley Girl boots. I look ready to run from a John Hughes film casting call to a date with one of the guys from Devo.

Skinny jeans? Sure, I wore them. From the front they were fine. From the back I appeared to have a sizeable hematoma distending from the base of my spine. Leggings and leg warmers? I had dozens of them in a variety of stripes and solid colors that I paired with cut-up sweatshirts. After all, who didn't want to look just like Jennifer Beals? I even recall making the leap from *Flashdance*-inspired fashions to cat suits and ankle boots, all the while wondering if, when I graduated, I could wear the stuff to work. (The answer: yes, if the job involved prowling the stairwells of the New York Port Authority during nonpeak hours.) What a feeling indeed.

As for the dolman-sleeve tops the stores and catalogs are carrying again, I confess, I owned several. My favorite was a black-and-white-striped number that gave me a wingspan a wandering albatross would envy. They're not something I'm buying now, though. These days if I want my triceps to flap in the breeze, I'll simply strip down to my bra.

Maybe it's just me, but I really think that if designers are going to pursue the "fashion backward" business, they should be required to add at least one modern enhancement to the clothing they pull out of the past.

For example, if Stella McCartney or Michael Kors insists on reintroducing the aforementioned skintight turtleneck mini at the Paris collections, New York Fashion Week, or wherever, the new version has to come with a nuclear-power thigh slimmer and a two-pack of Gas-X attached to the tag (because if you bloat while wearing that baby, it's over).

You see what I'm getting at here? If stuff's going to come back, it's got to come back better.

Don't give us run-of-the-mill leggings. Give us *miracle* leggings. The kind you slip on, and in seconds have gams that should be insured by Lloyd's of London. You want us to wear skinny jeans? Make them with magic fabric that prevents the Pear in a Sausage Skin syndrome so many of us regular gals suffer from. Or somebody's going to be sorry.

Of course there are certain looks that should never make a comeback. I'm talking about things like pants with waists so high you can rest your boobs on your belt, and tartan plaid ponchos with coordinating kilts. I imagine such Emerald Isle style is appropriate if you're applying to be Grand Marshall of the St. Paddy's Day parade, but other than that, why cough over twenty-two hundred bucks to dress like a bagpipe player?

Frankly I can't believe I just spent forty dollars on fashion magazines and am still completely clueless as to what I should be wearing. The upside is that I know what I never want to be caught dead in (besides the bib overalls Hemingway won't let me take back).

Leopard-print bustiers and cuffed wool shorts come to mind, as do cropped sailor pants, flowy dresses that make even the most Mary-Kate and Ashley Olsen–esque among us appear pregnant, and rabbit fur jackets with raccoon trim.[184]

---

184. I wore one of those patchwork rabbit fur horrors in junior high, and to this day I've got guilt over it. And the thought of all those dead bunnies makes me feel bad, too.

Maybe my decomposing pants aren't so awful. They're not fashionable, but they fit. And that prevents me from walking around naked, which I will be if my only other choice is a huge sweater cinched with a belt the width of a Great White, opaque leggings, and leg warmers paired with pumps. What's next? A Farrah Fawcett 'do à la Carmen Electra on the cover of *Cosmo*? Now, there's a look that'll send sales of Aqua Net soaring. Again.

It's sad to say, but the creator of Style Smackdown has yet to win a round. That could all change if bouclé comes back big, but that's pretty far off on the fashion horizon.

What's closer are clam diggers and fringed jean jackets, denim skirts edged with cotton eyelet, and a whole lot of *Desperately Seeking Susan*–inspired clothing and accessories.

While I find it tough to believe a new generation of boy toys will be wearing fingerless fishnet gloves, I admit I'm considering purchasing a pair. No, I'm not suffering estrogen-depletion dementia, just looking for a stylish way to hide my hands. Thanks to a sudden influx of age spots (that I'm certain I've developed from handling those damn hens), I've now got my own animal-print accessories at the ends of my arms. Which, come to think of it, could actually complement that leopard-print bustier.

Do you think I could wear it with cords?

Chapter Thirty-two

MUSTANG SUZY

$\mathcal{I}$ have a confession to make: I'm no Sir Isaac Newton. If you want proof, just ask the poor kids in Cuyler's second-grade class, whom I attempt to help with science every Wednesday at one o'clock.[185] Of course, I may actually be getting better at the subject, as I'm pretty certain I've come up with a whole new spin on the gravity stuff.

Just to be clear, it's a marketing spin (which means you can take the girl out of marketing, but you can't take marketing out of the girl), and I really believe it'll help single chicks stick out in the sticks.

My experiment was thoroughly inadvert, but last Saturday afternoon I proved that if you combine one blonde (me) and one laser-red Mustang convertible[186] (Hemingway's) that won't start, you can make men fall from the sky.

---

185. Being able to help out in my kids' schools has long been a dream of mine. Now that we live on a farm and I have free time, I'm realizing I'm really too stupid to be of any assistance.

186. The key here is the convertible. Ditch the Dodge Ram. Trade in your Toyota Tundra. And forget that titanic Chevy Tahoe. Think small. Sexy. "Topless." Trust me; it's an attention getter.

To be honest, they didn't exactly come crashing down from the clouds. But they certainly materialized out of the ether as if they could hear the non *vroom* of my V8 engine. Really. I don't know how to explain it. I wasn't crying or kicking the tires or cursing like Tony Soprano. I wasn't doing a little damsel in distress dance or banging my head against the steering wheel. I was just sitting in the car, trying to turn the key. Sure, I whispered the occasional "Uh-oh. I broke Hemingway's sweet 'Stang," under my breath, but frankly that was all.

And yet they knew.

One after the other, they began zooming into the never bustling (unless you're a blonde in a comatose convertible) Marshall Shopping Center (where the draw is a huge Tractor Supply, and the supporting players include a dry cleaner's and an Alcoholic Beverage Commission store), and parking next to my dead drop-top. It was as if they were picking up signals via ESP or satellite or even Santa Claus.[187]

There were men in pickup trucks, vans, and sport utility vehicles. Men on motorcycles and crutches (though not the same men, mind you). Men in sports cars and, yes, convertibles that were actually functioning on that fine day. And they weren't just coming off the street. They were streaming out of the stores.

Men in John Deere baseball caps with broken arms corralling kids munching Subway sandwiches. Men leading large dogs out of Best Friends Animal Clinic ("Here,

---

187. Why not? If he sees you when you're sleeping and he knows when you're awake, then he probably knows when your car is acting up, so don't curse at it, for goodness' sake. Or really, you're never going to get that Gucci bag you've been after.

hold my massive Mastiff, Cody, while I try to start your car"), and others carrying coffee from Freestate Coffee Company.

There were men toting takeout from China Wall, and others lugging large Luzianne iced teas from Foster's Grille. One man ran over from Radio Shack ("Here, watch my remote-control Ford Ranger while I try your car"), and another cruised my way from the Mac store next door.[188]

There were men bearing piping-hot pizzas from Anthony's ("Are you hungry? How long have you been sitting here?" Not hungry. Not long. Thanks), and men carrying DVDs, videos, snack foods, and game rentals from Movie Gallery. ("Have you seen *Half Nelson*?" Yes, trust me; it's not worth the whole two hours.)

At one point there were about eight guys standing over me, Red Man moist snuff stuffed in their cheeks, giving me directions. "Lift the steering wheel. Lower the steering wheel. Now try the key." Nothing. "Put it in gear. Put it in neutral. Now try the key." Nothing. "Turn on the lights. Tap the brake. Now try the key." Nothing.

When none of these tips did the trick, they began taking turns getting into the car and attempting to start it themselves. They forced the steering wheel right and then left. They jiggled the clutch. They popped the hood and poked around. They climbed back in and stared at the dashboard, the ignition, and the key. And then they leaned back, pondered my predicament, and rendered their opinions in a language I simply don't speak. "Maybe the en-

---

188. Please don't tell Hemingway. He's a PC guy with a massive distrust of all things Apple.

gine's seized." (The engine seized? Seized what? What could an engine possibly take?) "I think the starter's shot." (Starter? Isn't that a line of athletic apparel?)

As the number of white knights who rode to my rescue swelled into the double digits, I toyed with the idea of jogging over to the supermarket to buy beer. After all, it was hot, they were trying to help, and the whole endeavor had taken on the air of an impromptu car-care party not unlike those I used to host when I was the marketing director for *Popular Mechanics*.[189]

Anyway, while they made manly conversation about my cute coupe, it dawned on me that, if I were single, this would be the perfect way to meet men. Forget blind dates, bars, clubs, Match.com, and all that crap. Simply buy, borrow, or steal a convertible, cause it near-irreparable damage, then sit in it and wait.

Like I said, this old marketing chick's no Newton. But I think I've finally found an experiment I can do with Cuyler's class. In fact, we'll make a field trip out of it. The heck with hitting another cavern or corn maze, tractor pull or pig race, poultry show or 4-H petting zoo. We'll simply head straight to a mall, disable the Mustang, and test my theory on Guys and the Gravitational Pull of Ragtops That Won't Run. If it works, great. If not, we'll all take the school bus back. I've got a case of Coors we can split.

---

189. Yes, I directed marketing for that magazine for two years. No, I never actually read a page of it. Obviously.

Chapter Thirty-three

HOW YA GONNA KEEP HER DOWN ON THE FARM ONCE SHE LEARNS TO DRIVE TO D.C.?

*F*or some reason the theme from *Love Story* has been playing in my head since I awakened early this morning. Normally this would annoy me, but when I went to get a spoon to stir my coffee, new words to the first verse sprang to mind. My revised and ready-for-the-recording-studio version goes like this:

> *Where do I begin?*
> *To tell the story of the field mouse that's moved in.*
> *He's taken residence in my utensil drawer.*
> *I know because he's left me mouse droppings galore.*
> *And he must go.*

In all seriousness, there's nothing quite as stomach turning as discovering tiny turds sprinkled among the silverware. Cuyler splattered in chicken crap comes close, but even that doesn't pack the wallop of wondering whether any of us have unwittingly ingested the "gifts" our uninvited houseguest has given us.

Speaking of houseguests—the welcome kind—my

dear friend Trish paid us a visit this week. I haven't seen her in a year, so when she called to say she'd be in Washington for a meeting, I knew immediately it was time to make my virgin visit to MapQuest. I pulled down directions, gassed up the 'Stang, and left Hemingway pacing the porch, muttering, "How am I going to keep her down on the farm once she learns to drive to D.C.?"

He needn't worry.

Washington is nice, but it's just not New York. Sure, there's ample opportunity to plow down pedestrians who disregard the DON'T WALK signs, and a Starbucks[190] beckons on almost every block, but there's no obvious shopping. And I know because I conducted cutting-edge consumer research. With my eyes.

As I sat illegally parked and praying a police officer wouldn't boot me from my spot and send me back into the land of NO LEFT TURN and unlimited opportunities to get lost and miss retrieving my pal, I looked around. The office buildings and crowded sidewalks gave the District a somewhat New York feel, and the well-worn, fluorescent-lit dry cleaners and delis, color copy centers and shoe repair shops, banks and burger joints, nail salons, pawn shops, and tattoo parlors added to the almost Big Apple–like ambience. But the lack of a single clothing store was where D.C. and NYC really parted company.

I learned later that in D.C. the stores are in malls. But who has time to run to a mall? I need a Talbots on the corner. A Banana Republic just steps away from my subway stop. An Ann Taylor, or at least an Ann Taylor Loft, tucked

---

190. Be still, my latte-loving heart.

inside the lobby of my office building. The lack of easy-access retail makes me wonder how working girls handle such fashion crises as salad dressing–stained blouses or chocolate-smudged skirts.[191]

Clothing calamities aside, without as much as a J.Crew or Kenneth Cole within walking distance, what do D.C.'s professional women really do for lunch every day? And please don't tell me they eat.

During the long ride from the city back to the sticks, Trish and I had plenty of time to discuss the topics nearest and dearest to our hearts: kids (she has two; I have two), husbands (can't live with 'em, can't kill 'em), parents (there's no keeping up with them; they're worse than the kids), work (we're against it, particularly housework), friends (thank God for them), former co-workers (without them we'd be completely lost and out of the loop), the latest issue of *O, The Oprah Magazine* (and how something as simple as refusing to do laundry five days a week can go a long way toward helping you "live your best life"), the power of the Pottery Barn catalog to make us want to set fire to our homes, sea salt pedicures, facials, favorite steak houses, and most important, recent footwear purchases.

Now, one of the things I admire most about Trish is the restraint she displays in the shoe department. Unlike my immediate declarations of love for every Jimmy, Salvatore, and Manolo I meet, Trish plays the footwear field, coolly refusing to commit to so much as a flip-flop before survey-

---

191. Not to mention the sudden, sickening realization that the suit and pumps that exuded power and confidence in your bedroom mirror at six a.m., as little as four hours later actually make you look like a cross between an escort and one of Santa's elves in the conference room.

ing the store's entire selection. While I'm busy whispering, "We could be so bad together" to a pair of four-inch stilettos in strip-club scarlet, my much more practical pal is mentally flipping through her suit collection to determine which pumps, loafers, slides, slingbacks, sandals, or mules would make the perfect match.

And if she doesn't make a match, she does NOT make a purchase. I swear it's true. I've seen her not do it.[192]

As it turns out, Trish's latest buy was the boots she bought to tour our farm. And I never thought I'd hear the end of it.

"Look at this!" howled Hemingway. "She doesn't even live on a farm and yet she has the good sense to bring the proper pair of shoes! Susan, these are boots. Boots, this is Susan. Maybe someday you'll both meet again in a place called Tractor Supply." Sure, hon. And maybe someday you'll be able to get a tailgate protector for the pickup truck and a multipack of pig ears for the dogs at Neiman Marcus. But until that time, nothing doing.

In the end, we tooled around the farm in the aforementioned pickup, and our tootsies never even touched the ground. So what did it really matter if any of us were wearing boots or bedroom slippers? Despite my pointing out the property's problems[193] my dear friend found it breathtakingly beautiful. She even promised to come back this summer and bring her family. If I know Trish they'll all have boots, so I have about six months to get some.

---

192. And she's seen me buy the stilettos that to this day remain in their box, begging for a night on the town or even an afternoon of aerating the garden.

193. Lack of a Starbucks, hair salon, and shoe store to name three.

Finally it was time to cruise back into the capital and find Union Station. I was following MapQuest's exhortation to "Make a SLIGHT RIGHT,"[194] when I realized that doing so would result in the car being surrounded by a SWAT team guarding a slightly ominous government building. Now, I love a man in uniform as much as the next girl, and I don't think we looked suspicious, although if we'd been in New York without so much as a big brown bag from Bloomies between us we'd have been photographed and fingerprinted faster than Paris Hilton can run in her Prada pumps, but I didn't want to take any chances. I veered out of the turn, stayed straight, and drove us directly into the land of bodegas and abandoned vans.

Eventually I found Union Station. Trish made her train, and I made my way home, Keith Urban, Dixie Chicks, and Martina McBride taking turns blaring on my CD player. You'd think with all the country music that's become the soundtrack to my life lately, the field-mouse ditty that keeps playing in my head would have a whole Hank Williams thing happening. So maybe I'll rework it to the tune of "Hey Good Lookin'" and sing:

> *Hey, little field mouse,*
> *Why you in my house?*
> *How 'bout takin' your turds and leavin' town?*

Or maybe I'll just go buy a mousetrap.

---

194. What in hell is a "slight right"?

Chapter Thirty-four

45 IS THE NEW 35

*H*aving worked in magazines, I know better than to buy the bunk they splash across their covers. Lines like STROLL AWAY TWO SIZES! and NO-SWEAT SUMMER SLIM-DOWN! are designed to make you part with your money, but they'll never help you part with those extra pounds. For starters, strolling doesn't burn fat. Speed walking and running from incensed flank steaks do. And if you're speed walking[195] you're sweating, so there goes headline number two, no?

You understand what I'm talking about. Lines like BATHING SUITS FOR EVERY BODY mean they're showing Hefty sacks that cinch at the waist, or worse, real women in real bathing suits they really shouldn't be seen in. Admit it; you'd rather be subjected to those annoying Victoria's Secret Angels bursting out of bikinis than some Nancy from Next Door packed into one to prove "it can be done!" despite having six kids.

I know I would.

I also know that after more than twenty years in

---

195. Or running—let's not forget the running!

magazine marketing I should be smarter than to be sucked in by the words framing Oprah's smiling face. Specifically the words 45 IS THE NEW 35! God help us all. Particularly those of us who are forty-five.

Do they have any idea of the maintenance mania that headline has unleashed? From cow country to the West Coast, women in their midforties are kissing their families good night and disappearing into their bathrooms for up to two hours of cleansing, moisturizing, exfoliating, toning, applying, removing, smoothing, patting,[196] and praying. Oh yes, they're praying. They're praying the hundreds of dollars in skin-care, preservation, and rejuvenation products they're using actually work. And that their husbands don't complain, when they finally come to bed, that it's like sleeping with a baby seal.

Of course Hemingway doesn't complain. He likes that I look like a kid. He thinks it gives him permission to keep acting like one.

But I digress.

In addition to the wrinkle-defying feats taking place in powder rooms from the Atlantic to the Pacific, the hinterlands to high-rises, there's teeth whitening, callus buffing, and pedicure repairing. There's cuticle pushing, elbow sloughing, and a whole lot of loofah-ing. There's hair removal, cellulite fighting, and moisturizing bronzer applications that miraculously make pockmarked thunder thighs look lots thinner.[197]

---

196. Gently, please.

197. I don't know how this works, and I don't want to know. I just want the folks at L'Oréal to know that should they ever stop making Sublime Glow there'll be nothing sublime about the response from me and my millions of cottage cheese–addled pals. Why? Because we're worth it.

Of course the worst part isn't the beauty routine that routinely takes all night. It's deciding what to buy. The $100 "teenage skin in a tube!" miracle serum that promises to make me irresistible to acne-flecked high school freshmen (thanks, but I think I'll pass), or the similarly overpriced line filler that claims to turn back the clock with one swish of what looks to be a putty knife slathered in Burger King's special sauce. (Fast food on my face? On second thought, I'll take one of those teens.)

Frankly it's all so exhausting. And that may be the skin-care industry's ultimate evil plan. If they can deny us our beauty sleep in the name of looking young, lovely, and rested, we'll become increasingly dependent on their magic microspheres, elastomers, and GABA, their bio-maple compounds, peptides, and antiglycation serums. We'll keep spending exorbitant sums on these snake oils. We'll stay up into the wee hours applying them[198] and in the end, despite devoting half our lives to de-puffing and plumping, resurfacing and restoring, freezing and hydrating, lifting, smoothing, and de-sagging, we're going to look nothing but beat. Why?

Because we're never going to get to bed.

Thanks to the 45 IS THE NEW 35 headline, I expect to soon see one that says MISSING: 45-YEAR-OLD WIFE AND MOTHER. LAST SEEN ENTERING BATHROOM BEFORE *AMERICAN IDOL* AND STILL NOT BACK AT BREAKFAST. Could she be covered in moisturizer, enveloped in Saran Wrap, and tucked into the tub? She could. Or maybe she simply decided to save her sanity, embrace her smile lines, and take off out

---

198. And, if you're like me, wondering who the hell concocts words like *glycation*.

the window to meet the girls for margaritas. Now, that would be the smart move.

The other bone I'd like to pick with the magazine industry is in regard to the current trend of telling women of a certain age (aka my age) that the only makeup they need to look their best is moisturizer and a little mascara.

I've seen this nugget of nonsense in no fewer than five women's publications. And please don't tell me it was their annual MEN EDIT THE MAGAZINE! issue, or we're going to have much bigger problems than being encouraged to forgo our foundation.

Have you ever tried this moisturizer-and-mascara-only trick?

I have. The very same day I received my subscription to one of the afore-alluded-to magazines, I listened to its obviously sleep-deprived beauty editor and went cosmetics commando.

I scrubbed off my base, blush, eye shadow, and lipstick, slathered on enough moisturizer to polish our pickup, and touched up my mascara. I even pulled my hair back with a headband to highlight my "healthy glow." Then I stepped out of the bathroom and scared the hell out of sweet Hemingway.

"Cramps, huh?" he asked, all bear hugs and blustery concern. I looked at him like he was nuts. I felt fine; dewy-fresh and fabulous. I had no idea that to him I appeared to be glistening with the fever that foreshadows an Ebola breakout.

Undeterred, and clueless to my striking resemblance to *The Scream*, I took off to run errands.

At the bank, my favorite teller skipped the style small

talk we usually make and instead asked how my family was faring with the "flu thing." I replied that we hadn't had it. And she said, "Oh, well, get ready."

At the feed and grain co-op, the cashier wanted to know if the "chest thing" was going through our house. I swear I heard her mumble, "Must be somethin'," when I said no.

At the post office, the clerk saw me coming and reached for a fresh pair of plastic gloves. Since this is pretty much the norm, I didn't take it personally. But when he asked if I had the "bad cold" he and his co-workers were coping with, and I replied in the negative, he actually slipped on a surgical mask.

It went on like this at the video store, gas station, and dry cleaner's, where the owner pointed first to her face, then to mine, and whispered, "Oooooh. You have skin like Sleeping Beauty!" Initially I took it as a compliment. But then I wondered, Wasn't that poor kid in a coma?

I was beginning to feel like an unwitting participant in some covert study of communicable diseases when it hit me: My makeup-free face was freaking people out.

What was I thinking, listening to some self-proclaimed magazine beauty pro? I was in the magazine business. I should know better. They come up with an idea (think cuffed wool short-shorts, halter tops, and spiked heels "Perfect for your big sales presentation!" or modified mullets and green mascara—"He'll love your new look!") then perpetrate it on the American public. Trust me when I tell you they don't wear the stuff themselves.

And they don't run around naked faced.

I can't believe I was out and about with my complexion

as "rosy" as a clove of garlic. I raced home to my mad scientist assortment of drugstore and department store cosmetics, locked myself in the bathroom, and didn't emerge
until I'd L'Oréal-ed and Lancôme-d, Maybelline-d, Trish
McEvoy-ed, Revlon-ed, and MAC-ed my way back.

And, boy, was Hemingway happy. "Whew! For a
minute there you looked like Snow White," he said. First
Sleeping Beauty and now Snow White. When will I learn
not to take beauty advice from Dopey?

Of course when magazines aren't pushing their 45 is
THE NEW 35! and moisturizer-and-mascara mantras, they're
devoting feature after feature to saving face the newfan-
gled way: with needles. And I confess, they've got me seriously considering my nonsurgical options.

With a pretty significant birthday staring me in the
face, and the lines on my forehead forming a six-lane free-
way with little off-ramps headed toward my hairline, I've
recently come to the conclusion that the only way to rectify
my sad state of facial affairs and survive the big day is
with—dare I say it?—a bit of Botox.

Toward that end I've found a doctor (a local one; just
because I've learned to drive to D.C. doesn't mean I want
to), booked a free consultation, and pillaged our mutual
funds in preparation for bankrolling my body work. I think
that's fair. After all, that money was earmarked for the
kids' college. So even if Casey and Cuyler can't go, at least
I'll look young enough to.

All kidding aside, I hate birthdays. Particularly "land-
mark" birthdays family and friends fuss over. You know;
the kind of milestone event that elicits covert phone calls
and furtive whispers as people try to decide what to buy
me to cushion the blow.

Of course no one says that, but it's what they're thinking. Only on big birthdays do people proffer trips and shiny trinkets, spa days and designer handbags. On regular birthdays it's a coup just to get a card.

And frankly this year I'd even be happy to forgo the Shoebox Greetings.

There's really nothing anyone can give me that I haven't already got. Flabby abs and stretch marks? Check. Under-eye bags the size of breasts? Mine are at least a B-cup's worth of badness. Saggy lids, adult acne, spider veins, and the luster-free skin that's the hallmark of the hot-flash set? Trust me; I'm a dermatologist's dream.

Clearly I've got it all, so there's no need to buy me anything.

There is, however, one gift everyone can give me that requires no shopping, no wrapping, no rushing to make sure I receive it on the exact day the earth was graced with my wiseacre attitude, and no wondering if I'll like it. Believe me when I tell you I'll love it. Are you listening?

A lie.

Not a big, soul-blackening lie. A small lie. An itty, bitty, teensy-weensy white lie. The kind of insignificant, inconsequential prevarication I'm pretty sure even God would give a pass to.

You can tell it whenever you want to whomever will listen. And all you have to say is, "Wow, I can't believe my _____ [insert how you know me here: friend, wife, mom, daughter, sister, favorite fake farm girl, Jazzercise buddy] Susan just turned *thirty-five*." (Rest assured; this is an improvement.) "She doesn't look a day over thirty."

Easy to recall and recite, it's a one-size-fits-all fib. And it's available for you to give to me with virtually no worries on your part. Unless you're afraid God really will be galled. Then you might want to give me money.

If my family and friends won't advance my falsehoods, I'll have to hire the doctor I'm due to see. Sure, it'll be tough on my sweet sons, but there's a discount on Botox, Restylane, and collagen if I pay cash.

Chapter Thirty-five

THE CATTLE GOT NOTHIN' ON MY KIDS

Warning: As beautiful and picture-postcard-perfect as the country is, it *is* as bad as it can smell.

Consider for a moment the scent of steaming horse poop on a hot and humid June day. Now imagine it filling your nose while you're stuck, with your drop-top down, behind Seattle Slew and his fancy-pants mistress as they trot their way oh, so slowly down Main Street in Middleburg.

The worst, right? Wrong.

On the Barnyard Aroma Richter Scale, the odor of bloating roadkill[199] beats fermenting horse feces. And the gag-inducing scent of the girls' "gifts," strewn over every inch of the great bovine bathroom I call home, takes the top spot.

That is, until my kids enter the competition.

Tough as this is for me to admit, my sons get the gold

---

199. Will someone please teach the damn deer to look before they step out into the street? And as long as you're giving lessons, try talking some sense into the squirrels, groundhogs, and foxes, too. Don't bother with the turkey buzzards, though. When I'm zipping along and discover them munching on an eviscerated buck in the middle of the road, I hit the gas just to nail their nasty butts.

in the Stink Olympics. Their ability to wield a body odor is enough to make your eyes bleed. And I'm not talking strictly about the stomach-turning scent of Eau de Shower-less eighth-grader after a day of both phys ed and football practice. I'm talking about their passion for bad-breath burps and a love of farting on each other that I will never fathom.

If you've got little boys, you're hoping like hell I'm making this up. If you've got big boys, you're wondering if I've been stalking your loved ones and for how long. Trust me, I'm not making it up, and I don't need to look any farther than my own backyard[200] to state some universal truths about sons and stink.

For starters, their love of "letting one rip" is unrivaled. I swear Casey saves up every nasty gas bubble in his body for the moment he steps into the Durango, and then lets loose with such strength and stench I've more than once been forced to pull over and flee the vehicle. And if that's not bad enough, Cuyler then feels compelled to make his own award-winning contribution, and I wind up suffering their fraternal flatulence in stereo.

They also like to play the "Guess what I had for lunch?" game in the car. This spectacular scent offensive (part of the Bombard 'Em with Body Gas competition, and an event in which Casey's never scored less than a perfect ten) is almost as disgusting as the aforementioned fart festival.

We'll be driving along like a regular family, with Casey punching buttons on the radio and Cuyler kicking the seat

---

200. Which is where I'd keep my two animals if I could ever pry them off the PlayStation.

and screaming, "Stop! I like that song! Stop! I said stop!" when suddenly Case will shout, "Guess what I had for lunch?" Before I can shove my right hand over his mouth (because, believe me, I know what's coming), and while holding fast to the steering wheel with my left and trying desperately not to drive off the road, he lets out a belch that could shatter the windshield, and exhales the last (God willing) scent of his lunch. "Mmmmm. Hot dogs!" he announces. Like I needed to be told.

Clearly their behavior in the body odor department is abhorrent. But it's got nothing on their frightening fascination with body parts.

It seems every time I turn around, breasts, butts, "baginas" (as Cuyler so sweetly puts it; when he outgrows his little-boy lisp I'm going to cry), and of course penises are the preferred topics of conversation.

"Do girls have penises?" my little man asks while playing with his own over breakfast one morning.

"No," I tell him for the hundredth time. "Now take your hand out of your pants and finish your pancake." Sounds disgusting, I know, but if I made the kid stop and wash between every bite and fondle, he wouldn't have finished a meal in his entire life. Keeping his hand down his sweats, he segues to his next-favorite subjects—babies and "baginas."

"You don't spit a baby out of your mouth, do you, Mom?" he says, stuffing a mouthful of pancake into his. "'Cause it would get covered in germs, right?" (Honey, you don't know the half of it, I think to myself.)

"Right," I answer, just as he exclaims, "Babies come out of baginas!"

The big swig of half-caff swirling in my mouth comes streaming out of my nose. "Baginas, huh?" I say, scrambling for a napkin and wondering how he knows this, who told him, and how much jail time I'll get for killing that person. "Interesting," I respond, trying to regain my composure.

"Or butts," he says sweetly, wiggling his own off his chair. "Babies come out of butts." Now, there's a nice clean place for them, I think to myself with a sigh of relief. Anything but "baginas."

A short while later I'm at my desk, giving half my attention to drafting a direct-mail piece I'm certain will go directly into the garbage pails of all those who receive it, and the other half to watching Hefner have his way with a harem of hens, when Cuyler pops up at my elbow. "Hey, Mom," he asks, "what are these?" I turn and there's my baby, bare-chested and pulling at his little-boy breasts.

"Those little circles are part of your chest and the dots in the middle are nipples," I reply.

"Nipples?" he cries indignantly. "*Nipples* like on a *baby bottle*? I'm not a baby!"

"No, no, not like that," I respond, but it's too late. He's trying to rip his right nipple off his body and bellowing with every tug.

Suddenly he stops and screams, "Why do boys need nipples, anyway?"

"Hell if I know, honey," I say, and he's stunned. He could care less about nipples now that he's got the goods on Mom.

"You said 'hell,'" he says, eyes wide.

"I sure did," I admit.

"Can I say it, too?" he asks.

I pause. "Just till Dad comes home, OK?"

"OK!" he says, running from the room to find his big brother, and yelling, "Casey! Casey! Where the *hell* are you?"

Maybe you think I'm nuts, but the way I see it, there's nothing like a little well-placed profanity to prevent a trip to the emergency room. (Or with my sons, the psych ward.)

"Mom, why are Quentin's mom's breasts so much bigger than yours?" Cuyler asks innocently during dinner one night.

"Yeah, hon, why are they?" cracks Hemingway from the head of the table.

Before I can respond, Casey adds his two cents with a snicker: "Lots of my friends' moms have bigger breasts than Mom. Heck, lots of my girlfriends do, too, and they're only thirteen!"

"But *why* are they bigger than Mom's?" my little guy persists.

"Because," I begin to respond, shooting Hemingway what I hope is a look that says "Speak, and you're on the sofa" but there's no stopping Mr. Smart Mouth.

"Because Mom was supposed to be a boy!" he says suddenly. "But at the last minute God changed his mind and made her a girl."

Now Casey is completely cracking up and, I confess, so am I, but Cuyler is buying it by the bushel. "So he only had time to give her tiny ones?" he asks matter-of-factly.

"That's right." Hemingway nods sagely.

"And no penis, either, huh, Dad?"

"Nope, son, no penis, either," Hemingway agrees, shaking his head in mock sadness.

"Poor Mom," Cuyler says, pondering my sad state of flat-chested affairs. "Well, at least you *almost* got to be a boy, Mom," he adds, patting my arm consolingly. "From the looks of Quentin's mom's chest, I bet she never even had a chance."

I guess it's pretty obvious that in our house, it's all about being a boy. I'd describe it as penis-centric, but penis central is more like it. That fact is never clearer than during football season. Every Sunday afternoon you can find my sweeties stretched out on the couch, watching the game. They've got their six feet atop the ottoman, their left hands cradling a Coke and their right hands tucked down their pants. Now, there's a family photo for you.

I've tried the "Hey, guys, that's gross" routine and gotten nowhere. I've tried ignoring them, but that hasn't worked, either. So finally I decided, if you can't beat 'em, see what happens when you join 'em. I squeezed onto the couch, put my feet up, stuck my hand in my pants, and cleared the place faster than Casey after his first encounter with Thai food. (Who knew beef satay could smell so good going in and so bad coming out?) In less than ten seconds I had the room, the remote, and the fabulous Brett Favre all to myself.

Sometimes my sons' barnyard behavior really works in my favor. But most times it just gets my gag reflex going.

One night not too long ago I was standing in the kitchen, whipping up dinner (which, to the chickens' great relief, was not a poultry recipe), when suddenly Cuyler came speeding toward me with a golf ball–size boogie stuck to the tip of his index finger.

"Mom, check this out!" he shouted, like he picked the winning lottery numbers and not his nose.

"Yup, it's a biggie," I responded, backing away from the greenish-brown specimen he seemed to be trying to stick in my eye.

"It's way bigger than the others," he continued excitedly.

"The others?" I asked, my stomach turning at the thought of a full-blown boogie collection somewhere in the kid's room.

"Yeah, they're too small. I'm only gonna keep this one. Come see!" And then he was off and running to his bedroom, cradling his precious booger like a baby.

Of course I was hot on his heels, and not two steps through the doorway I glimpsed a display of fresh snot streaks on the wall next to the self-portrait he did in his other favorite medium, marker.[201] "At first I thought this was the biggest," he said, using his flashlight to highlight the first of four rows of yellowish goop, each topped off by a dollop of mucus so massive I felt my stomach flip. "But then this one was bigger," he continued, spotlighting boogie number two. "And these two were even bigger than the others," he concluded, shining his flashlight on boogies three and four before flipping it off dramatically and turning to me. "But now I've got the biggest booger ever born, right, Mom?"

---

201. Black marker. On a white wall. Is it any wonder I keep my painter and not my pediatrician on speed dial?

"Right, hon," I responded, wondering how one gets mucus off Benjamin Moore.

Unfortunately, while I was lost in thought, he leapt onto his bed and began scanning the room for the perfect spot for his perfect pick. "Wait!" I cried, desperate to prevent the desecration of another wall. "Why not keep it in a container? I mean, if you put it on the wall it could dry up and fall off"—(please God)—"but if you keep it in some Tupperware you can . . ."

"Take it to school for show-and-tell!" he cheered, springing off the bed and barreling back to the kitchen. Not exactly what I had in mind, but hey, if it saves my house and what's left of my sanity, I'll take it.

Not five minutes later, the World's Biggest Booger was safely ensconced in a plastic container and tucked inside his backpack.[202] Feeling slightly more in control of the situation, I decided to broach the topic of basic hygiene with my younger son. (Further proof that any sanity I once possessed passed along with the placenta.) "Sweetheart," I began, "you know it's really not hygienic to pick your nose and wipe it on the wall."

He furrowed his brow. "*Hygienic?* What's *hygienic?*"

"Clean," I continued. "*Hygienic* means 'clean.' It means using a tissue to wipe your nose, and washing your hands after you use the bathroom."

"Sounds like heinie. HYGIENIC HEINIE!" he says, flopping to the floor in hysterics.

"What's up with him?" asks Casey, who's suddenly

---

202. I know he can't bring live animals or toys for show-and-tell, but sweet Mrs. Harrison's *never* said a word about bodily secretions.

clomped in from football practice, covered in mud (but not manure, thank God) from his cleats to his Giants cap, and looking pretty unhygienic himself.

"I've got a hygienic heinie!" Cuyler replies, roaring.

"Trust me, bath-free boy," I interject, "you've nothing of the kind."

Now my big guy is completely confused. "What's a hygienic heinie?" he wants to know.

"*Hygienic* means 'clean,'" I begin to respond, "but . . ."

"There's no way *his* heinie is clean!" Casey howls, and that's it. He's thrown down the gauntlet, and Cuyler's up and chasing him from room to room.

"Is so clean!"

"Is not!"

"Is so!"

Last I saw, they were running around the chicken coop, trying to pull each others' pants down. I'd have stopped them, but I was too busy trying to bleach boogies off the wall.

Having been raised in a house with three brothers, I know there are degrees of disgusting, and my sons' performance pales in comparison with that of their uncles.

Growing up, I used to watch in horror as the three maniacs I'm related to by blood wrestled each other to the living room rug on a regular basis. This in and of itself was fine. But the fact that the "match" was over only when the weaker sibling was butt-bombed *in the face* by the stronger sibling—who'd deftly positioned his derriere directly over the nose of the brother beneath—made it a perfect ten in the disgusting department. On more than one occasion I watched my poor mom use a wooden spoon to beat the offending victor off his perch atop the proboscis of the screaming victim, in a futile attempt to get my gasbag brothers to break it up.

At the time I was certain the whole scenario had scarred me for life. I also thought that only my brothers behaved this way, and that when I finally met my Prince Charming, he'd no sooner lift a cheek and let one loose than my brothers would lift a hand to help around the house.

But it was not to be.

The man I met, fell madly in love with, and married is the absolute king of breaking wind, the president of passing gas, and the grand titan of the sneak-attack toot. I can't tell how you many times I've been quietly reading a book, only to suddenly find myself surrounded by an aroma so awful I'm sure the cat is decomposing under the couch. Then I look up, and there's my Hemingway, snickering away behind his book, pleased as punch with yet another SBD[203] delivery.

As you can imagine, between my husband and my sons I really have to work to keep the house from smelling like the public restrooms in Central Park. That means scented drawer liners, potpourri closet caches, air fresheners in every room, and a growing tolerance—even pursuit— of odors other women find repulsive. The pungent smell of cooked broccoli? Bring it on. The nose-wrinkling tang of canned tuna? I'll take it. The overpowering stench of cabbage, salmon, and tripe cooked stovetop? Let's make two pots!

The way I see it, the stronger the stink, the greater the

---

203. Silent But Deadly.

odds I'll actually disguise the heady "bouquet of boy" that fills the house.[204] Of course I've yet to find the right combination of food and/or air fresheners that does the trick, but I'll keep trying. I've no illusions of ever beating them in the body odor game, but if I can win the occasional round—like when company's coming—then at least I can finally stop using clothespins as party favors.

204. If I ever hit on the right recipe, I'm giving it a shot on the "girls."

And Now for an Insect Aside...

TO: Friends & Family
FR: The Virgin of Upperville
Date: Sunday, 8:30 p.m.
Subject: Nervous Ticks

Up until this morning, I was a tick virgin.

Then Cuyler came in from the fields with one wedged in his upper back. Why am I sharing this horrifying tidbit? Because gross as it was, it was fascinating to watch.

First, I thought the tick was a chunk of dirt, so I tried to wipe it off. Nothing doing. Upon closer inspection (and in my advanced myopic condition, I do mean nose-to-skin, squinty-eyed action), it appeared the dirt was *moving*. Kicking its back legs, to be exact. That's when it hit me that my poor baby wasn't covered in ordinary farm filth, but in fact had a creepy-crawly bug breaststroking its way into his sweet shoulder blade.

Having made this discovery (and yes, the legs twitching in the wind was what gave it away), I did what any dyed-in-the-wool suburbanite would do: I screamed. Then Cuy screamed. And I'm sure the tick let one loose when I tugged it out with the tweezers.

A hot shower, complete alcohol rubdown, and healthy dose

of Neosporin later, my little pajama-clad man was watching TV, and the tick (what tick?) was a pest of the past.

Tonight I retire a titan of tick extermination. Who says I can't master this sticks stuff Suzy style?

Love,

Susan

Chapter Thirty-six

THE SECRET'S OUT

It's no secret how I feel about Victoria's Secret. When I'm in the store, a forty-five-minute trip from Nate's Place, so I don't go too frequently, or curled up with my morning coffee and the brand-new sale catalog, I feel a rush of hope so intense you'd think the Capri pant had finally been declared dead. As I prowl the aisles and peruse the pages, my whole being tingles with the sense that anything is possible, that life *is* beautiful, that tomorrow truly could be a brighter day. Particularly if I buy the Body by Victoria Padded Demi with Secret Embrace Technology today.

Right now, for a mere twenty-eight bucks, I can get boobs. Something I've wanted since my best friend Roma returned from summer camp with cleavage three days before we started seventh grade. I spent every morning that year stuffing balled-up Saran Wrap down my starter bra, and every evening massaging Miracle Gro granules into my sweaty chest. Afterward I'd stand in the shower and pray while, apparently, the fertilizer pooled in my posterior. Thirty years later the real miracle is finding pants that fit my 38DD derriere.

Anyway, this darling bargain demi promises to boost my boobies a full cup size without anesthesia and a cosmetic loan from Capital One. That makes Hemingway happy, particularly since he thinks the five grand I'd like to spend on breast augmentation would be better invested in replacing his knees. So what he can't get around? At least I'll look like I do.

Obviously surgery is out of the question, and frankly I worry about having something unnatural in my body again. (The jury's still out on the two boobs I've given birth to.)

If you're thinking I'm a shallow, self-involved wife and mother who should learn to see the glass as half full, think again. I'm actually a shallow, self-involved, flat-chested wife and mother who's sick of seeing her Maidenform half full. Clearly, Victoria's not the only one with a secret.

To satisfy my quest for breasts I'm buying the adorable demi in Buff, Whisper Pink, and Miami Tan. If it came with Jamie Foxx or Colin Farrell from *Miami Vice*, that would be the best, but as we've already seen, you can't ask for miracles. Unless of course it's the original Miracle Bra. With its removable pads and contoured underwire cups it's more than manna from heaven. It's manna for hooters.

I figure once I'm through purchasing all the turbocharged mammary maximizers Victoria's Secret stocks and I'm pushed up so far my chest protrudes from my cheekbones, it'll be time to tackle my aforementioned gluteus maximus. I'd kill to make it more minimus, and the VS Uplift Jean could do just that. For sixty-eight dollars the pants promise to shape, firm, and lift, something I didn't think could be achieved without our hay elevator, several

Jaws of Life–type tractor attachments, and power-assisted liposuction. I plan to purchase several pair; I just need to decide what style: the Sexy, the Ultra Sexy, or the Hipster. I'm leaning toward the Sexy (hey, you've got to walk before you run in your four-inch Steve Madden stilettos), and as far away as humanly possible from the Hipster. I may be foolish enough to want to dress like a twenty-five-year-old, but at forty-something it's just tempting fate to wear fashions that practically invite fractures.

Despite Hemingway's stance on elective surgery, I spend an inordinate amount of time thinking about tummy tucks, body contouring, and boob jobs. I fantasize about being sucked in, pushed up, and slimmed down. Of walking into a spectacular "spa-maceutical" complex I've dreamt up, which I call the Center for Surgical Magic, and selecting Jessica Simpson's figure, Sienna Miller's face, and Kate Hudson's hair from an à la carte menu of unlimited options. I'd have a quick consultation with the *Nip/Tuck* dudes, be whisked off to the OR for a complete overhaul, and awaken the world's hottest woman.

But of course that's all just a fantasy. One that would cost me about three hundred grand and my sixteen-year marriage. Better to stick with Vicky and the Very Sexy Seamless Collection. Unless I discover its very special ingredient is sticky Saran Wrap. It's no secret how I feel about that stuff.

Chapter Thirty-seven

MEET THE LOB SQUAD

It all started when I made the mistake of recently reminding Hemingway that I've always wanted a tattoo. "Susan," he replied, his face contorted like he just found a spider in his Stoli, "a tattoo shows a distinct lack of breeding."

Excuse me, but did he just diss my mom and dad, my Irish-Italian upbringing, and my steadfast conviction (pounded into me by both my parents) that penne Bolognese is an acceptable breakfast food?

I think so.

Offended but undaunted, I broach the topic of tattoos with the one clique I count on to help make all of life's crucial decisions (i.e., highlights or lowlights, Botox or bangs, six weeks or six months of sleep-away camp for my crotchety eight-year-old): the girls.

Every day I thank God for my girlfriends. All of them: my old friends up North, and my new ones here in horse country. When the chips (and salsa) are down, and it's time to choose between a fourth margarita or a first mojito, my girlfriends order the former and tell me it's the latter. And what do I know? It's my fourth margarita.

Anyway, we're racing down the highway in my friend Deb's Excursion, a vehicle so massive I have to wonder how she handles it (particularly since she's about as big as her own eight-year-old), when I announce that I want a tattoo.

No response.

Considering there are four women in the car, all of whom are doing their most passionate Pink impression, laughing and sampling each other's lip glosses, and generally celebrating the fact that for the next few days they're free from playing farm wife, chauffeur, and head chef, this doesn't surprise me.

So I say it again. Loud. And this time I connect.

"Houston, we have a redneck," says Jenn, the youngest and most conservative of the crew, and the only one we practically had to hog-tie and toss into the car. Why? It seems she'd never left her kids in her husband's care for more than a day. Why? She said she was worried they'd subsist on peanut butter sandwiches, but I think she was afraid they'd Gorilla Glue the goat pen. Again.

"Me, too! Me, too!" shouts Deb, flicking the iPod off so fast I'm sure she's going to flip the space shuttle spiriting us and two hundred pairs of shoes, T-shirts, shorts, sweatpants, sweatshirts, blow dryers, curling irons, flat irons, several bottles of tequila, a gallon of margarita mix, a case of chardonnay, and a cardboard box bursting with Cheez-its, Doritos, Tostitos, and all manner of no-nos for our "yes, yes!" girls' getaway weekend. "I always think about getting one!"

"If you want one, get one. What's the holdup?" snaps Diana, Deb's younger sister, and the only one among us who's single, childless, and completely unaccustomed to having to make decisions by committee.

"The holdup is Hemingway," I respond, clutching the dashboard and wondering how Deb's managing to do ninety in the left lane while craning her head around to catch every morsel of conversation, and if it's really going to hurt when we hurtle into the median. "He's completely anti-tattoo. He says it shows a distinct lack of breeding."

"Houston, we have a blue blood!"

Did we have to keep invoking Houston? For a split second I secretly hope Jenn's little guys are enjoying a farm-wide Krazy Glue free-for-all, and then I catch myself. She's a dear friend. And no one deserves to find a frog in the freezer. Again. "Trust me," I reply, "Houston cannot help us."

"A lack of breeding!" Diana bellows. "He's what, related to the royals or something?"

Bingo. My mother-in-law, God rest her soul, was a Brit. She wasn't related to the Queen Mum, but from the way she talked about Diana, Charles, and their two princes you'd have thought they were old cricket partners.

I share this tidbit with my friends and watch happily as it completely unhinges them. In seconds we're all laughing and chanting, "Lack of breeding! Lack of breeding!" and listing things and activities we love that attest to our spectacularly poor pedigrees.

Ankle bracelets. Cobalt-blue hair extensions. Cold pizza and beer for breakfast. Black nail polish. (Trust me: There's nothing like the reaction folks give a Goth mom.) Spiraling into hip-shaking, sexy-pout-making, disco mode in the middle of the mall at the first Muzak-y strains of

"Let's Stay Together." (And continuing to dance no matter how fast our mortified offspring freak out and fly into Aeropostale. *Puh-leeze.* Like they weren't headed there, anyway.) Toe rings. Trashy novels. And of course, tattoos.

Clearly we were a quartet of classless acts.

And if you're going to have an act, you've got to have a name. In honor of the fact that we all suffered from a Lack of Breeding (proving once again that birds of a trashy feather do indeed flock together), we christened ourselves the LOB Squad. We selected a mascot, the lobster, and several questionably conducted hours later (sorry, true LOBsters don't transgress and tell) began our assault on the sleepy hamlet of Nags Head.

As the lead LOBster, I took it upon myself to set the tone for the weekend. Upon arrival at Deb's beach house, I dashed to the third-floor deck and proceeded to dance atop the picnic table. Sure, drunks do this all the time. But only those whose lineage is seriously suspect can strut their stuff sober. (Belated apologies to Deb's husband, Mark, for the stiletto scratches he was forced to sand, and thanks to her sweet son Camden for returning my feather boa. Beats me how it got into the hot tub.)

After this, it was all downhill, which is how we LOBsters like it. I have a vague recollection of the four of us collecting seashells after too much chardonnay, attempting to affix a gargantuan plastic lobster to the Excursion's grille, and consuming at least our respective body weights in Bombay martinis and scallops soaked in garlic sauce.

At some point we got really crazy and took a whole bunch of pictures in which we actually all look good. To my mind this can only be credited to the amazing feats digital photography lets you perform in terms of erasing orange Doritos stains from the sides of people's mouths. And Corona bottles from their hands. And the wall clock that mars the snapshot of *somebody's* mom dealing black-jack by giving away the precise, pre-dawn time that particular Kodak moment was captured.

The only thing we didn't do was get tattoos. We plan to when the four of us return for the Second Annual LOB-ster Fest in a few weeks. Or, I should say, Diana, Deb, and Jenn plan to. I got mine a month ago. The timing was never right when I wrote ad copy out of our home in Ridgewood, and when I was running the corporate rat race, top jobs and tats just didn't mix. At least not in my mind.

One of the best things life in the boonies has given me is the chance to be myself: the fake farm girl in the tight jeans with the beautiful orange-and-yellow butterfly on her right shoulder.

I'm sure my virtually blue-blooded better half would've preferred it someplace more discreet, like my inner ear, but I opted to wear it loud and proud.

After all, I'm a LOBster. What I lack in breeding I more than make up for in brass.

Chapter Thirty-eight

DOWN THE RABBIT HOLE

$\mathcal{F}$or as long as I can remember, the change of seasons has made me sad. Deeply, painfully sad. And not just because at some point I have to put my peep-toe stilettos and lightweight bib overalls[205] away for the winter. Getting the blues is how I'm built.

Spring to summer is relatively easy, and the start of football season makes summer to fall bearable.[206] Fall to winter is when things begin to get dicey. And winter to spring? Hurts like a pair of supertight Spanx at a sit-down dinner.

If you've never been depressed, you're probably wondering what I'm talking about. Depression is more than feeling down. And teary. And irritable. And hopeless. And overwhelmed. And indescribably exhausted. (And yet ready, willing, and somehow able to bite somebody's

---

205. OK, I confess. Putting these suckers away does not sadden me. I won't wear them, but Hemingway insists they hang in my closet "just in case." Just in case what? Just in case I finally suffer a massive head injury and spend the rest of my life wearing "mom jeans" from John Deere?

206. Until the day Brett Favre retires; after that, all bets are off.

head off for something as small and inconsequential as allowing—no, encouraging—the chickens to roost in the window boxes you just planted with two hundred dollars' worth of Gerbera daisies, petunias, and impatiens.) Sorry. I think I already mentioned feeling irritable.

Depression is also physically painful.

At my most depressed my legs and back suffer like a piñata at one of Cuyler's birthday parties. The soles of my feet hurt to the touch,[207] and my upper arms ache and twitch as if the alien baby from *It's Alive* is incubating in my biceps. It wants out. I want it out. But all I can do is wait it out.

When I was first diagnosed and still couldn't quite believe that I, a card-carrying class clown and resident funny girl among my friends, was depressed, I was certain these symptoms signaled the flu. I recall going to the doctor on at least three change-of-season occasions and demanding drugs. I wanted relief and I wanted it now. Each time I showed up, my doctor checked me over from head to toe. He did blood work. And he listened to my list of ills, all of which were highlighted prominently on the WARNING SIGNS OF MAJOR DEPRESSION poster on the back of the examining-room door. And then, in the absence of fever, chills, and the other fun stuff that accompanies influenza, he gently reminded me to take as good care of myself as I do my family, try to do less, and take my Lexapro.

Hello, my name is Susan and I take happy pills.

Now, if the mere mention of antidepressant medication gets you going all Tom Cruise, my advice is that you stop

---

207. Which makes taking the pedicure cure impossible.

reading right here. If you're one of those folks who'd rather have a loved one go around nearsighted and walking into walls than give them glasses, put this down. If you're still wondering why people with skyrocketing cholesterol need Lipitor or Zocor or Crestor or any one of those "ors" and not just a little self-discipline in the diet department, please take your club and go back to your cave. We'll call you the day the wheel makes its debut.

I love my antidepressant and have written long imaginary letters of gratitude to its inventor. This isn't to say it always works perfectly. As I've mentioned, the change from winter to spring hurts with the ferocity of realizing I'll never own a Birkin bag, a Porsche Boxster, or even a few of the five hundred acres on which we reside. But *I* work a heck of a lot better with my daily ten-milligram dose than I ever did without it.

Some people experience major depression at the death of a loved one, a big move,[208] the loss of a job, or the birth of a baby. With the help of talk therapy and occasionally a course of (please, don't tell Tom) medication, they get better and that's that.

Others, like me, are born without the ability to produce enough serotonin,[209] and with a smaller-than-normal hippocampus.[210] According to medical science, both of these differences are irrefutable proof of depression.

I wish I'd known all this when I was twelve. At least

---

208. Like to a farm—hint, hint, Hemingway! Just kidding. Our move to the hinterland has actually been very good for my head.

209. The chemical in the brain that makes you feel good.

210. The area of the brain that stores memories.

then I would have understood my freakish response to the first blush of spring. While my friends took off to hit tennis balls, hang out at the pizza parlor, and spy on cute boys, I hid in my room, under my desk, crying into a dog-eared copy of *My Darling, My Hamburger*. Years later I read that Helen Gurley Brown once did something similar. I still felt like a mutant, but it's comforting to have something in common with the original *Cosmo* Girl.

Despite myriad advances in medical science, there's nothing anyone can do about my humble hippocampus. This is actually fine with me; it's nice that some part of my person is petite. But my serotonin level is a whole different story. My antidepressant acts like a push-up bra for my brain. It boosts, pads, and pumps. It adds, if you will, a full cup size to my serotonin stores. The result, to paraphrase Billy Crystal's famous Fernando, is that most days I not only feel good, but I almost think I look good, too.

So why am I telling you all this? Because I'm one of those people you'd never suspect gets depressed. So if it can happen to me, it can happen to anybody.

Hemingway describes me as exuberant, fun-loving, and always laughing. My staff at *Family Circle* gave me a charm bracelet inscribed with the words SUZY SUNSHINE as a going-away gift. And several of Cuyler's second-grade buddies refer to me as the silly mommy who can't do science but tries, anyway.

Maybe not the most mature reputation, but I like it.

Most days I'm fine. But there are times, like when the leaves fall off the trees and a dead one shows up in my living room (demanding, in that passive-aggressive manner Scotch pines have perfected, to be decorated), that I can't fathom how I'll muster the strength to make merry (or make the beds, for that matter). I always come out of it, thank God and the nice folks at Forest Laboratories, and I find it helps to tell my better half, and sometimes a girlfriend, how I'm feeling.

It doesn't stop me from heading down the rabbit hole, but at least somebody's there to toss me a bag of baby carrots and a copy of *Vogue*.

Chapter Thirty-nine

JERSEY GIRL

$\mathcal{Y}$ou can take the girl out of New Jersey, but you can't take New Jersey out of the girl.

Seems every time I go home to visit,[211] I come back with hair as big as a round bale and a North Bergen accent so thick it clears the cows from my path faster than a cattle prod.

On the ride up, I belt out a duet with Keith Urban during my fantasy debut at the Grand Ole Opry. (I have to admit, I'm a crowd pleaser in my Lucky Brand jeans, black leather top, and four-inch stilettos.) On the way back, it's me, Bon Jovi, and the Boss in an imaginary SRO performance at the Stone Pony. (Same outfit, in case you're wondering. I'm a firm believer in sticking with what works.)

And while I'm actually in New Jersey, I do Jersey girl things.

---

211. Which is a lot lately. See, there is this wonderful little publishing house called Penguin and they've offered to buy a book I've written. This book, in fact. For some reason they think my new life in the country, on a cattle farm, with nary a Starbucks in sight, is funny. So now I get to head north for meetings and lunches, the likes of which I'd never ditch in favor of managing my minibar. If I still had one, that is, which I don't. And I don't think my Snow Day Survival Kit counts.

Like test drive Corvettes and Camaros with salesmen who look more than a little like *The Sopranos'* Christopher Moltisanti. Then I come home and try tearing around on our New Holland Quicke, which never works, as that tractor is totally misnamed.

I also play a little game I made up called Spot the Guido. With the influx of Egyptian, Indian, and Greek men, who are as strikingly dark and swarthy as the Italian boys I grew up with, it's getting tougher and tougher to tell the wiseguys from the wannabes. Tougher, but not impossible.

For starters, when a group of PGs[212] strut into the diner where my cousin Lisa and I are simultaneously scarfing down chicken Caesar salads and tearing into all the great stuff we just got at Guess? ("Don't you just love this sweater dress? And what about these boots? Feel these boots! Careful! Don't drop 'em in the dressing!"), their cooler-than-thou attitudes, leather jackets, and tans immediately trip my "game on!" trigger.

Me, looking nonchalantly in the direction of the PGs: "What do you think?"

Lisa, giving them a split-second once-over and concluding: "The leather's fake."

Me: "The tans are real." I pause to surreptitiously stare, chew, and dump what has to be the sixteenth whopping dollop of Caesar dressing on my "dietetic" lunch. "God, don't you wish you could get that in a bottle?"

---

212. Possible Guidos. Let's keep up here, people!

Lisa, who can eat, drink, and even lick her lips without removing a single layer of her forty-dollar Chanel lipstick, stops and looks at me in total exasperation. *"You can.* I keep telling you. Mix Aveeno with Neutrogena, and bam, you're bronze."

I won't bore you with the rest of our girl talk, but suffice it to say that those guys were not Guidos.

The track-suited sextuplet in the booth behind us, however, sure was. What gave them away? Maybe it was their velour outerwear and tight, wife-beater tees. Or maybe it was their booming loud "business" conversation, bellowed into their cell phones ("Whadda I look like? A geriatric transportation service? You want me to take Nana to see Aunt Grace, ya gotta give me gas money, Ma"). Or maybe it was simply the fact that they were each wearing what had to be the entirety of Target's gold jewelry department on their person. Take your pick. In the end, it all points to GUIDO.

When I'm not test driving cars or forcing friends and relatives to play the silly games that go running through my head, I like to stock up on stuff I just can't get down south. This includes all manner of New York Giants gear, Italian cold cuts (like Provolone and prosciutto. Correct pronunciations: pro-vah-*loan* and pro-*shoot*, not pro-*shoot*-o, thank you very much), and holiday gifts for my Jewish pals.

I'm not kidding. When I'm in Jersey, I make it a point to pick up as much Jewish paraphernalia as possible. Hanukkah-candle gift packs. Blue and silver wrapping paper. Bags of chocolate coins wrapped in gold foil. Why does this make me so *mashugga*?[213] Because frankly I still haven't recovered from my first holiday in the hinterland when I discovered that the local Wal-Mart offered a whopping two Hanukkah cards from which to choose and not a single roll of appropriate gift wrap. I should've known I was going nowhere when I asked a salesperson for assistance and he responded, "You know, I don't think we celebrate that holiday here."[214]

I also like to pick up presents for my new southern girlfriends. And to be honest, it's not so much about the gift as it is where I get it. Like the costume accessories I found for a friend's party at The Fun Ghoul.

Mush all three words together and say it really fast: *TheFunGhoul.*

That just kills me. I mean, who can resist shopping at a place with a name like that? I'd planned on bringing flowers or dessert or a few dozen of Hemingway's organic eggs, but when I passed a billboard that screamed, THE FUN GHOUL COSTUME COMPANY. WE SWEAR OUR STUFF'S THE SCARIEST! all other hostess-gift options went out of my head. I raced in and rang up fifty dollars' worth of horns and halos, thrilled that my passion for Italian invectives had led to a purchase that would surely give my new pals the giggles.

My other favorite hotspot is Capo Vino.[215] Yes, I can get

---

213. Yiddish for "crazy." For a real *freyd* (joy, delight, treat) pick up a little tome called *Yiddish with Dick and Jane.*

214. Looking for a true exercise in futility? Try finding a Passover card in cow country. Go ahead. Try. I hate e-greetings, but sometimes there's simply no other way to say, "Happy Seder!"

215. *Capo* is Mafia slang for "captain" or "crew leader." The aforementioned Christopher Moltisanti is a capo. Can you say "Suzy loves *The Sopranos*"?

La Crema Chardonnay and Kendall Jackson Merlot at my local Giant. But it's the customized Capo Vino bag, emblazoned with the words #1 WITH A BULLET that makes a gift of their grape a big hit (pardon the pun).

Of course the one place I no longer shop is Made Menswear. The last time I was there I bought Hemingway the one and only flannel-lined denim work shirt they had on hand, and he hated it. "Sue," he said, opening the bag and pulling out what I thought was the perfect find for my farm boy, "this is Guido gear."

"What?" I replied, practically deaf from the crunch of the Aussie Sprunch coating my mane and cementing it into the biggest head of curls south of Seaside Heights. "What are you talking about?"

"I'm talking about the fact that there's a zipper where the buttons should be. And look at this," he continued, cracking up, "there's a Kangol cap attached to the tag."

"Correction," I responded, "a *fuzzy* Kangol cap." I was laughing so hard I could barely breathe. "Hold on to your hay bales, hon. You're the Godfarmer!"

Oh yes, each time I go north I bring a bit more of the Garden State back with me. Right this instant I've got huge hair, a rejuvenated Jersey "honk," and a hankering to pierce my belly button. I'd get a gold hoop, but then I'd look like one of our bulls.

It's bad enough I'm going Guidette. But I draw the line at bovine.

Chapter Forty

GO AHEAD, MUDDY MY DAY

$\mathcal{I}$ have a confession to make: I'm starting to enjoy farm chores.

I'd appreciate if we could keep this tidbit between us, as around here I've got a "too cool for agricultural school" reputation and I don't want the barn cat out of the bag just yet. I also don't want Hemingway getting the crazy idea I'm ready to ditch my low-slung Lucky jeans for flannel shirts, overalls, and muck boots. When the fashion magazines feature the stuff, fine. Until then, Farmer Suzy's herding cattle in couture.

Why are farm chores suddenly so much fun? Because the other day I got to play in the mud. Being a red-blooded, chardonnay-drinking, *Desperate Housewives*–addicted American woman, mud is a substance about which I have mixed emotions. Mud applied to my body, in the warm cocoon of a four-star spa, makes me swoon. Mud on the dogs, the kids, and the kitchen floor makes my blood boil.

And as my sons will tell you, you should never, ever get mud on Mommy.

I was lunching with a dear friend when Hemingway

called to say he was stuck. Since my better half is a writer who also has a bad back, being stuck could have several connotations. Was he stuck on a line of dialogue or a specific detail? Or was he flat on the floor, unable to get up?

Neither, it turned out. He'd driven the pickup into a far field to check a pond or fence or some such foolishness and gotten stuck in the mud. Why he was telling me I couldn't imagine, and since my soup was cooling, I was pretty hot to hang up. I offered one more half-listening, but loving-wife "Oh, dear, I'm so sorry," and was signing off when I heard him say, "I need your help."

My help? My help? Who is this again?

"I'm going to have to pull it out with the tractor," he continued, "and I need you to steer." Steer the pickup? The thing's the size of a school bus. And besides, it's in the mud. "Sweetheart," I said, "did you mean to call *me*?"

Forty minutes later I was standing on the steps of the tractor, my honey at the helm, winging my way across the pasture. *Winging* is probably pushing it, as our New Holland Quicke doesn't move faster than five miles per hour. But in any case, we were heading out through the mud toward more mud.

And frankly, I was having a hard time acting put-upon.

Oh, sure, I kept my petulant-princess puss on my face, and threw in a good deal of eye rolling to reinforce my disdain at having been dragged home for such a dirty endeavor. But the fact is—and please, this has to stay here—I was having fun.

It was sixty degrees and sunny, our two sopping-wet mutts were racing ahead of us, and with every turn of the gigantic tire to my right I was *thwapped* with mud. It was in my hair, in my hood, and all over my cute little BARN BRAT cap.

I was a complete *Glamour* "don't," and I didn't care.

Finally we reached our destination: the mud-stuck pickup truck. Hemingway positioned the tractor in front of it, affixed the tow rope, and told me to keep the windows open so I could hear him. Famous last words. I turned the ignition and hit the gas. The wheels spun like my head at a designer handbag sale. In seconds I was splattered in slime.

I took several whopping chunks to my cheeks and direct hits on both eyebrows. I had long, goopy drips down my neck and in my ears. But the coup de gross was an oversize molelike dollop near my mouth that gave me a quasi–Cindy Crawford–like sex appeal, if you could get past the fact that I was probably covered as much in manure as I was mud.

At some point during my baptism by grime we managed to free the truck. I was still in the driver's seat, frosted in filth, when I felt Hemingway watching me. I'm sure he was wondering how long it would be before I completely flipped out.

But I didn't.

Instead I peeked in the rearview mirror and played connect the dots with the muck on my mug. I swirled and smooshed and patted it deep into my pores. It wasn't exactly a mud pack at the Ritz-Carlton, but it served its purpose: I popped my head out the window, came nose to nose with one of the cows that had come to watch, and giggled as it recoiled in horror.

You know you look bad if you can give cattle the creeps. And what's more fun than that?

Suzy's Top Ten Farm No-Nos

According to some insurance company quoted in *Progressive Farmer*, a magazine I now read concurrently with *Vanity Fair* and ask myself such crucial questions as "Which bush hog would Sandra Bullock buy?" and "How is it no one's ever suggested Burt's Bees for poor Orlando Bloom's chapped lips?" farming is third in dangerousness behind oil rig operator and fireman. And this makes me wonder if, when Denis Leary's done with *Rescue Me,* he'll do *Harvest Me*? Might make a nice follow-up, no?

All kidding aside, this frightening fact has spurred me to pen a list of the top ten things you should never do on a farm. Maybe it's a little odd for me—a Jersey girl who wasn't raised among beef cattle and bush hogs, and whose closest contact with a farm animal was the rooster on the cover of a Corn Flakes box—to do this, but I think my brief tenure here in tractor land makes me the perfect person to expound on this subject. Particularly since I've done almost all the dumb things described here and can tell you in no uncertain terms: Don't try this at home.

1. *No "dynamic duo on the tractor!" tricks.* Hemingway and I should never have been on the New Holland together. It's just plain dangerous. In fact the majority of accidental farm deaths are caused by people piling onto tractors. If the folks at your house have a penchant for riding around in pairs, get a bicycle built for two.

2. *Don't chase chickens.* See how they run when you

approach? That's chicken speak for "Back off, buster, or I'm breaking the eggs." Those feathered fiends can be pretty feisty, so keep them away from kids' eyes. (Not to mention fresh manicures; trust me when I say that pockmarked polish is not pretty.)

3. ***Don't forget to buckle up.*** For about ten minutes Hemingway and I thought it was fine to go sans seat belts as we raced around our back forty. (Hey, it's not the highway, so it's OK, right? Wrong.) One good smack to the skull later, I learned the hard, headache-y way that buckling up in the farm truck might save me from being killed if the thing overturned. Plus I wouldn't have to live on Tylenol.

4. ***No scaling the grain silo.*** You'd think Casey and Cuyler were training for the X Games the way they gravitate toward our abandoned grain silo. Twice I've caught them trying to climb it; once with a "parachute" they concocted in case they fell. No one should ever hike a grain silo or hide inside one. That trick's best left for when your mother-in-law comes to town.

5. ***Power tools are not movie props,*** no matter what your budding horror movie maker says. Casey insists he's on his way to being the next Wes Craven. This means he likes to scream, "Action!" and chase Cuy around with a chain saw. Why he can't remake *Scarface* and practice with the plastic AK-47s we have piled high on the porch I'll never know.

6. ***The barn is no place for a barbecue.*** Sure, this statement seems obvious. But if you haven't made it clear to your kids that hay bales, wooden ladders, and rafters ignite pretty readily, take it from me (and Ladder Co. No. 3): tell them today.

7. ***Don't join the cattle for a cold one.*** To cows, the water in that stream is free-flowing Poland Spring. To humans, it's more likely a massive case of E. coli. Why? Because cattle use streams for a whole lot more than quenching their thirst, if you get my drift. Unless you're up for some serious gastrointestinal distress, resist the temptation to drink with your ruminants.

8. ***A farm is not a petting zoo.*** You may be surrounded by the most docile cattle, sheep, and donkeys. But even laid-back livestock will flip if besieged by a group of seven-year-old boys at a birthday party. (Right, Cuy?) Encourage your kids to speak softly to farm animals, stand far from their hind legs, and remember: Baby bulls are best left unleashed. (If you take nothing else from number 8, that tidbit's the ticket.)

9. ***Don't hop the electric fence.*** Or the barbed wire or four-board fence, either. Hurdling anything on a farm is asking for trouble (and quite possibly a tetanus shot). Save it for the track.

10. ***Use your head; wear a helmet.*** To me, the idea of racing around on my four-wheeler without my matching

helmet makes about as much sense as going barefoot in a ball gown. I simply believe in the power of accessories. In this case, one saves your look; the other, your life. See, there really are benefits to having been raised reading *Vogue*.

Chapter Forty-one

SOOZAPALOOZA

When I'm not pretending to be put-out by doing farm chores,[216] I'm back to doing the three things I love most but didn't have time for when I was running to and from *Family Circle* every day.

Like writing humorous, slice-of-life essays and ad copy. The ad copy pays well, is great fun, particularly for those of us who enjoy playing *Name That Tune* with words, and I get to work for several of my dear friends without having to leave my living room. So what's not to like?

The humorous, slice-of-life essays do not pay well, if they pay at all, and in fact typically leave me in a state of high anxiety and abysmal self-doubt as I await my next rejection letter from some newspaper or magazine. So why do I do it?

Because what I really want is to be the next Nora Ephron.

And the only way to do that is to get published. And the only way to get published is to start by getting rejected. And that part I've got down cold.

---

216. A secret, may I remind you, that stays here.

In fact right this second I am waiting for a rejection letter. Not just any rejection letter. The mother of all rejection letters, particularly as it pertains to those of us who write funny stuff, or at least attempt to.

I have been awaiting this rejection letter for twenty-six days now. Which means it's six days late. The people from whom I'm expecting it are typically mercifully quick and like clockwork in telling me to take a hike. If I mail them a piece on the first, I have their "Maybe your friends think you're a riot, but they're wrong" letter by the twenty-first. Twenty days on the dot. I know because I send them one of my demented diatribes once a week. And so far I've received a rejection—within twenty days—to every single one.

That's not to say I'm not making progress. I am. My first thirty-five rejection letters were standard photocopied form-letter fare. But of late each has had a personal note scrawled in the corner. Stuff like "I really liked it!" and "Keep trying!"

So I do. I do keep trying.

That's why twenty-six days ago I sent them a few more of my "female funnies," as Hemingway calls them. And that may be the problem. There are two editors of this publication, a man and a woman, and I write mainly for those with uteruses.[217] It's a good bet the gentleman calling half the shots doesn't share my fondness for shoes, fashion, and fine-needle injectibles, or my fear of having a thirty-five-dollar pedicure pecked to death by a bunch of churlish

217. I'd say breasts, but since there are plenty of guys who'd benefit from a little Victoria's Secret Ipex action, it's safer to go with something gynecological.

chickens, which means the chances of my getting the green light are slim, but you never know.

What I do know is that I get a lot done while waiting to be spurned by this and other magazines.

Last week I washed the windows. Not most people's favorite task, but my particular take on it made it a bit more bearable. I started using the old newspaper and vinegar trick. Then, in a burst of inspiration, I switched to vinegar and a bunch of my *Good Housekeeping* "Your drivel will never see the light of day" communiqués. Nothing I've written has gotten their seal of approval, but that sparkle sure gets mine.

Just this morning I replaced the drawer liner sheets in my shoe cubbies. I skipped the lavender-scented Laura Ashley sheaths in favor of several "Get lost" missives from *Working Mother*, *Cosmopolitan*, and *More*. Their brightly colored logos look pretty peeking out from beneath my footwear. And seeing my four-inch stilettos stabbing their editors' signatures gives me a certain perverse sense of satisfaction.

Occasionally I even wrap gifts in rejection letters. *Red-book*'s are particularly perfect for this application, as they're printed—big surprise—on red paper. Sure, they bellow "YOUR STUFF STINKS," but topped with a shiny bow they make any present look pretty. (Plus they let me off the hook for not having bought something more expensive. Obviously I can't afford to.)

It's reached the point where my bills and rejection letters arrive in lockstep. If I open my post office box to find an invoice for our health insurance premium, I can be sure a rebuff from *Reader's Digest* is tucked somewhere in there, too. If it's time to pay *Cingular*, *DirecTV*, or *MasterCard*, it's time to be snubbed by *Seventeen*, the *Saturday Evening Post*, and *Prevention*.

The combination of bills and bad news would depress most people, but not me. My work has actually begun to get picked up more frequently, and that makes me feel good. Optimistic. Hopeful that Nora Ephron–greatness could one day be within my grasp.

I do think, however, that it's human nature to dwell on the rejections, the ones that got away, the ones that didn't want you for whatever ridiculous reason.

Like my high school boyfriend, Donny. He dumped me for a redhead. No offense, folks, but when does a blonde get dumped for a redhead? At my last class reunion I learned the poor guy had gone legally blind. Frankly I saw that coming senior year.

In all seriousness, getting the kiss-off from dozens of popular publications doesn't bother me. What bothers me is the waiting. And since I can only do so much with my collection of rejection letters, I'm free to spend hours at a clip indulging the third of my long-dormant passions: playing the piano.

Have I mentioned the piano? Hemingway bought it for me as a birthday gift.[218] I've played every single day since I was four, except for the 4,745[219] we didn't have one while we lived in Ridgewood.

If you recall, part of the appeal of Nate's Place is that it

---

218. The kids got earplugs.

219. For the mathematically challenged (like me), that's thirteen years. And thirteen years is a long time to go without tinkling the ivories, particularly if you're one of those people who's used to tinkling every day.

had a wall I could dedicate to a piano.[220] Add to that the fact that I'd actually have time to play it, and you can see why the prospect of living on a farm didn't totally freak me out. I figure Hemingway came here to make hay. I came here to make music.

And a name for myself as the next Nora Ephron.

But back to the piano.

I love playing it, but lately I find my nose pressed so close to the music I can practically feel Beethoven's breath on my face. Sad to say, but it's gotten to the point where I might need peepers.

Now, I adore accessories as much as the next woman, but to me these magnifying glasses masquerading as eyewear simply scream "middle age." And I don't need any help advertising my descent into the physiological horror show of hot flashes, night sweats, insomnia, age spots, midmonth migraines, progesterone creams, and a growing obsession with cardigans.[221]

But really, back to the piano.

It's a fifteen-year-old Baldwin upright in excellent condition, except for the abuse it takes from me. And I do dish it out. One day I'm mangling Mozart's *Sonata in C*, and the next I'm beating Billy Joel's "My Life" to death while the crowd in my head cheers and flicks their Bics, begging for an encore.

One evening I got so carried away I thought I could

---

220. The wall just happens to be in the living room. This allows me to bop back and forth between my piano and my laptop all day long. When I can't write, I play. When I can't play, I write. Clearly moving to the farm has cured me of the Clean Sweep!

221. Although a few pair in Burberry plaid might make the whole thing more palatable, not to mention chic.

hear them chanting my name—"Soooo-zin! Soooo-zin!" It
turned out to be Hemingway calling me from the kitchen.
I raced in to discover that dinner had turned to charcoal on
the cook top. Twenty-five minutes and one frozen pizza
later,[222] I was back at the piano. All this practice means I'm
sounding better, but the house has hit a few clunkers.

Mealtime mishaps aside, having the piano has actually
made me a better parent. Thanks to it, I've found the perfect way to propel my two surly spawn off the PlayStation
and onto the five hundred rolling acres on which we reside: I simply play *and sing*.

I stumbled upon this particular technique one weekend when, while pounding out Keith Urban's "Days Go
By," I heard bedroom doors slamming upstairs. At first I
was miffed and immediately decided my two dunderheads
would not be invited to my Mamapalooza concert debut. I
also thought, if I sound that bad, why don't they either put
in the earplugs Hemingway the wiseguy gave them, or go
outside?

And then it dawned on me: I just didn't sound bad
enough.

So I started to sing. Loud. I wasn't three bars into it
when "Days Go By" became boys rushing by carrying
more sports equipment than Modell's.

Maybe spending so much time outdoors will net them
pro football, basketball or baseball careers, which will result in multipage profiles in *Sports Illustrated*. And when a
reporter asks them, as one undoubtedly will, what inspired
them to practice, practice, practice, they'll simply say: my
mom's singing. Now, won't that be nice?

---

222. How did we survive before DiGiorno?

Speaking of practice, I need to get back to the piano. I've been working on some classics by Queen and Elton John. And of course I always practice *the* classics. Like Chopin's "Minute Waltz." I'll never be able to play it in sixty seconds, but I have perfected clearing the house of husband, kids, and dogs within the first four measures.

It's nice to be back to doing what I love, from the comfort of my living room, with a full view of frolicking—and occasionally fornicating—farm animals. Talk about inspiration! I still haven't heard from the "Number 1 humor magazine in America"[223] but I'm sure I will shortly.

I'm also sure that when I do, it won't be funny. It will, however, be a relief. No one likes being rejected, but at least you know where you stand. Or in my case, sit. Sometimes at my piano, but most of the time at my laptop.

Look out, Nora Ephron.

---

223. *Funny Times*. It's the gold standard of humor writing. And no, they still haven't published any of my stuff.

Chapter Forty-two

GET YOUR NEW YORK ON

$\mathcal{A}$s I mentioned a few chapters ago, I recently sold my first book. (Look for my second, *When Suzy Met Nora*, in bookstores soon!) Of course, when I sold it, it wasn't a book. It was a blog. And before that it was just a once-a-week e-mail update I sent my friends, family, and former colleagues, who were waiting, I'm certain, for me to snap and say, "I'm outta here." (Particularly when I couldn't force any of the farm animals, including those I've given birth to, to kickbox with me, and plans to build a Target in town fell through.) Amazingly, though, I didn't snap. I stuck it out. And as the great Frankie S. would say, I did it, not to mention documented it, my way.

What you don't know is that the day after a major chunk of New York City exploded,[224] killing one person, maiming dozens of others, and forcing many of my friends and former colleagues to work from home as their offices were in the "frozen zone," I had to travel from the bucolic

---

224. A pipe blew up under Forty-second Street. It wasn't a terrorist act, thank God, but it was terribly frightening and reminiscent of September 11 nonetheless.

backcountry into the Big, once again bruised Apple for my first meeting with my editor.

Like I wasn't nervous enough. Now I didn't just have to worry about blowing it; I had to worry about being blown up on the way to blowing it. Wasn't it stuff like this that forced me to flee the city for the sticks in the first place?

Now, what you've probably already figured out about me, and I promise this will all tie together shortly, is that I'm one of those people who likes to talk to people. Even if I don't know them. I always think, You're a person; I'm a person. We share the same planet; maybe we can be pals. So I strike up conversations. Here in the South, this trait does not immediately paint me as mentally suspect. But in New York, among my fellow straphangers on the Grand Central shuttle, it always did.

Once while riding the subway, I saw a woman wearing the most beautiful pair of pumps. I couldn't help staring at them. And then she started staring at me staring at them. I didn't want to make her uncomfortable, so I decided to put her at ease by doing what I do best: hurtling into fast-forward-friendly mode.

"Your shoes are beautiful," I cooed. "Are they Prada? No, no. Let me guess. They're the new Kate Spades, aren't they? I saw them in *In Style*. Did you get them at the downtown store or Saks? I love Saks, but they just don't have the selection, you know?"

I took a brief pause to breathe (but somehow managed not to take in the mounting fear on her face) before plowing on. "They look great on your feet," I gushed, leaning in so close I could literally smell the leather. "I'd kill to have such high arches. Have you worn them with jeans? I've got a pair they'd be perfect with. What about the bag? Did you get the matching bag?" This was followed by yet another split-second stop while I caught my breath, but not the fact that she'd tucked her feet—and those perfect pumps—all the way under her seat.

"So, do they run true to size?" I blathered on, oblivious to her DEFCON 4–level freak-out. "I'm a seven. Did you know that seven is the most popular size? It is," I added, gazing fondly at my fabulous, and fabulously pricey, Stuart Weitzman stilettos and wondering just for a sec if she'd swap shoes. "Do you think they have any sevens left? I'm sure they don't. I'm sure they had a bunch, but they're probably out, right? Right?"

Surprisingly, she never actually replied. She simply reached down, plucked those puppies off her feet, and ran, carrying them, into the next car.

It's unfortunate, the freakish response some people have to friendliness.

Of course this friendliness is something my buddies frequently badger me about. They want me to knock it off and get my New York on. For the uninitiated, this means snarling and not smiling; being taciturn, not talkative. And absolutely, positively not offering condolences to a Pakistani cab driver who bemoans the state of his beloved country, leading me to believe he means the war and strife and poverty of the place, when in fact he's just grumpy because they haven't got a Gap.

Believe me when I tell you it was tough extricating myself from that conversation.

In my defense, I must say that I really do know how to

New York. I went to college there and I worked there. I can fend off a homeless person making a lunge for my morning mocha from fifty feet, and I've perfected the art of using my briefcase as a battering ram. I can run in the aforementioned stilettos (and whip 'em off and wield 'em like a butcher knife in a nanosecond), jump a turnstile in a skirt (which is the price you pay for spending your last dime on designer footwear), and snag a cab on Fifth Avenue at the height of the holidays. (If you're thinking I'm about to tell you that wearing a short skirt and high heels helps, you're right. I am. In fact I just did. So do it. You went to see the tree go up. Do you still want to be there when it comes down?)

Clearly I'm able to get my New York on. I just don't like to, and living in the serenity of Nate's Place for the past two years has helped me come to terms with that personal tidbit. Right now all I want is to window shop my way through the West Village, revel in the fact that Denise and Angeline (numbers 27 and 93, in case you can't recall), don't smell nearly as bad as the subway stop at Broadway and Canal, and wow the woman willing to take a chance on a counterfeit farm girl. What I don't want is to get blown up on my way to the most important meeting of my life.

Of course, acting New York City–surly won't save me if terrorists have other plans. And since I've no clue what those cretins are concocting, I've made an executive decision. I'm going to act natural. Not a state I can claim for my hair color, but that's a discussion for another day.

I'm going to forgo the tough city-chick bit and simply be me. Overly friendly, fast-talking, and even faster-walking me. I'm going to quiz the guy pushing pretzels in front of the Le Parker Meridien Hotel about how often he's got to redo his dreads, and hand my skim, half-caff, extra-whip mocha to the first homeless person who hones in on it. I'm going to wolf whistle right back at the construction workers on West Forty-third, and help the obviously lost gaggle of European, backpacking, guitar-toting twenty-somethings find Madison Square Garden. In short, I'm going to get my New York on the only way I know how to wear it: with a dippy smile and an incurable case of flap jaw.

Now that I think of it, maybe I am mentally suspect. Or maybe I'm more of a country chick than I ever thought I'd cop to. In either case, promise me you won't tell my editor?

Part Five

EPILOGUE

(OR, AS I LIKE TO CALL IT, GROUNDHOG DAY, PART DEUX)

"What are you doing?"

I was standing out on our lawn, listening to the crickets and contemplating the front of Nate's Place. With its dahlia-, petunia-, and vinca-filled window boxes hanging off the porch, lush green ferns dangling from the ceiling, sweet white rocking chairs, and steps piled high with straw roosters, cement turtles, and freshly picked pumpkins,[225] it is my always-and-forever favorite spot on the 110-year-old tenant house in which we reside.

I was lost in a wild fantasy in which I convinced the frugal farmer to whom I'm married to permit the purchase of black shutters, something he's loath to agree to, as he thinks they should be white, which I think will make our farmhouse-red abode look swathed in surgical bandages, so why bother?, when he snuck up and startled me with those four little words.

"What are you doing?"

---

225. I know; it's summer. Hemingway got a little ahead of himself in the planting department. Again.

"Waiting," I replied.

"For what?"

"For death to overtake me." You didn't actually think I was going to launch into my pitch about the exterior adornments I so desire, not to mention deserve, now, did you? After all, and this I neglected to mention, I had just snuck out on the poor guy and left him alone with a kitchen full of dirty dinner dishes. I tend to doubt he put them in the dishwasher, but I'm certain he stacked them neatly on the counter after encouraging our two canine garbage disposals to lick them clean. If I didn't get in there quick it was quite possible Casey would think they'd been washed and would put them away.[226]

"Why?"

"I just ingested a totally Stu-grown salad and I figure I have about a half hour before it hits my large intestine, brings on a bout of diarrhea I wouldn't wish on a turkey buzzard, and leaves my lifeless body clinging to the commode."

"Well, you are always complaining you're . . . you know."

"Oh, so your little rancid romaine, cherry tomato, and cucumber concoction is just what the doctor ordered? Doctor Kevorkian, maybe."

"I'm crushed."

"Don't be. It was actually delicious. Going down. Coming up could be a completely different story."

"Oh, so now it's coming up."

"Please, could we just enjoy the view?"

"Of the house?"

---

226. Again.

"Of the house."

"What's wrong with it?"

"Nothing. I've just always liked this view of Nate's Place."

"Two years later, you're still calling it Nate's Place."

"I guess it's because the house has so much history. So many other people have lived here. It's like it's Nate's, or somebody else's, but not ours."

"It isn't ours. It's Doug's."

That startled me. I looked away from the house and at my husband, aka Hemingway, aka hon, aka He Who Was About to Give Me Very Bad News. "Oh, my God. You got fired."

"What?"

"You're standing here, ruining my pre-death experience with all this ghastly gastrointestinal chatter because you're trying to work up the nerve to tell me you got fired."

"I didn't get fired."

"Oh, well, of course. Doug did just retire, and he probably doesn't need us babysitting his property anymore. It really makes so much sense." I glanced around at the henhouse, the hog pen, the springhouse, the pasture where the hay bales burned and the cattle ate them, anyway. I loved bitching about this place, but that didn't mean I was ready to leave it. "I don't know why I'm getting so worked up. I mean, I always knew this day would come. I just, well, somewhere along the way I forgot. Alright, so you got fired. It was bound to happen."

"I didn't get fired!"

"Then he's selling the farm. Duh. Why didn't I think of that? And we need to move. And since he's selling the farm he won't need a farm manager anymore so it's kind of like you got fired or downsized or whatever."

"Susan, Doug's not selling the farm, and I didn't get fired."

"So you're hovering over me because why? You lost a bet and you get to tell me I have a brain tumor or the big C or something? Please. I already told you. I'm dying of Stu salad."

"I'm here because I thought my salad would taste better with chunks of salmon."

"Anything not to kill a chicken."

"Chicken wouldn't be bad. But salmon would be good, too."

"Trust me; chicken's the way to go."

"You just don't like them because they peck at your feet."

"Excuse me for wanting to protect a thirty-five-dollar pedicure."

"Try a pair of boots."

"Now, there's a look. Boots with shorts. Works in the chicken coop and on the street corner!"

"Very funny."

"Don't you think the house would look better with black shutters?"

"The house would look better with water."

"What, the well pump's out again? I'm getting a little tired of using all our Poland Spring for the boys' baths."

"The pump's fine. I've just been thinking how great it would be to be completely self-sustaining. You know, to live off the land. We already grow our own produce. The chickens give us plenty of eggs. The next logical step is salmon."

"I'd think the next logical step would be pigs. Then we'd have a little bacon to go with our eggs. And then we could open a diner."[227]

"I'm trying to talk seriously with you about this."

"You seriously need salmon?"

"Yes."

"So walk down the cellar steps to the freezer and get some."

"I'm talking about raising our own."

"Don't you need water for that?"

"That's what I'm saying. Hey, where are you going?"

"To cancel your subscriptions to *Hobby Farms, Progressive Farmer,* and that *Organic Living* newsletter that claims it can be used as toilet paper after you're done reading it. Which I guess is only fitting, since first it fills your head with crap and then it helps get rid of it on the way out."

"Susan, I'm trying to talk to you about living on the water. Don't you remember telling me you wanted to do that?"

You know the movie *Groundhog Day*? Well, it seems that every two years I have a sort of Groundhog Day of my own. Granted, there are twenty-four months between each, but still it's as if I wake up to find myself in the middle of a conversation about a conversation I have absolutely no memory of. You'd think there would be medication for this, and maybe there is. I just can't seem to remember to ask my doctor about it.

But back to this particularly stressful moment in my life.

"Of course I want to live on the water. I'm a Pisces. I'd

---

227. We're not Greek, but it could work. After all, our last name does end in a vowel.

live in the tub if the kids didn't need to stand in it for their once-a-month whether-they-need-it-or-not showers. So sure, I probably mentioned it. Just like I also probably mentioned how much I'd like to run away for a weekend with John Cusack. But I don't suppose that little request's about to resurface, is it?"

"Funny, I thought you were a George Clooney fan."

"John Cusack. I've had a thing for him since *Say Anything*."

"His movies you can remember. Our conversations you can't."

"Forgive me for not wanting to drop everything and run off to a lake or wherever it is you need to go raise salmon. I'm sure I said that *one day* I'd like to live on the water. But what makes you think that one day is today?"

"I found the perfect lake."

"I had no idea you were looking."

"Think of it as my contribution to keeping the mystery alive in our marriage."

"The mystery is how I haven't killed you yet."

"Come on, admit it. You want to know about the lake."

"OK, mystery man, where is this lake and how do we raise salmon in it?"

"You don't raise them *in* the lake. The lake just provides the water for the big tanks that we'll put in the backyard."

"I take it there's a house involved."

"Your favorite kind."

"Waterfront, with a view of Neiman Marcus?"

"Like I said, you'll have to see for yourself."

"Hmm. A house on the water with something other than a Tractor Supply nearby. Dare I even inquire as to the status of a Starbucks?"

"I dare you not to."

"Get out. You're either making this up or I'm having some kind of pre-death brain fart brought on by your damn salad.[228] I swear, in a minute I'm going to hear a voice telling me to walk toward the light and then you and your house on the shores of fabulous shopping will disappear and I'll be dead."

"Are you done now?"

Is he kidding? Of course I'm not done. How can I be done? We just got here. In fact we still have boxes in the Butler building that we haven't unpacked. The kids are finally settled. I've just made friends. And I'm just catching on to this farming stuff.

After eighteen months, I now know the difference between a steer and bull, and I can hold an intelligent conversation about the pros and cons of making hay. In addition, I know more than any DKNY-wearing former magazine marketing pro should ever have to know about pastured poultry and rotational grazing. And I'm finally comfortable with the fact that *bush hog* is spelled with two words.

And now he wants me to move.

"Alright, here's the deal. I'll see the lake, the house, the whole shebang. But I'm not making any promises."

"That's all I ask. I'm telling you, you're going to love it. There's room for the chickens and a big vegetable garden.

---

228. Oh, God, I am so shallow. Other people have their lives flash by. I have visions of the perfect lake house.

And I'm going to raise the most delicious salmon you've ever tasted. You know what else? We can get a motorboat. And you know what that means, right?"

"What?"

"You can finally learn to water ski."

"Water ski? Me?"

"Don't you remember telling me you wanted to learn?"

Bill Murray, where are you?

THE IMPRACTICAL GIRL'S GUIDE
TO FARM SPEAK

*N*oah Webster I'm not. But if you've ever entertained the idea of ditching the city or the suburbs for the back o' beyond, you'll need to know some farm speak. You'll also need to know how to parallel park a pickup truck, but as I can't maneuver the Mustang into a space without mangling the meters on both ends, I think it best to leave that lesson to the pros. For a crash course in talking country, see below. For tips on finagling your Ford F-150 into a Prius-size spot, call your local driving school.

Barn—Large, airy building perfect for rebirth as a mini mall, day spa, or Designer Shoe Warehouse.

Brush Cutter—Unwieldy, self-propelled device that "goes where your bush hog's never been!" which means it can fit into tight spots around places like the springhouse, chicken coop and hog pen. (Come to think of it, maybe I should try it in the small space between Casey's bed and the wall. I'm unsure what's growing there, but I believe it began as a pair of boxer shorts and several manure-encrusted sweat socks. In any case, "it" is starting to bloom, and since bleach and a touch of Round-Up didn't get rid of it, it might be wise to bring in the big guns. Failing that, I could simply set fire to the room and move my slob, I mean son, to the barn where he belongs.) Anyway, the brush cutter is great for mowing down the scratchy, stalky stuff that sprouts purple buds in a desperate attempt to convince us it's a flower and not the weed we know it is, as well as thistle, weed bushes, and the occasional black snake. But it's even better at getting away from Hemingway (remember, it's self-propelled), turning around, and chasing him across the field while the kids and I watch, horrified and hollering, "Run, Daddy, run!" from the safety of the front porch.

Burn Pile—Forget hauling your refuse to the recycling center (because, remember, there's no garbage pickup here). Simply toss it in the burn pile on your property. First, tell the kids you're putting in a swimming pool, then dig a huge pit. Next, throw in all your household crap: broken coffee tables, crushed cereal boxes, mangled lawn chairs, empty snack packages, old sofas, decade-old tax documents, even rugs decimated by pup-regurgitated potpourri (sorry, Mom!). Hand your kids a couple of packages of marshmallows and some long twigs, and set the whole kit'n'kaboodle ablaze. Sure, they'll be pissed it's not a pool, but it's nothing a few s'mores can't cure.

Bush Hog—Basically a massive lawn mower. The major difference is you don't ride it and you don't push it. You pull it behind a gigantic tractor. And this is what makes the testosterone heavy among us very happy. To Hemingway, there's nothing better than a day spent sitting at the helm of the New Holland, pulling the bush hog over the pastures, cutting swaths of grass the width of an airstrip and the height of a Marine recruit's haircut. In short, the perfect piece of equipment for keeping husbands busy between ball games.

Bush Hog Repairman—A frequent visitor during the spring and summer months, when Hemingway inadvertently uses the bush hog to find tree stumps, rocks, and the rusted remains of long-lost farm equipment.

Butler Building—A prefabricated metal building. Farmers use it to store equipment and protect it from the rain. Pigeons use it to roost in the beams and poop on the equipment, which then has to be washed—usually with recycled rainwater.

Cattle Guard—A series of thick metal slats that run the width of a farm road. There are just a few inches of space between each slat; enough to catch the hooves of an escaped cow and prevent it from running out into the street and becoming hamburger. The cattle guard's also primo at snagging the wheels on my Rollerblades and snapping the heels off my suede Louboutin boots. The damn thing treats my stuff like chopped liver. So why I should care about the cows becoming chop meat is beyond me.

Chicken—Feathered egg-laying machine that frolics in its own filth, snatches hot dogs from the hands of children, and pecks fresh pedicures with a vengeance. Synonyms for *chicken* include *fowl*, *pullet*, *hen*, *banty*, and *friggin' bird*.

Chicken Tractor—A chicken coop on wheels. Makes moving the pullets to fresh pastures easy, and trips to the butcher a breeze.

Cow—Massive ruminant (mammal with four stomachs) weighing about 1,500 pounds, despite being a vegetarian. Can be used to simultaneously mow and fertilize grass, attract flies for chickens to eat, and, ultimately, as the main course at a barbeque. Common cow terms include: *heifer*, a cow that's never had a calf; *calf*, a baby cow; *bull*, a male cow; and *steer*, a bull caught hanging with the heifers and consequently castrated.

Cow Wintering—When I first heard about cow wintering, I thought, "Unfair! Unfair! Chickens get a customized RV to take them places (see *Chicken Tractor*) while the bovines get to hit Miami Beach. What do I get to do? Stay here in the frozen sticks!" As it turns out, the chickens may be headed for a hot spot (like my broiler), but cattle spend the frigid winter months in the fields, munching dead corn stalks in the snow. Not exactly the Bovine Spring Break I believed it to be.

Deer—Overgrown rodent with a talent for making kamikaze attacks on cars. A perennial favorite of both hunters and auto body shops.

Dual-Purpose Cows—The hardest-working bovines in the farm business. Used first for dairy production; once they run dry they make their debut in the butcher department.

Farm—A pastoral setting bedecked with fences, livestock, tractors, and barns, many of which are unused, so why one can't hold an Ann Taylor or a Starbucks is beyond me.

Four-wheeler—Synonyms include *ATV*, *Japanese Quarter Horse*, *Quad*, and the *Second Most Popular Form of Farm-Style Suicide*. (Number one is stupid tractor tricks.) Typically ridden sans helmets (no matter how much your kids promise they'll put them on) and at high speeds over unfamiliar terrain, four-wheelers are fun for the whole family. If your idea of fun includes concussions, crushed bones, and blood loss. Use your head. Wear a helmet.

Hay—What some folks in the sticks make while the sun shines. Comes in square bales and round bales, and the good stuff (yes, there's such a thing as "good" hay) is snapped up by the horse folks, who buy only the best for their million-dollar mounts. The dregs wind up at nurseries in suburbia, where minivan-driving moms pick it up along with pumpkins for their Halloween decorating endeavors. Guess who pays the highest price per bale?

High-Speed Internet—A fabrication of the Hughes-Net folks. Here at Nate's Place, we connect to cyberspace via satellite. First I click on Explorer, then I shower, dress, put on my makeup, straighten the kitchen, and kick the dogs out for the day. By the time I'm back at my desk, my MSN home page is just opening. I highlight "Horoscopes" and go make more coffee. Clearly the connection's not fast, but it's certainly accelerated my multitasking skills.

Horse—Massive mammal that's as much work as a newborn. Folks in this neck of the woods pay millions for their mounts and house them in stalls as luxurious as four-star hotels. Live here awhile and you'll realize it's not a dog's life you're after; it's Affirmed's. (Affirmed was the eleventh American Triple Crown winner. He and his rival, Alydar, went at it tooth and nail. Kind of like the Yankees and the Red Sox, if you know what I mean.)

Hydraulics—In a nutshell, hydraulics is the science of operating machinery via the pressure created by forcing a liquid like water or oil through a narrow pipe. Rather like shooting collagen through a tiny needle and into your lips to make them more luscious, or counting on a bra with a built-in water pump to give you cleavage. Not that I have firsthand experience with any of that stuff, but you know what I mean.

Manure Management—A tad bit different from upper management (but not by much), manure management is the process of spreading cow crap over the fields upon which dairy cattle dine. This popular organic approach results in milk that's better for you, if you can get past the fact that its extra-special ingredient is feces.

Organic Gardening—Using dead things to grow live things. Hemingway fertilizes his impressive harvest with food scraps, leaves, grass, cow manure, crushed eggshells, and chicken droppings. Then he sets our fowl free on the garden to do bug patrol. After that, the trick is in the timing: He's got to pull the chickens off the job the moment they've cleared the place of creepy-crawlies and before they begin pigging out on the produce they were used to protect.

Pastured Poultry—The practice of letting chickens graze where they like, as opposed to being confined in a coop. The organic farming militant to whom I'm married believes free-ranging fowl will make for a more delicious bird. I can hardly wait to conduct *that* taste test.

Pickup Truck—The local antidote to a minivan. If you live in the country, your preferred mode of transportation is a massive pickup with vanity plates, and a dog to do the driving while you fiddle around with the gun rack.

Range Cubes—The dog biscuits of the bovine world. Only cattle are more likely to shit than sit at the mere sight of these snacks.

Rotational Grazing—The practice of moving cattle from one field to another on a regular basis so the grass in the original field can regenerate. Think of it as going to a different restaurant each month with your girlfriends, then working your way back to the first spot once the drink specials have changed.

Skid Loader (aka Skid Steer Loader)—Basically, an electric chair on wheels. You climb in through a hatch and squeeze into a seat surrounded by a steel cage. (Kind of like Hannibal Lecter's lockup.) Hand grips control the wheels:

push them forward to go forward; pull back to go in reverse. Push one forward and the other back and you're spinning in a circle. You know, like a preschooler in a Fisher-Price race car. Foot pedals operate the bucket, which I imagine is there to catch the prisoner should he or she pitch forward from the force of the electricity. Hemingway says I'm overreacting to the precariousness of this contraption, but in my opinion, the skid loader alone is the reason farming's the nation's third-most-dangerous profession. Obviously I'm having a tough time shaking that little tidbit of information.

Tractor—The pickup truck's big brother, complete with a never-ending variety of attachments, all of which can kill or maim in a never-ending variety of methods. Hard-core owners insist on open cabs so they can battle sunstroke and frostbite on even terms, while softies prefer closed cabs that muffle the screams of those about to be crushed beneath the bush hog.

Tractor Supply—The Saks of the sticks. No Ralph Lauren, but a full selection of ladies' insulated bib overalls, matching goatskin gloves, and rubber muck boots. (Personally, I'm waiting for ones with a peek-a-boo toe before I even consider buying a pair.) The first stop for dual-lid full-size truck toolboxes, llama food, cattle dewormer, ear tags, and udder wash, if that's what trips your trigger. And no, they don't sell hunting supplies.

Weed Whacker—Now, I know what you're thinking. You're thinking, Oh, a weed whacker. Big deal. We have one of those. No, you don't have one of these. You could

take out a redwood with this sucker. It's huge. It's powerful. It's best used in the morning, when the farmer slinging
it is sober. But you can't tell that to my man. Occasionally
Hemingway gets it into his head that weed whacking in
the twilight after a couple of vodka tonics is a commend-
able undertaking. So then I, in an effort not to need an un-
dertaker, grab my wine and the portable phone and head
to the front porch. There I sit, watching and waiting, with
bated chardonnay breath, for the weed whacker to take off
his toes, hack off a hunk of heel, or amputate his entire foot
at the ankle. Should it happen I'll certainly call an ambulance. And maybe they'll even take him to the hospital. But
probably not before telling us about some poor bastard
who lost an ear and a chunk of scalp while whacking weeds
country style.

Work Boots—The stilettos of the farm set (aka not
something Suzy's slipping into). Hemingway, on the other
hand, has become the Imelda Marcos of the work boot
world. He's got a fancy "dress" pair with steel-reinforced
toes (in case a waiter drops a drink on his foot), and at least
a dozen others for every day. Waterproof. Slip resistant.
Thermal insulated. Some cinch, some tie, some light up
when he walks. Just kidding. They don't make those in
men's sizes. But if they did he'd definitely own a pair.

Acknowledgments

$\mathcal{I}$ have a confession to make: There would be no book if
there were no farm, and there would be no farm without
my brother-in-law and sister-in-law, Doug and Nancy Mc-
Corkindale. Thank you both for making possible the country life I love to pooh-pooh.

And speaking of *poo-poo*, I must take a moment to thank
those who've been putting up with my bellyaching and BS
longest: the Ridgewood Junior Football crew (the Benin-
tendes, Biagis, Caramannas, DeVitas, Edelbergs, Egans,
Grafs, Grundys, Krausses, Marchliks, Morminos, Rotas,
and Wades); the stars I had the honor of working with at
Family Circle (Barbara, Cory, Janine, Kim, Lisa, Rich, Ryan,
and Whitney); and all my friends in New York, New Jersey,
Connecticut, California, and Australia. Please forgive me
for not listing each of you here. I am blessed to be able to
say that there's simply not enough space.

My deepest and most heartfelt thanks go also to the
beautiful and talented Noel Cody, without whom I never
would have met my wonderful agent, Abby Koons. Thank
you, Abby, for embracing my "voice" (even if I do sound

like Carmela Soprano) and working tirelessly to find the perfect publisher for *Confessions*. I swear never again to get tattooed during contract negotiations, but I can't make any promises about body piercing.

Kara Cesare, what can I say? You get me better than I get myself. Thank you for your on-the-mark editorial direction, unabashed enthusiasm, and willingness to teach me the ropes (and not let me hang myself with them). I hereby anoint you and Abby honorary LOBsters. Just let me know how you take your morning margarita.

Special thanks to Lindsay Nouis for answering my six million silly questions, and to Anthony Ramondo, art director extraordinaire, for the cover of this book. You hit the high heel right on the head.

I'd like also to take a moment to thank the *Fauquier Times-Democrat* for running my column (despite my penchant for writing about barnyard animals and breasts, but not barnyard animals *with* breasts), and the two talented women who gave me my break there: Robin Earl and Laura Lyster-Mensh. If I ever grow up, I want to be like both of you. That's not likely to happen, but a girl can dream, can't she?

To all my new Southern gal pals, including but by no means limited to the Marshall Mafia, the LOB Squad, the Jazzercise chicks, and the crew at Claude Thompson Elementary School: Thank you for embracing this high-energy Jersey girl. I love you, too.

If you laugh at my stuff, and Lord knows I hope you do, it's because I was lucky enough to learn from the masters. To the funnymen I call family—my dad, Gene Costantino, and my brothers David, Nick, and Dan—thank you for your encouragement and faith. You are my humor heroes.

And of course I can't thank my dad without thanking my mom, Joan Costantino. You gave me my first notepad and pencil (anything to shut me up!), and I've been chasing you around demanding you read my drivel ever since. Thank you for believing in me and for all your emotional and financial support. (If I could get the next check before Neiman's annual shoe sale, that would be super.)

As I said before, there would be no book if there were no farm. But I could never have written (and written and rewritten) about the farm without the love, friendship, and five thousand daily phone calls and kicks in the butt from my best friend, Trisha Clark; my cousin and soul sister, Lisa Orban; and my patient, prescient therapist, Ellen Dolce. (Like you didn't know I was nuts.) You three are the reason I lived through the past twelve months. I promise: next book, no nervous breakdowns. Unless Escada stops making my size.

In closing, I've got to acknowledge my beautiful boys, Casey and Cuyler. For your patience with this whole process and your pride in me, you have all my love and most of my advance. (OK, all of my advance. Just remember: When you're done with the video games, go milk the goats!) No book means more to me than the two of you do.

And finally there's the guy who's been with me the whole way. I've loved you since I was seventeen, Stu. Only you know how counterfeit this farm girl really is, and yet you still love me. How did I get so lucky? If you'll permit me one last confession, Farm Boy, I've got to tell you: I'd follow you anywhere. Now, I believe you were saying something about salmon?